FIRE ENGINES FIREFIGHTERS

FIRE ENGINES

FIREFIGHTERS

The Men, Equipment, and Machines, from Colonial Days to the Present

by Paul C. Ditzel

with special photography by
John Garetti and Jeffrey Kurtzeman

Bonanza Books
New York

This 1984 edition is published by Bonanza Books, distributed by Crown Publishers, Inc. by arrangement with Crown Publishers, Inc.

Manufactured in Italy

Library of Congress Cataloging in Publication Data

Ditzel, Paul C.
Fire engines, fire fighters.

Bibliography: p.
Includes index.
1. Fire-engines—United States—History.
2. Fire prevention—United States—History. 3. Fire-departments—United States—History. I. Title.
TH9371.D57 1984 363.3'7'0973 84-20420

ISBN: 0-517-460041
h g f e d c b a

CONTENTS

PROLOGUE

If Prometheus was worthy of the wrath of heaven for kindling the first fire upon the earth, how ought all the gods to honor the men who make it their professional business to put it out?

—*John Godfrey Saxe, American journalist, poet, and lecturer, ca. 1850*

There are today more than 1,200,000 firefighters in the United States who make it their business to put out fires that occur at the rate of more than three hundred every hour. Theirs is the most dangerous job in America. One firefighter is killed on the average of about every three days, and around half the nation's firefighters are injured each year. Despite the dangers—and government figures show they are far worse than those faced by police officers—these firefighters continue to follow a tradition of public service that goes back more than two hundred years.

The complete history of American firefighters—the fires they fought and the development of their apparatus—has never before been told. This is not to suggest that there is a dearth of books on the subject; but the many books that have been written tell the history only in bits and pieces, usually focusing upon one city or area. *Fire Engines, Firefighters* fills this void by presenting a comprehensive account of the fire service in the United States—the men, the equipment, the techniques—from colonial times to the late twentieth century.

America's fire problems have changed greatly during those years. Colonial fires were caused mostly by chimneys that threw sparks on thatched or wood-shingled roofs. In most communities households were required to maintain one or more fire buckets, and nearly all citizens—men, women, and children—were expected to help fight fires with their buckets. Since this method was not very effective in the case of large fires, burning buildings were often abandoned to the flames, and instead efforts were concentrated upon saving adjacent structures by throwing water at safe distances from the fire. Organized fire protection was a highly essential need in early America, and in fact it became commonplace long before the organization of other public services such as police protection or water supply.

Fire problems in America worsened after the American Revolution. Buildings were constructed increasingly taller so that the top floors were beyond the reach of most fire ladders. Water supplies were inadequate and alarm systems slow. The growth of industry created new fire hazards in factories and commercial structures. Growing cities needed better apparatus. The ingenuity of American volunteer firefighters led to many improvements in equipment and helped to spawn the country's fire apparatus industry, which one day would become the supplier to the world. Better hose and more powerful pumpers—pulled to fires by the volunteers and operated by hand—enabled the volunteers to carry the attack inside buildings to the heart of the fire. However, with interior firefighting came greatly increased dangers to firefighters.

Volunteer fire companies afterward proliferated, and healthy rivalries developed between them, with neighborhood outfits devising faster ways to get to fires, better ways to fight fires, and more highly decorated apparatus to outshine that of other companies. Out of all this came a uniquely American institution: the volunteer fire company as the social and political hub of the city. Friendships formed during firefighting, and the pride in belonging to an élite company of hell-for-leather firefighters exerted strong influences upon the social, business, and political fabric of nineteenth-century America.

The camaraderie of early volunteer fire companies provided springboards to better jobs—not to mention political office. Firefighters could be expected to vote as a bloc for a fellow volunteer; their votes helped elect seven mayors in New York and eighteen in St. Louis. But around 1835, gangs of toughs began to infest the volunteer companies in downtown areas of major cities. What had begun as healthy competition gradually devolved into mayhem and murder as the unruly volunteers, now politically entrenched, became powers unto themselves.

The firefighting scene began to change around midcentury, with the development of the steam-powered fire engine. Paid departments now became feasible, because steamers could be operated by far fewer firefighters than those required by hand pumpers.

Fire problems continued to accelerate, especially as Americans, including many volunteers, moved west. As western cities prospered, buildings were slapdashed together to handle the rapid growth of business and the sudden influx of immigrants. Chicago became a tinderbox of wooden buildings and shabbily constructed commercial structures that could not withstand flames. The Great Chicago Fire in 1871 proved that. The rush to the California gold fields made San Francisco, with its wooden buildings, a boom town as well as another fire breeder. Conflagrations raged in San Francisco with predictable frequency after 1849. Rebuilt each time, the wooden city, prosperous as ever, was again ripe for burning, when the April, 1906, earthquake shattered water mains and kindled dozens of fires that joined virtually to destroy the city.

An examination of the history of fire protection in America shows a constant lag behind the need, especially in safety laws. The myth of the fireproof building was shattered during the 1903 Christmas holidays in Chicago, when 602 people, mostly women and children, perished in the Iroquois Theatre fire and stampede. Early twentieth-century industrialization bred sweatshops and death traps such as the Triangle Shirtwaist factory that burned in New York in 1911 with the loss of 146 lives.

As America continued to grow upward and outward and as new industrial processes multiplied hazards—not the least of which was the age of petrochemicals—still better protection was needed. Gasoline-powered apparatus replaced the steamer engines. Powerful engines were needed to conquer fires in large buildings and industrial complexes. Aerial ladders grew longer and water towers offered an answer to the problem of providing large volumes of water at high pressures for fighting fires on top floors.

What a distance American firefighters have come since those days when they formed bucket brigades to dump three-gallon buckets of water on fires! One New York City fire engine, the mightiest in the world, can now pump 8,800 gallons a minute. Apparatus and firefighting techniques have evolved to a high degree of sophistication. About the only thing that has not changed radically is the firefighter.

Given the dangers and the increasing fire hazards, why do firefighters continue to pursue their calling? It is a question that is often asked, but no one has ever come up with a complete answer. It is not a matter of the aura of bravery—a word rarely heard in firehouses—that attracts them. Nor is it a male "ego trip" nor the fulfillment of a boyhood wish born from watching the glamorous firefighters rush into battle. Anybody who has crawled along a tenement corridor filled with smoke at 3 o'clock in the morning to douse a smoldering mattress knows there is little glamour to it. Is it then simply a career that offers excitement and challenge? Partially. Is the job security and the guaranteed pension part of it? Yes, though in these days of municipal layoffs the firefighter's job security is not what it used to be. We may come close to an answer by noting that firefighting is one of the few jobs that provides a deep sense of personal satisfaction, one derived from the knowledge that a person is helping his fellow human beings.

Whatever the motivation for getting out of bed in the dead of night, sometimes in a blizzard, to make rescues and fight a fire at great personal risk in somebody else's house or place of business, firefighters are a very special breed. This distinction was made in Philadelphia in 1975 after eight firefighters were killed in an oil refinery fire. Five of them perished while trying to save three others trapped in a blazing sea of flames. This episode is one of the finest examples in American fire-service history of instant, unhesitating, and unquestioning bravery despite terrible odds.

Again we may ask the question: Given the chance that one of them will be killed while fighting a fire somewhere in the United States during the next few days, why do they do it? Chief Edward F. Croker of the Fire Department of New York put the case very well in February, 1908, after a deputy chief and four firefighters lost their lives.

"Firemen are going to be killed," said Croker. "When they join the department they face that fact. When a man becomes a fireman his act of bravery has already been accomplished. What he does after that is all in the line of his work. They were not thinking of getting killed when they went where death lurked. They went there to put the fire out, and got killed. Firefighters do not regard themselves as heroes because they do what the business requires."

To paraphrase John Godfrey Saxe: If not the gods, how ought we to honor these men? This book is a beginning.

1

BOSTON: "THE HAUGHTY FLAMES TRIUMPHED"

Boston was built to burn. Early that Thursday, March 20, 1760, some sixteen years before the Declaration of Independence, the town's 15,600 people were jam-packed into block upon block of houses and tenements. Only about half the buildings were brick; the rest were wooden with shingled roofs. Some stood three stories high, taller than any fire ladder could reach. Many were more than a century old.

Residential districts were tucked among a hodgepodge of similarly constructed warehouses, shops, tanneries, breweries, rum distilleries, bakeries, furniture factories, carpentry and carriage works, codfish and whale oil processing plants, shipyards and timbered wharves, alongside of which stood dozens of ships. There was hardly a building or ship in Boston that was not a breeding ground for fire.

Boston was a firefighter's nightmare, and fires were commonplace in the seaport. Most were caused when sparks from faulty chimneys landed on the wood-shingle roofs. Narrow streets lacing the town enabled flames to go leapfrogging from one block to another. Boston had experienced eight conflagrations in its 130-year history. Some residents this blustery night could recall the worst, the Great Fire of 1711. Starting in Cornhill Street about 7:00 P.M., October 2, that fire had lasted eight hours, destroyed one hundred buildings, and killed about a dozen people. Cornhill had been rebuilt, and now, nearly half a century later, it was ready to go up in flames again.

Boston, seen here in a 1768 view, was a firefighter's nightmare. The city's buildings were a hodgepodge of stores, tenements, factories, and warehouses. Nearly all had wood roofs, which were often ignited by chimney sparks. There was hardly a building in Boston or a ship in the harbor that was not a fire-breeder.

A foretaste of what was to be known as the worst conflagration in America up to the Revolution was given on each of the three days prior to that Thursday. Unusually warm winds from the north had made the town tinder-dry. Before noon on Monday, flames destroyed a carpentry shop in the west end of the city. The fire was battled by the entire fire department—more than a hundred men and nine pumpers. The engines were rectangular wooden water tubs in which hand pumps were mounted. Water was supplied by bucket brigades formed by area residents, who were directed by a firewarden. Despite their efforts on Monday, strong northeasterly winds pushed the flames into a large adjoining house, which was destroyed. Several nearby buildings were severely damaged.

Tuesday, at around 10:00 A.M., fire was discovered on James Griffin's wharf in a building occupied by the British Royal Artillery. Exploding gunpowder rocked the town, and five men were hurt. Flames spread to an adjoining carpenter's shop and a blacksmith's. The loss would have been worse had it not been for a high tide, which provided an excellent water supply. The wharf would be rebuilt, to become, thirteen years later, the site of the Boston Tea Party.

On Wednesday, the cry of fire called out the engines five times. Boston firefighters were exhausted, and most of them went to bed early.

The wind had calmed by 2:00 A.M., Thursday, when somebody discovered flames shooting from a large house on Cornhill Street (now Washington Street) occupied by a well-to-do widow, Mrs. Mary Jackson, and her son, William. Cries of fire awakened the neighborhood. Firefighters of Marlborough Engine, No. 5, hastily dressed, ran from their homes to the shed housing their pumper, and hauled it north to Cornhill. From the time of alarm until they got to the fire, at least ten minutes elapsed. The Jackson house was now beyond saving. They would have to try to save the houses on either side.

As the Marlborough firefighters pointed their rig at the fire, neighbors under the direction of the district firewarden quickly formed bucket brigades, passing water from a nearby well to the last person in line, who dumped it into the tub. The empty buckets went down the other side of the line for more. Firefighters stroked the pump handles, and water jetted from the long nozzle on top of the water box. More fire companies arrived, but despite their efforts, the intense heat ignited the houses next to the Jacksons'. With luck, the firefighters hoped they could put out the fire by checking the north-south spread. But luck was not to be with them this night. In a few minutes a fourth house was burning.

And then, with horrifying swiftness, the wind picked up and grew into a sharp gale from out of the northwest. Flames jumped from narrow Cornhill into the next street east, Pudding Lane (now Devonshire Street). Firefighters were quickly joined by the rest of the department: the Great Fire Engine, No. 1 (so named because seventeen men were assigned to it, more than to any other in town); North Copper Engine, No. 2; Old North Church Engine, No. 3; Engine No. 4; Hero Engine, No. 6; Old Prison Engine, No. 7; Cumberland Engine, No. 8; and West Engine, No. 9. Also arriving were members of the Boston mutual fire societies, elite organizations of property owners who ran to fires with buckets and salvage bags and protected each other's property.

Firefighters quickly took up new positions as the wind drove the flames into still more buildings. Before they could get up water, another entire block of houses and stores would blossom into flames. King Street, site of the Boston Massacre ten years later, was next to go. Soon, all houses, shops, and three warehouses on the south side of King were blazing. King pointed to the waterfront, about a quarter of a mile to the east. Barring a miracle, nothing could stop the fire from spreading into the warehouses, docks, and ships. From King the flames swept into other streets, lanes, and alleys. In Quaker Lane (Congress Street) all was ablaze: houses, tenements, a barbershop, a gunsmith's, several chair-making shops, three sail lofts, a barrel factory, two blacksmithies, and the fish market.

"Then was beheld a perfect Torrent of Fire bearing down all before it; in a seeming Instant, all was Flame," wrote Town Clerk William Cooper. Samuel Savage later recalled: "I can say without exaggeration that I never in my life was in a greater storm of snow or knew it snow faster than the fire fell all around us."

The gale sucked up chunks of blazing shingles and broadcast them far in advance of the flames. The firebrands rained down upon more wood roofs, took root, and sprouted into still more fires, which quickly melded into the holocaust. Upper and lower Water Street erupted in flames as more houses, shops, and woodworking plants were steadily consumed. To the south, Milk Street and Battery March quickly took

The first practical fire engine in America was this hand-operated tub, which Boston imported from London and put into service on January 27, 1678. Water was dumped into the wooden box, which was about three feet long and eighteen inches wide. Inside the tub was a pump that fed a flexible, snakelike nozzle. The engine was carried to fires by hand.

fire. The flames would destroy virtually all buildings along the streets: tanneries, a bakery, houses, tenements, two shipbuilding yards, and a rum distillery. Fire spilled out onto Wendell's Wharf and destroyed all buildings and large quantities of warehoused merchandise as well.

The narrow streets were now clogged with the homeless and soon-to-be homeless, who grabbed whatever they could and fled. "The distressed Inhabitants of those buildings, now wrapped in Fire, scarce knew where to take Refuge from the devouring Flames," said Cooper. "Numbers who were confined to Beds of Sickness and Pain, as well as the Aged and Infant, then demanded a compassionate Attention; they were removed from House to House, and even the dying were obliged to take one more Remove before their final one." A pregnant woman was helped to the slopes of Fort Hill, where she went into labor and gave birth in an open field lit by the glare of the flames.

It was frustratingly slow going for the nine companies of firefighters, who bullied their way through the mob in desperate attempts to take up new battle positions ahead of the flames. The gale turned their ineffective streams into spray and blew it back into their faces. Many firefighters knew their families were in danger, that their homes and places of work were threatened, but they stayed with their rigs and tried to keep the searing heat from blistering their faces. And then, to further mock their efforts, the wind capriciously changed and turned the flames around. The whirlwind of fire fed upon buildings that it had earlier missed and then continued its rampage into the waterfront.

There was great alarm near the southeast perimeter of the fire, where enormous quantities of gunpowder were stored in the South Battery. Townspeople and British troops quickly began moving the powder to safety. But they were not fast enough for the speeding flames. A massive explosion rocketed debris high into the boiling clouds of smoke and flame. The ground's trembling was felt throughout Boston; many thought an earthquake had struck.

The glow from burning Boston was mirrored in the harbor waters and could be seen far out to sea and for nearly fifty miles north in Portsmouth, New Hampshire. Help came from dozens of the suburbs ringing Boston. Charlestown firefighters loaded their engine on a boat, rowed across to Boston, and joined the battle. Rich and poor stood side by side as they helped firefighters. "The People in this and the neighboring Towns exerted themselves to an uncommon Degree, and were encouraged by the presence and Example of the greatest Personages among us, but the haughty Flames triumphed over our Engines—our Art—and our Numbers," said Cooper.

The fire raged for ten hours until, about noon, it ran out of buildings to burn. Miraculously, nobody was killed, and only a few were hurt. But the fire had destroyed 349 buildings, about equally divided between residential and commercial structures. More than half a dozen ships, schooners, and sloops were burned to their waterlines. The homeless included "243 wealthy, 468 poor and 314 middling class," a total of 1,025 people. Losses ranged between 100,000 and 300,000 British pounds. None of it was covered by insurance, an idea that had earlier been discussed but had never taken hold. The fire victims mostly had to rely upon relatives and friends for food, clothing, and shelter until they could rebuild their lives.

The town treasury, depleted by an earlier fire, contained only 3,000 pounds for relief, and this was quickly distributed. Donations came from the governors of many colonies as well as from businessmen and clergymen throughout America, Nova Scotia, and London. But even that did not come close to meeting the need. A petition for financial aid was sent to the king. The reply—which was two years in coming—stated simply that the petition "had been graciously received by his Majesty." And that was the end of that. The indifference of King George III would long be remembered by Bostonians, who were learning that their best hope for help was to be found at home.

America's earliest fire engines were imported from Europe. The best were built by Richard Newsham in London, like this one, whose pumping handles were operated with hands and feet by means of treadles. Newsham's engine could shoot water four times farther than any competitor's and delivered up to 170 gallons per minute.

Bitterness was all the greater, considering that the Massachusetts Colony had provided the king with about two thousand men to fight in the French and Indian War. No colonial city had contributed more to the war effort and had less to show for it. Noting that the fire had occurred "after the exhaustion of war," the *Boston Post Boy* said in a prophetic editorial: "This once flourishing Metropolis must long remain under its present Desolation."

Although Boston would not incorporate as a city until 1870, the town had every look of a city and most of the problems of twentieth-century urban America. Wealthier citizens were buying homes in the dozens of suburbs around Boston. The central part of town was decaying. There was runaway inflation, a mark of the war. With the approach of the end of the war in 1760, there came an economic slump. The sagging economy and growing unemployment had caused many property owners to delay needed building repairs, notably to chimneys. Dozens of complaints of faulty flues were made to town selectmen. Housing, moreover, was at a premium. Many families crowded into buildings intended for only one or two. With some houses having as many as seven fireplaces, and all in almost constant use, there were plenty of places for fires to start.

Because Boston had been built out on a spit of land, there was no longer much room for expansion to build the town's economy and to broaden its tax base. Citizens were taxed to the hilt. The war had, moreover, cost the lives of many of its young men. Many widows on the public dole added to an already burdensome welfare problem that was caused by high unemployment.

Boston selectmen spent much time worrying about fire protection and wondering how to find ways of funding it while meeting other increasing public service needs of the town. Aid, if it came at all, was grudgingly given by Parliament and the Crown. England, meanwhile, continually increased the burden of taxation and imposed new demands on the colonies.

An investigation into the Great Fire of 1760 failed to determine its cause. As would be typical of later investigatory bodies, the investigators looked for ways to prevent a repetition of the disaster while neglecting to cure the situation that had caused the problem in the first place. Blaming the rapid spread of flames on narrow streets and wooden houses with their cedar shingle roofs, the selectmen decreed that no new buildings in excess of seven feet would be permitted unless constructed of stone or brick with slate or tile roofs. This law was similar to one passed half a century earlier but not rigidly enforced.

The seven-foot exemption was intended to apply to privies. It would have been absurd, the selectmen contended, to insist upon brick outhouses. The selectmen also voted to widen the streets; to increase by two the number of firefighters assigned to each engine; and to acquire one additional fire hook for pulling down walls and one more ladder for each rig.

All well and good. But they never got around to making stone or brick construction and fire-resistant roofs retroactive. Perhaps, in light of the economy and the fact that building stone was not of high quality, any strict enforcement would have been utopian. In any event, fire-prone housing remained and Boston continued to burn.

On a freezing January night ten months later, in 1761, flames swept through a row of wooden stores and into a produce market. Only its brick walls remained standing, and these had to be propped up with ladders. Over the vigorous opposition of many who thought the market not worth saving, Faneuil Hall was rebuilt and became the Cradle of Liberty. At the rate Boston burned, it is a miracle that anything remained to be designated a historical monument.

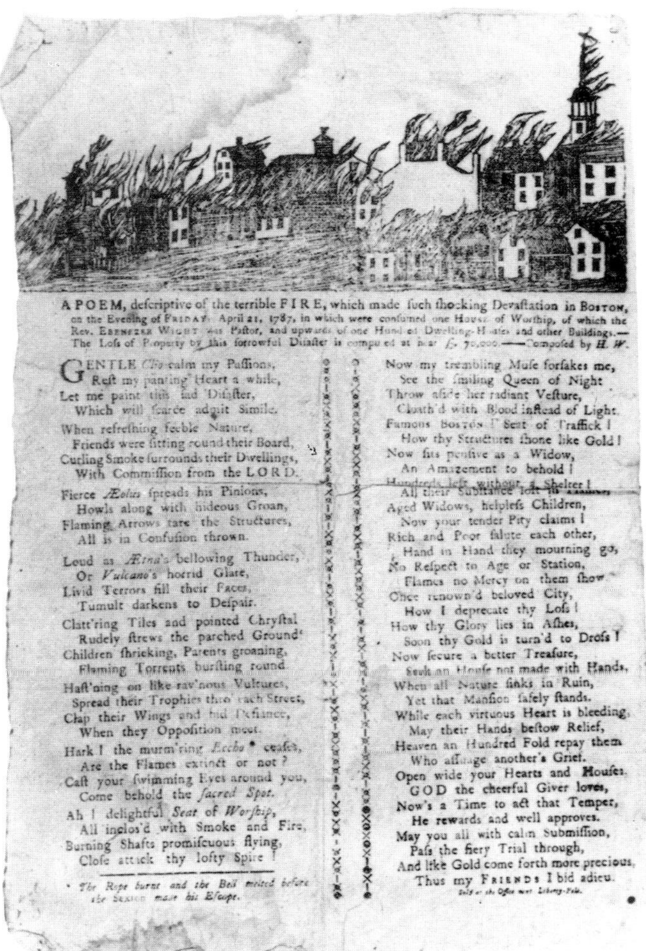

A POEM, deſcriptive of the terrible FIRE, which made ſuch ſhocking Devaſtation in BOSTON, on the Evening of FRIDAY April 21, 1787, in which were conſumed one Houſe of Worſhip, of which the Rev. EBENEZER WIGHT was Paſtor, and upwards of one Hundred Dwelling-Houſes and other Buildings.—The Loſs of Property by this ſorrowful Diſaſter is [illegible] at near £. 70,000.——Compoſed by *H. W.*

GENTLE *Clio* calm my Paſſions,
Reſt my panting Heart a while,
Let me paint this ſad Diſaſter,
Which will ſcarce admit Simile.
When refreſhing feeble Nature,
Friends were ſitting round their Board,
Curling Smoke ſurrounds their Dwellings,
With Commiſſion from the LORD.

Fierce *Æolus* ſpreads his Pinions,
Howls along with hideous Groan,
Flaming Arrows tare the Structures,
All is in Confuſion thrown.

Loud as *Ætna's* bellowing Thunder,
Or *Vulcano's* horrid Glare,
Livid Terrors fill their Faces,
Tumult darkens to Deſpair.
Clatt'ring Tiles and pointed Chryſtal
Rudely ſtrews the parched Ground
Children ſhrieking, Parents groaning,
Flaming Torrents burſting round
Haſt'ning on like rav'nous Vultures,
Spread their Trophies thro' each Street,
Clap their Wings and bid Defiance,
When they Oppoſition meet.
Hark! the murm'ring *Eccho** ceaſes,
Are the Flames extinct or not?
Caſt your ſwimming Eyes around you,
Come behold the *ſacred Spot.*
Ah! delightful *Seat of Worſhip,*
All inclos'd with Smoke and Fire,
Burning Shafts promiſcuous flying,
Cloſe attack thy lofty Spire!

* *The Rope burnt and the Bell melted before the Sexton made his Eſcape.*

Now my trembling Muſe forſakes me,
See the ſmiling Queen of Night
Throw aſide her radiant Veſture,
Cloath'd with Blood inſtead of Light.
Famous BOSTON! Seat of Traffick!
How thy Structures ſhone like Gold!
Now ſits penſive as a Widow,
An Amazement to behold!
Hundreds left without a Shelter!
All their Subſtance loſt [illegible]
Aged Widows, helpleſs Children,
Now your tender Pity claims!
Rich and Poor ſalute each other,
Hand in Hand they mourning go,
No Reſpect to Age or Station,
Flames no Mercy on them ſhow.
Once renown'd beloved City,
How I deprecate thy Loſs!
How thy Glory lies in Aſhes,
Soon thy Gold is turn'd to Droſs!
Now ſecure a better Treaſure,
Seek an Houſe not made with Hands,
When all Nature ſinks in Ruin,
Yet that Manſion ſafely ſtands.
While each virtuous Heart is bleeding,
May their Hands beſtow Relief,
Heaven an Hundred Fold repay them
Who aſſuage another's Grief.
Open wide your Hearts and Houſes,
GOD the cheerful Giver loves,
Now's a Time to act that Temper,
He rewards and well approves.
May you all with calm Submiſſion,
Paſs the fiery Trial through,
And like Gold come forth more precious,
Thus my FRIENDS I bid adieu.

[illegible]

Left: *This map of Boston shows the dates and locations of major fires in the town from the 1650s to 1722.* Above: *A Boston fire on the evening of April 21, 1787, was the inspiration for this poem.*

"BURNINGS BEWAYLED"

The distinction was dubious, but Boston historically had more fires and worse fires than any other colonial town. Before the Revolution, it experienced nine conflagrations, while America's two larger cities—Philadelphia (second in size only to London in the British Empire) and New York—had yet to have one. Why? Luck played a role. Fire was no less a threat in Philadelphia and New York, and their luck would one day run out, too. The main reason for Boston's sorry record was its flammable construction and the lax enforcement of fire-prevention and building laws.

More reasons come into focus by examining the history of America long before the Great Boston Fire of 1760. There was no room for fire apparatus aboard the crowded ships that brought the early colonists. Even if there had been, it is unlikely the settlers would have brought any. European-style pumpers were crude and ineffective, in any case. Firefighting apparatus had changed little since three hundred years before the birth of Christ.

Colonists followed European tradition when building their settlements. Structures went up, not out, and were clustered side by side. Tightly built colonial settlements offered protection against Indian raids. But early building materials—thatch for rooftops and wood for chimneys—created severe fire hazards. Boston began to have chimney-caused fires almost immediately after the town's incorporation on September 7, 1630. Thatch and wooden chimneys

Like the seaport of Boston, shown here in a view from about 1730, most colonial cities were fertile grounds for fire. With its wooden roofs, flimsy construction, and poor enforcement of fire prevention laws, Boston experienced more severe fires than any other city. It had nine conflagrations by the outbreak of the American Revolution.

Below: *A 1948 postage stamp honors the organization of the first volunteer firefighters—actually fire prevention officers—by Peter Stuyvesant.* Opposite: *Fire engines received their water from bucket brigades formed between the engine and the source of the water. Loaded buckets went up one line; empties came back down the other for refills.*

In case of alarm, however, New Amsterdam residents—like those in other colonial communities—were expected to turn out of bed and run for the 250 leather fire buckets—each about three gallons in size—plus the hooks and ladders that were strategically placed around neighborhoods. Fifty buckets hung outside City Hall and about ten apiece were located at various other well-known buildings, including a tavern and several houses, the sheriff's being one of them.

Colonists were often required by law to buy their buckets and to keep them in repair. These buckets were frequently decorated with the owner's name, address, type of business, and sometimes the family coat of arms. The number of buckets required could depend upon the fire risk to the building. In 1687, New Yorkers with no more than two chimneys needed but one bucket. A baker had to have three, a brewer six. From this tradition stemmed later fire regulations stipulating the number of fire extinguishers and other apparatus to be located in various types of commercial and public buildings.

In Boston and elsewhere, townspeople were ordered to place buckets of water on their doorsteps at sunset in case of predawn fires. During daytime hours or at night, the cry of fire, followed by "Throw out your buckets!" would be further spread by ringing bells in churches, forts, and town halls. The colonists first put out their buckets to be picked up and run with to the fire by people already on the streets. They were then expected to follow and to bring any remaining buckets.

Two lines of people quickly formed from the fire to the nearest well, pump, or river. One line passed along full buckets, which were dumped on the flames. The empty bucket would then be passed across to the other line, usually consisting of women and children, and the bucket went back for more water. Nobody was permitted to cross the brigade line. Anyone who tried or who refused to fall in and lend a helping hand would get a bucket or two of water dumped over him.

When the fire was out, buckets would be taken by cart to a common meeting ground. The town crier's bawling, "Hear ye! I pray ye, Lord masters, claim your buckets!" was the signal for townspeople to retrieve theirs. Sometimes the call touched off a scramble or a fight among children to retrieve buck-

ets belonging to wealthy citizens, for the reward could be a coin or a piece of cake.

If fires could be legislated out of existence, then Boston would have been spared. More laws followed when the town was hit by a conflagration at midnight, January 14, 1653, which leveled the most densely settled part of town and killed three children. The selectmen ordered every householder to provide himself with at least one ladder "that shall reach to the ridge of the house." Also ordered were poles "of about 12-feet-long, with a good large swab at the end" for beating out roof shingle fires. The selectmen purchased six "good and long" fire ladders to be hung outside the meeting houses, along with four new hooks, all to be branded with the town mark to deter thieves.

The selectmen then hired Joseph Jynks (or Jenks), an ironworker of nearby Saugus, to build "ingines to convey water in case of fire." This is the first recorded mention of a fire engine in America. There is conjecture whether the "ingines" were pumpers or only water-carrying tubs. Some lean to the idea that they carried a syringe, or siphon, of the type first developed around 300 B.C. and later used extensively in the Roman Empire. Water was ladled into the top of these cannonlike contraptions. The operator pushed a plunger and the water squirted out.

Still Boston burned. An early-morning conflagration destroyed about fifty homes and warehouses on November 27, 1676. Clearly, something better was needed than Jynks's "ingines," and the selectmen voted to buy the very best London had to offer. The best was not good. America's first practical fire engine—actually a device for pumping water, operated manually—was put into service on January 27, 1678. It consisted of a wooden box about three feet long and eighteen inches wide, standing on four legs, with protruding front and rear handles that enabled it to be carried to fires. Mounted inside was a pump that fed a flexible, snakelike nozzle, the water being supplied, as usual, by the bucket brigade.

Unlike latter-day fire engines with such romantic names as Lady Washington and Excelsior, this first engine was inelegantly named "ye Engine by ye Prison," for the obvious reason that it was located in a shed close to Boston's jail. The selectmen appointed America's first paid firefighting officer, Thomas Atkins, to captain the rig. Atkins's prime qualification was his carpentry trade—he could keep the thing in working order. Atkins appointed twelve assistants: Obediah Gill, John Raynsford, John Barnard, Thomas Eldridge, Arthur Smith, John Mills, Caleb Rawlings, John Wakefield, Samuel Greenwood, Edward Mortimer, Thomas Barnard, and George Robinson. Together they formed America's first paid fire department, a statement that must quickly be quali-

Opposite top: *Salem, Mass., volunteers pulled this engine to fires around 1748. Since the wheels did not swivel, the firefighters picked it up to turn round a corner.* Opposite bottom: *Scene with an early pumper imported from Holland.* Right: *Rattle carried by watchmen to report nighttime fires.*

fied. It is likely they got paid by the fire, plus something extra to keep the machine fit and to "exercise" the pumper in monthly training sessions. Boston's plan was the start of the American fire service's "on-call" system of firefighting, still used by many departments in smaller communities to assist paid men.

The selectmen later began another American fire service tradition by excusing firefighters from civic duties, including jury and military service. Faster responses to fires were encouraged, starting in 1739, by awarding a bonus of five British pounds to the first company to get water on a fire.

Boston's optimism that at last it had found a way to solve its fire problem was short-lived. A few months after the first fire engine in America was purchased, the pyromaniacs were active again, and despite "ye Engine by ye Prison," the city lost eighty houses and seventy warehouses in just one fire. Soon after the Great Fire of 1711, the selectmen—recognizing the great confusion resulting from the lack of organized and directed firefighting efforts at the scene of fires—appointed ten unpaid firewardens, one for each ward of the city.

Firewardens' duties were similar to those of today's fire chiefs, with a measure of police work thrown in. At fires, their authority was supreme. They directed firefighting and salvage. They could order a building to be hooked down or blown up. In each ward, they could order citizens to form bucket brigades, fine anyone who refused, and arrest looters and anybody who interfered with firefighting. Later, when "curiously cloaked ladies" distracted firefighters, a law was passed "which makes no Discrimination of Person or Sex." Any prostitutes loitering around fires would hereafter be ordered by the firewardens to help fight the blaze. To discourage looting, another law ordered Indians and blacks off the streets whenever fires occurred. Still, the problem remained.

The firewardens' badge was a five-foot-long pole, red in color and topped by a six-inch flamelike spiral of bright brass. The emblem embodied the English tradition of the mace carried by English Lord Mayors and the marshal's baton, an idea that perhaps explains how policemen came to have billy clubs. Edward Tufts, in his delightful monograph "Douse the Glim," says the firewardens' prickly pole "was not only a colorful badge of duty but came in very handy for an occasional push or prod to keep the crowds in line."

Perhaps of deep significance in explaining Boston's fire epidemic was the town's attitude. The Puritans believed that God used fire to punish sins. It was a belief rooted in centuries of religious tradition. Following the 1653 conflagration that killed three children, Governor John Winthrop said, "The Lord sanctifieth His hand to us all." The Puritan outlook was best summarized by Preacher Increase Mather in his sermon "Burnings Bewayled," which he delivered immediately after the Great Fire of 1711:

"Has not God's Holy day been prophaned in New England? Has it not been so in Boston this last summer, more than ever since there was a Christian here? Have not burdens been carried through the streets on the Sabbath day? Have not Bakers, Carpenters and other tradesmen been employed in servile work on the Sabbath day? When I saw this . . . my heart said, will not the Lord for this kindle a fire in Boston?" If Mather was correct, the instrument of that divine hand was a Scottish immigrant, Mary Morse, an indigent who started the fire—some say she was drunk—while working in her backyard slum in Cornhill.

Years later, Savage said the Great Fire of 1760 was "the Lord's doing." The conflagration was a blessing in disguise, he said, because it told Bostonians to mend their sinful ways. Savage's name, however, does not appear on any list of those 1,025 people who lost everything. Nobody thought to get their reactions.

3
PHILADELPHIA'S FIREFIGHTIN' BEN

That farsighted city planner, William Penn, never achieved his dream of a Philadelphia with houses built in the middle of squares and surrounded by trees and shrubs, "so that it may be a greene country towne which may never be burnt." But he came close enough. By the time of Boston's Great Fire of 1760, Philadelphia's buildings were mostly of fire-resistant brick and stone with slate roofs. The first bricks came as ballast in ships bringing the settlers. By the time of the Revolution, Philadelphia's brick industry was prospering, and the city's preponderance of brick buildings earned it the name, the Red Brick City.

Philadelphia was nearly half a century old in April, 1730, when it experienced its first major fire. The blaze on Fishbourne's Wharf destroyed some houses and warehouses. By Boston standards it was not much of a fire. But it was enough to prove that the City of Brotherly Love needed more than its lone fire engine, now twelve years old, to protect it.

Benjamin Franklin, who had lived in Boston prior to moving to Philadelphia in 1723, had had plenty of opportunity to see what fire could do and was not at all hesitant to exhort the readers of his *Pennsylvania Gazette:* "It is thought that if the People had been provided with good Engines . . . the Fire might easily have been prevented from spreading, as there was but little wind." Responding to this call, the Town Corporation ordered four hundred buckets, twenty-five hooks, and three new fire engines. One

Because of its predominantly brick construction, Philadelphia escaped the many serious fires that plagued other cities. When there was a fire, it usually was severe, such as this blaze that destroyed a new Lutheran church on December 26, 1794. The fire started at eight o'clock and raged out of control until midnight, when only the shell remained.

was purchased from Anthony Nicholls (or Nichols), a local mechanic, who doubtless built it along the European style.

The two other engines—both with wheels and pulled by hand—were ordered from Richard Newsham of Cloth-Fair, London, whose advertising broadside was widely distributed in the colonies. Newsham said he was an engineer, but some historians put him down as a pearl button maker. In any event, Newsham was not exactly a paragon of modesty. He boasted that his machine shot a stream with great force and would also water gardens "like small rain."

Newsham said, "All impartial Men of Art and Ingenuity will allow this, and the most prejudiced cease objecting when they see the effectiveness of this machine." The Londoner pointed out that he had "play'd these Engines before his MAJESTY and the Nobility at St. James's," and claimed that the king had immediately ordered one to protect the royal palace.

Newsham said the largest of his six sizes of pumps could squeeze through a three-foot passageway, which no other fire engine could do. The pump handles—also called brakes—could be worked either by hands and feet by means of treadles, or by hands alone. The pump could throw water four times farther than any competitor's pump. The four largest pumps were mounted on wheels; the two smallest were carried like a chair. Six men were required to operate the pump, three on each side.

The inventor said his machines were popularly priced because he had a "due Regard to the publick Good, as well as his own Profit." Prices ranged from twenty to seventy pounds. The pumpers could deliver from 30 to 170 gallons per minute (gpm) at distances ranging from twenty-six to forty yards.

Although there is no question that Newsham's pump was superior to anything available—faint praise, perhaps—credit must be given, too, to a mechanical genius of ancient Alexandria, named Ctesibius. Newsham's instrument was an improvement on that of Ctesibius, which was developed about 200 B.C. The Greek reputedly discovered the application of air as a motivating force in propelling water. Among his inventions were a water clock, an organ, and the pump.

Ctesibius's device was a two-cylinder single action pump shaped like an upside-down U. Forming the top of the ∩ was a pivoting crossbeam, or rocker, at the ends of which were attached the pump handles. The rocker was connected to the pistons or legs of the ∩. Both legs, each snugly fitted into a brass cylinder casing, stood in a tub of water. On the upstroke of the pump handle, one of the legs rose from the cylinder. Atmospheric pressure caused the cylinder to fill with water. On the downstroke, the water was driven from the cylinder and into an air chamber, or dome. The purpose of the dome was to smooth out the pulsations to create a steadier water flow.

The churning of the pistons up and down—alternately filling and emptying the cylinder casings—sent a continuous stream of water surging through the device, into the dome, and out the discharge opening. Newsham's device differed from Ctesibius's chiefly in its wheeled mobility. Otherwise, refinements were mainly cosmetic. The air chamber was concealed by a wooden housing at one end of the rig. Mounted atop this housing was a long, swiveling

Opposite: *Brass name plate* (top) *was mounted on rig of Philadelphia's Northern Liberty Company. Cape* (center) *is said to have belonged to George Washington, honorary member of the Friendship Fire Company, Alexandria, Va. Cape* (bottom) *is typical of those worn in parades.* Below: *Illustration from a 1725 advertisement for Newsham engines.*

gooseneck nozzle that connected to the discharge opening. The Ctesibius pump, in fact, was the basic principle behind every fire engine for more than two thousand years, until around 1920, when the American fire apparatus industry ceased the manufacture of hand pumps.

Philadelphia's fourth-size Newsham could discharge 90 gpm to a distance of 108 feet. The sixth size—the largest—had a discharge capacity of 170 gpm that went 120 feet. It was around seven feet long and just under two feet wide, with a deck standing twenty-five inches off the ground. Newsham's wheeled engines had one drawback, which he failed to mention in his advertisement—the handle for pulling it did not pivot. To turn the rig from one street into another, firefighters had to pick it up and swing it around.

The Quakers quickly compared the Newshams to their homemade Nicholls, and according to one account, the Nicholls won the day. The boast probably was pure hometown pride, because the Nicholls proved unwieldy, and the Newshams outlasted it.

While Philadelphia was buying its Newshams, New Yorkers were being swayed by the same advertisements. Some leaned toward first giving Zachary Greyaal's rig a chance. Greyaal offered a machine consisting of a large water barrel containing a gunpowder charge encased in thin metal. The inventor said that rolling the barrel into the burning building would cause the heat to ignite the powder. The explosion would release the water and the fire would go out. Skeptics asked what would happen if the fire gnawed a hole in the barrel and the water leaked out before the powder let go. That stumped Greyaal. New York decided to go with the Newshams.

On December 3, 1731, the city turned out to celebrate the arrival of the Newshams, aboard the *Beaver.* Like Philadelphia, New York bought a fourth- and a sixth-size. There was much speech making, and even the acting governor showed up. The Newshams—officially named Engine Company 1 and Engine Company 2—were paraded to their new sheds on the east and west sides of City Hall and put in service under the care of Aldermen Peter Rutgers and John Roosevelt. Four days later they got their baptism when they were hauled to a midnight fire in the attic of a carpenter's house. It was not an auspicious start: the house burned to the ground, and the one next door was damaged.

Thanks to Franklin's constant needling in the *Gazette,* Philadelphia could have been known as Fire Prevention City. While others were worrying about how to fight fires, Franklin was brimming with ideas on how to prevent them. "An ounce of prevention is

The Engineers and pipe men wher John Hay Jur
And Samuel Spangler. and the Company all
the Citizens at work. the had leather fire Buckets,
Hook.men-Michael Weitner. Laurence Jacobs, and
Joh Kraber. the ladder men Michael Schreiber.
Samuel Ilgenfritz. martin Smyser. all of the Citizens had
fire buckets in there houses. hanging up. Ready at the Alarm.

Above: *Early firehouses were little more than wooden sheds.* Right: *A portrait of Benjamin Franklin honors him for forming the first volunteer fire company in Philadelphia, though it shows him wearing a hat of nineteenth-century design. Franklin's Union Fire Company was organized on December 7, 1736. Its thirty members bought 180 leather fire buckets and sixty linen bags, "for preserving our own and our fellow citizens' houses, goods, and effects in case of fire." While some members of the Union Fire Company were fighting a fire, others would salvage as many of the victims' belongings as possible and put them in the bags. Franklin is credited with popularizing the concept of organized volunteer firefighting in America. He constantly crusaded for better fire protection and fire prevention laws through the pages of his* Pennsylvania Gazette. *Because of his efforts, fire prevention in Philadelphia was superior to that in any other city in the nation, and it remains outstanding to this day.* Opposite: *The city began to import Newsham engines from England around 1730. To send a stream from the nozzle, mounted on top of the engine, volunteers pumped the handles on each side. Newshams remained in use for many years, until manufacturers in this country began to build better apparatus.*

worth a pound of cure," he wrote around 1735, in describing the dangers of carrying hot coals in open warming pans from room to room. "You may be forced (as I once was) to leap out of your windows and hazard your necks to avoid being over-roasted."

Franklin campaigned for clean chimneys. "If chimneys were more frequently and more carefully clean'd," he wrote, "some fires might thereby be prevented." Franklin urged a system of officially appointed chimney sweeps who could be held accountable for their work. It took the aldermen nearly forty years to do it, but thanks largely to Franklin's persistence, they eventually licensed chimney sweeps and fined them if a fire occurred within a month of cleaning. Philadelphia's chimney laws differed from Boston's only in the degree of enforcement; no Philadelphian was immune. Five councilmen, two city officials, and even the mayor were found guilty of dirty chimneys. Franklin's suggested law became a model for other colonial towns.

Following much editorial urging for organized fire companies, Franklin and four friends formed their own on December 7, 1736. They called it the Union Fire Company. Membership was limited to thirty. Each agreed to buy six leather buckets and two linen bags to be marked with their names and company, "for preserving our own and our fellow citizens' houses, goods and effects in case of fire." The Union's articles provided that upon the outbreak of fire, members would put candles in their front windows to expedite the response of firemen through the dark streets. Union Fire members would, with buckets and bags, "immediately repair" to the fire. While some fought the blaze, others salvaged as many of the victims' possessions as possible, putting them in the drawstringed linen bags and then standing guard against thieves.

Franklin modeled Union Fire after Boston's mutual aid societies, the first of which was formed September 30, 1717, while Franklin was still a Boston

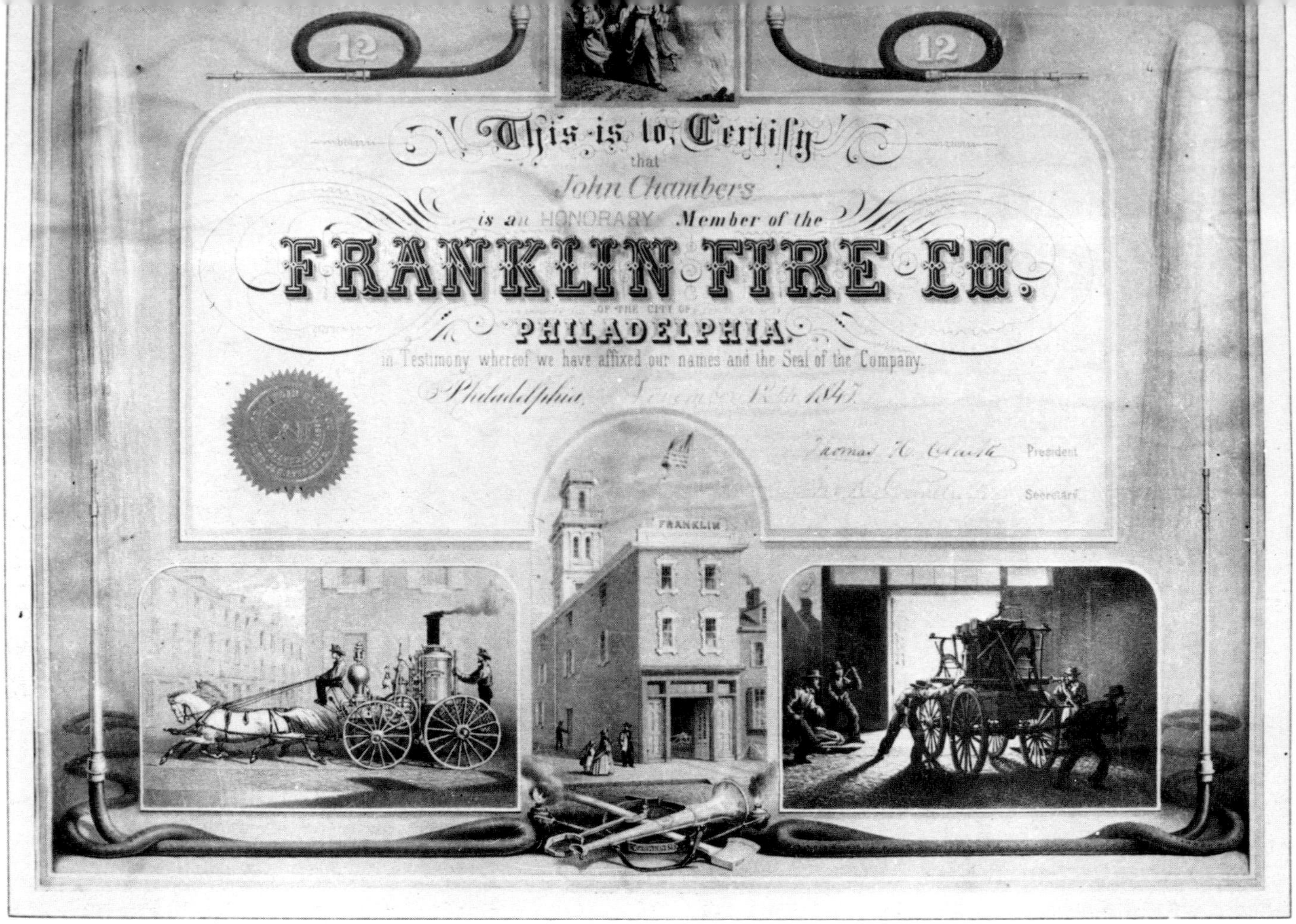

12 12

This is to Certify
that
John Chambers
is an HONORARY Member of the

FRANKLIN FIRE CO.

OF THE CITY OF

PHILADELPHIA.

in Testimony whereof we have affixed our names and the Seal of the Company.

Philadelphia, ... 1847

Thomas H. Clark President

Secretary

FRANKLIN

TO ASSIST THE SUFFERING AND PROTECT THE WEAK

INSTITUTED FEBRUARY 20TH 1752

INCORPORATED SEPTEMBER 20TH 1841.

THIS CERTIFIES THAT

Anthony Morin HONORARY Member

of the **Hibernia Fire Engine Company No. 1** of the

FIRE DEPARTMENT OF THE CITY OF PHILADELPHIA

Signed Active Roll March 30th 1840.
Transferred to Honorary R. Oct. 30th 1857

President.

Secretary

1752 1752

1

HIBERNIA

resident. Their purpose was "mutual aid in case it should please Almighty God to permit the breaking out of Fire in Boston." Like Franklin's Union Fire Company, the Boston societies mostly had limited memberships, usually prominent citizens such as James Otis, orator and lawyer who fought the Stamp and Townshend Acts, and John Cotton, famed Puritan clergyman. Each Boston mutual provided himself with two water buckets, two salvage bags, a bed key, and a screwdriver. (The last two instruments were used to take apart beds prior to their removal from burning buildings, for beds in those days had special meanings—a person could be born, procreate, and die in the same one.) Each mutual kept a book listing names and addresses of fellow members' homes and businesses. The Boston societies' primary purpose was to fight fires and save the property of fellow members. Franklin took the Boston idea one step farther and served everybody.

Like Boston societies, the Union Fire Company had business meetings eight times a year, followed by dinner and socializing. Members were fined for tardiness or failure to attend; the fines were used to replace equipment. (Franklin himself was to pay his share while he was attending to the business of the Continental Congress and serving as American representative in Paris.) The Union Fire Company remained active for more than eighty years.

Although Franklin popularized what was to become the concept of organized volunteer firefighting in America, he was not popular with one Andrew Bradford, editor of the rival *American Weekly Mercury.* In 1738, Bradford organized the Fellowship Fire Company. Fellowship's formation stemmed from Bradford's dislike of Franklin. If imitation is the sincerest form of flattery, Franklin should have been flattered. The articles of Fellowship were nearly identical to those of Union. But Bradford did Franklin one better. Fellowship upped its charter membership to thirty-five so that it could claim to be the largest fire company in the city.

Fellowship marked the only time a fire company was formed as a result of a feud between newspaper editors; it also began the rivalry that was to characterize American volunteer companies. The year after Fellowship was organized, the Union Fire Company—in a feat of one-upmanship—bought a pumper from London. Franklin was, of course, put in charge.

Twelve other Philadelphia fire companies soon were formed, including the Hand-in-Hand in 1742, whose members claimed they were "the most eminent men in Philadelphia, embracing merchants, physicians, lawyers, clergymen and citizens of wealth and refinement." By 1771, the mayor and nearly all members of the city corporation would belong. Companies proliferated up until the Revolution, often from common religious and business associations. The illustrious Hibernia, for instance, consisted of Protestants and second generation Irishmen. Philadelphia shoemakers formed the Cordwainers company before 1769.

In his *Autobiography,* Franklin could pridefully say: "I question whether there is a city in the world better provided with the means of putting a stop to beginning conflagrations; and in fact, since these institutions, the city has never lost by fire more than one or two houses at a time, and the flames have often been extinguished before the house in which they began has been half consumed."

More than two hundred years later, Philadelphia still enjoys the benefits of Franklin's fire-prevention legacy. A city with severe fire problems, it has nevertheless consistently won more national awards per year for fire prevention than any other major American city. In 1961, in honor of the hundredth anniversary of the paid Philadelphia Fire Department, the city honored its debt to Franklin by placing a large bust of him near the fire station closest to Independence Hall. The bust, by the sculptor Reginald E. Beauchamp, is covered with eighty thousand pennies donated by Philadelphia schoolchildren.

Opposite top: *Philadelphia's Franklin Fire Company was named after Benjamin Franklin, who constantly campaigned for better fire prevention.* Opposite bottom: *Hibernia Engine was one of Philadelphia's most illustrious fire companies.* Above: *Newsham pumper like those used in Philadelphia. It could discharge water to a distance of about 120 feet.*

4 START OF A COLORFUL ERA

On December 16, 1737, the New York General Assembly created an organization that, in the 127 years of its illustrious existence, became more famous and colorful than any other American firefighting organization. The act establishing the Volunteer Fire Department of the City of New York called for appointment of "strong, able, discreet, honest and sober men."

Thirty-five volunteers were initially appointed. In contrast to Philadelphia's silk-stocking companies of the elite, New York's was a blue-collar lot of carpenters, coopers, blacksmiths, gunsmiths, shoemakers, bakers, shipyard workers, and ropemakers. The man in charge was Jacob Turck, a gunsmith, who three years later devised America's first fire hat. It was made of leather with a high crown and a narrow brim.

The act formed the basis for rules and regulations in countless other cities and towns that would set up their own volunteer fire departments. "Upon notice of the happening of a fire," the act said of the volunteers, "they are to take the engines and assist in its extinguishment, and afterwards to wash the engines and preserve them in good order." If absent from a fire without reasonable cause, the volunteers would be fined twelve shillings. They were "once in each month to exercise the engines, so as to keep them in good order." Neglect of duty would cost the volunteer his appointment. Volunteers were exempt from serving in the "several offices of a constable, surveyor of the highways, juries, inquests, or doing military duty except in cases of invasion or other imminent danger."

In addition to the two Newshams purchased by the city in 1731, the volunteers started with a good supply of ladders, poles, hooks, and axes. New York was relatively free of fires during the first years of the company; but all that changed starting on March 18, 1741, when the fort and the governor's house were destroyed. A plumber's carelessness was blamed. A week later a house was damaged. Careless smoking next caused a storehouse blaze. Three days later came a hay fire. The volunteers were returning from that one when they got an alarm for a fire in a kitchen loft where a black man slept. The following day burning coals were discovered in John Murray's stable on Broadway. Further minor house fires occurred during the next two days.

Rumors spread that blacks were plotting to burn New York. While the magistrates were meeting to

Opposite: *The first fire mark of the Insurance Company of North America, used to identify insured buildings.* Below: *Charleston, S.C., volunteers pull down a flaming house.* Bottom left: *The cry "Throw out your buckets!" was the signal to fling buckets into the street. Runners took them to fires.* Bottom right: *Early fire axes.*

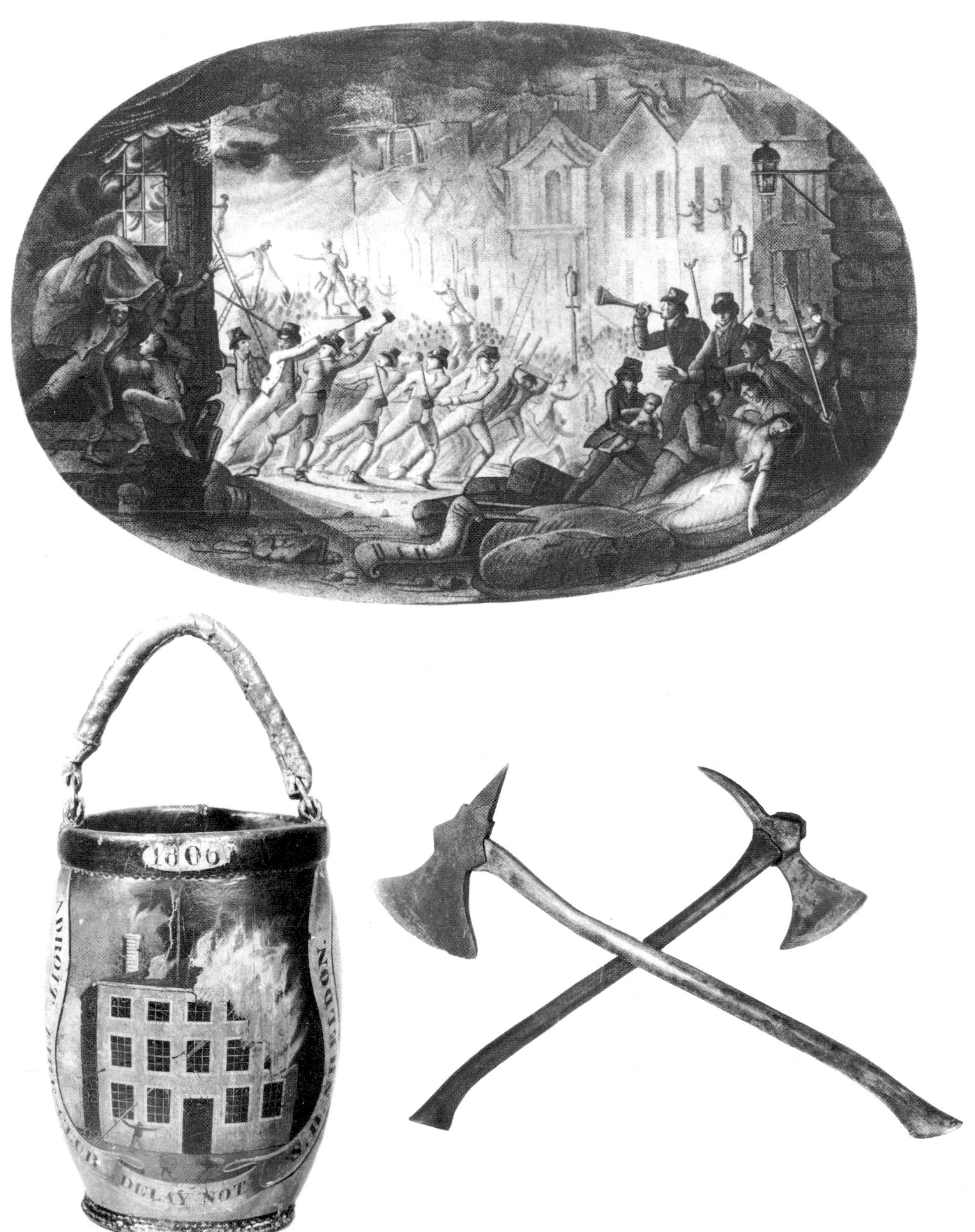

There was as yet no fire apparatus industry in America, aside from shoemakers, who fashioned the leather fire buckets; carpenters, who made ladders; and blacksmiths, who forged the hooks and axes. The slow start was partly due to English pressure on the colonies to buy British-made goods, and partly to the fact that technology was lacking. But however slow the start, America would one day become supplier to the world of the finest firefighting apparatus.

Before the Revolution, a number of makers began trying to improve upon the Newsham-Ctesibius design. Among them were David Wheeler, John Green, and John and Thomas Hill, all of Boston. One Bostonian came up with a horse-drawn rig, but it proved too cumbersome to be practical. Wheeler and Green supplied Boston with a pumper, which apparently met with such success that Charlestown acquired one, too. In New York, William Lindsay claimed his pumper could discharge "two hogsheads

investigate, flames were discovered coming from the roof of a storehouse. New York panicked. Blacks were jailed indiscriminately. The common council voted a one-hundred-pound reward and a full pardon to informers. One hundred fifty-four blacks were imprisoned. Eighteen were hanged, fourteen burned at the stake, and seventy-one deported; the rest were pardoned or freed for lack of evidence. During the same period, twenty-four whites were jailed, four of whom were executed.

Whatever the reasons for the epidemic of fires, it was plain that better firefighting apparatus was needed than the Newshams and other imported rigs. Newshams nevertheless continued to be popular and soon began arriving in Boston. In Charleston, South Carolina, poor whites and black slaves were forced to operate them. Refusal resulted in the imposition of a five-pound fine on whites; blacks suffered thirty-nine whiplashes.

Opposite top: *The mark of the Philadelphia Contributionship, America's first successful fire insurance company, formed in 1752.* Opposite bottom: *The mark of the Mutual Assurance Company, organized in 1784, also known as the Green Tree Company.* Below: *Richard Mason began to build end-stroke engines such as this one in Philadelphia in 1768.*

of water in a minute, in a continuous stream"; prospective customers were invited to call upon him at the Fighting Cocks Tavern, one of New York's notorious dives. Few American builders came up with anything near the equal of Newsham's engines or those built by Ragg (probably a Newsham partner) and Nuttal in London, or those built on the Continent, especially in Germany and Holland.

An exception was Thomas Lote, a New York cooper and boat builder. In 1743 he sold New York an engine shaped like an upside-down T. It, too, followed the Newsham principle, except that the covered air chamber was located in the center of the pump, with the pumping handles at the ends (instead of the sides, where Newsham put them).

The Lote engine was the first successful pumper made in New York. Although officially designated Engine Company 3, it was better known as Old Brass Backs, because Lote made extensive use of brass on the box that covered the pumping mechanism. It is

not known how many engines he made, if indeed he made more than one. The engine was stationed near Kalch-Hook Pond in lower Manhattan and was apparently manned by farmers, because the name Old Brass Backs eventually gave way to "Hayseeds."

Philadelphia was the site of the first successful American fire apparatus manufacturer. In 1768, Richard Mason—a carpenter and member of the Northern Liberty Engine Company—placed the pump handles on his engines fore and aft, just as Lote had done. This end-stroking made it easier for bucket brigade men to feed the pump's cistern; the resulting faster entry of water meant better pumping capabilities. Mason widely advertised that his engines were of white oak or cedar with "the joints of the cistern lined with copper." Interested parties could examine its virtues by visiting Northern Liberties Engine, one of the first to acquire a Mason.

Mason's prices compared favorably with Newsham's. His engines, moreover, carried a seven-year guarantee and came in four sizes. The smallest required six men, who could pump water 80 feet. The most powerful could shoot water 120 feet and needed fourteen men. In addition to its end-stroke design, the success of Mason's engine was due to a growing resentment in America toward British-made products.

End-strokers were dubbed "Philadelphia-style" engines and won a large following. Mason and his son, Philip, continued the business until around 1806. They are believed to have built at least 119 pumpers, which were sold throughout the United States and in the West Indies. As with Newshams, Philadelphia-style Masons spawned many imitators.

All this time, Benjamin Franklin was coming up with still more ideas about fire protection. On April 13, 1752, he became a founder of what most authorities consider the first successful fire insurance company in America, the Philadelphia Contributionship for the Insurance of Houses from Loss by Fire. Insurance was not a new concept in the colonies. Several companies had been formed on the model of those organized in England following the Great Fire of London, on September 2, 1666, which had destroyed thirteen thousand buildings. But apparently most, if not all, of the American companies foundered near their outset.

Following British practice, the Philadelphia Contributionship designed a distinctive mark, which was to be hung at the second-floor level of insured buildings. The company hired John Stow—who later recast the Liberty Bell to make it ring better—to cast one hundred leaden marks, which were mounted on small wooden shields. The design—four hands clasped and crossed—gave the firm its popular name, the Hand-in-Hand company. Today, more than two hundred years later, the Philadelphia Contributionship is still active, the oldest fire insurance company in the United States.

A rival insurance company—the Mutual Assurance Company for Insuring Houses from Loss by Fire—was formed in 1784 when the Contributionship refused coverage on buildings close to trees. The reasoning was that trees attracted lightning—Franklin's influence again!—and hindered firefighting, and that chimney sparks landing in them would cause fires to spread more rapidly. The mark of Mutual was a leaden tree mounted on the wooden

shield, and it henceforward became known as the Green Tree company.

In the years preceding the Revolution, insurance companies multiplied, and hundreds of distinctive marks were hung outside buildings throughout America. When the British occupied Philadelphia and New York, they seized the marks, melted them, and recast them into bullets. The marks were replaced after the Revolution, but they gradually disappeared with the organization of paid fire departments. Today they are highly prized by a host of collectors, who have organized a club, the Fire Mark Circle of the Americas.

Fire marks originally served several purposes. They discouraged arsonists—who set fires out of spite—by serving notice that the victim's property would be replaced by the insurance company. More important, as far as firefighters were concerned, the marks virtually guaranteed that they would receive a bonus for holding damage to a minimum.

Before volunteer fire departments were organized, fires often touched off pandemonium. All able-bodied men and women were expected immediately to drop what they were doing, grab their buckets, and rush to the scene, or help drag along the hand-operated pumper. Bucket brigade lines were quickly formed, and anybody crossing the line could expect a bucket of water to be dumped on his head. The absence of organization in firefighting was one reason for the massive spread of flames, as in this blaze, which has involved three big buildings and is threatening more. The Philadelphia-style end-stroke pumper (right center) *would be more effective if it were placed closer to the fire. And the two men who are chopping down the tree* (right), *perhaps in panic, would be more helpful if they joined in the rescue of the person trapped on the second floor of the building next to them. The scene took place in York, Pennsylvania, in 1805.*

5 THE FIERY SPIRIT OF '76

Snow blanketed Boston around 9:15 that night of March 5, 1770, when the Town House bell urgently began ringing out a fire alarm in King Street. Firefighters ran for their pumpers, while others brought buckets and salvage bags. Among them was Samuel Maverick, age seventeen, of North Cooper Engine, No. 2. Other townspeople quickly gathered near the King Street Custom House only to find that the alarm was false. It is unclear who turned it in, but many suspect the British troops of the Twenty-ninth Regiment. For months there had been frequent fights and rioting between troops and townspeople, and the redcoats personified a whole list of grievances against the Crown.

Some in the crowd that moonlit night turned for home, but most remained and began to taunt the Custom House sentry. Reinforcements quickly arrived: Captain Thomas Preston and a squad of eight redcoats. The taunting quickly escalated into a bitter exchange of threats; the redcoats fired into the crowd; and eleven townspeople fell, five of them fatally wounded. When the smoke cleared, the bloody body of Samuel Maverick lay sprawled beside his fire bucket and salvage bag. Maverick was the first American firefighter to fall in the cause of liberty. He would not be the last.

The Boston Massacre, as it came to be called, was not the start of the profound involvement of colonial firefighters in the events leading to the inevitable war.

The burning of New York on September 21, 1776, after Washington and his troops had evacuated the city. Firefighting was hampered because New York's fire engines had been sabotaged and holes had been cut in fire buckets. New York's first Great Conflagration destroyed nearly 500 buildings. The British executed many citizens found carrying matches.

Long before the Revolution, colonial fire companies had become power bases for rallying protests against the king and local Tories. In Philadelphia, the King George III fire company changed its name to the Delaware, and Lutherans scratched out the name of their fire company, Queen Charlotte, and adopted "Fame." Protesting the duty on wool with the passage of the Stamp Act, members of Philadelphia fire companies Hibernia, Sun, Fellowship, Crown, and Beaver vowed to stop eating lamb to promote the growth of homegrown flocks. The Hand-in-Hand Fire Company threw out member John Hughes, the Stamp Act agent in Philadelphia. Similarly, Boston's Free-American Fire Company booted out John Mein, a Tory printer. The Anti-Fire Stamp Fire Society said they would look the other way if fire happened to break out in Boston's Stamp Office.

Up to the Revolution, colonial firefighters had known only fires caused by defective chimneys, arson, carelessness, or punishment by the deity. But throughout recorded history fire has been a powerful weapon of war. Exactly how devastating it could be, patriots and Tories would soon learn.

With the approach of hostilities, colonial towns examined their fire protection for anticipated extraordinary wartime demands. Boston had nine companies and around two hundred firefighters to protect a population of 16,000. New York's 25,000 people had seven engines, two ladder and bucket companies, and 170 firefighters. Philadelphia, America's largest city with 40,000 people, had 170 firefighters, eight engines, and around twenty companies on the order of Franklin's Union Fire Company.

The colonists began beefing up their fire protection. New York started to build an eighth station but never finished it. In some cities, wealthy citizens bought pumpers and donated them to firefighters. John Hancock, while serving with Samuel Adams as a firewarden, presented a pumper to Boston and stationed it near Hancock's Wharf. Selectmen ordered that "in case of fire the estate of the donor shall have the preference of its service." The engine was named Hancock No. 10, and fourteen firefighters were appointed to operate it. A year following his famous ride in 1775, Paul Revere was appointed firewarden.

Baltimore apparently lacked a similarly public-spirited wealthy citizen. The town organized its first outfit, the Mechanical Fire Company, in 1763. For six years it had to rely solely upon buckets, ladders, and axes. A lottery failed to raise money to buy two fire engines. When a Dutch ship arrived in port in 1769, however, firefighters learned that an engine was on board, and that the captain was willing to sell. The firefighters scraped together ninety-nine pounds and Baltimore got its first engine, which was named Dutchman. Although Holland-made, the Dutchman closely resembled a Newsham.

Prominent citizens of Alexandria, Virginia, started that community's first fire protection with the organization on August 13, 1774, of the Friendship Fire Company. (The outfit still remains in existence.) Members ran to fires with leather buckets and salvage bags until a year after their founding, when they received as a gift their first fire engine. The donor was George Washington, who bought it for eighty pounds, ten shillings while he was in Philadelphia being named by the Continental Congress as commander in chief of the army. He became an honorary member of Friendship.

Washington had a lifelong interest in firefighting. Legend has it that as early as 1750, when he was eighteen, he occasionally galloped on his horse from Mt. Vernon to nearby Alexandria to help fight fires. He often visited local fire companies during his travels. In May, 1775, while en route to Philadelphia with delegates to the Continental Congress, the Washington party stopped in Baltimore. They were escorted to a reception at the Fountain Inn by the Mechanical Fire Company and three outfits of militia. For entertainment that afternoon, the Mechanical Company demonstrated how fast they could get the Dutchman into action and how far they could throw water.

Harper's Magazine in February, 1880, reported: "In the last year of Washington's life, a fire occurred near the Market House in Alexandria. He was riding down King Street, followed by his servant, also on horseback, and he saw the Friendship engine poorly manned. Riding up to a group of gentlemen, he said, 'It is your business to lead in these matters.' Throwing the bridle of his horse to his servant, he leaped down and seized the arms, followed by a crowd that gave the engine such a 'shaking up' as had never been seen before."

Boston simmered in the years leading to the ultimate break with England. A month following the April 19, 1775, skirmishes at Lexington and Concord, the city was swept by rumors that the Sons of Liberty planned to burn it down. The Liberties—a secret group whose members included Samuel

Following the American Revolution, volunteers frequently decorated their apparatus with paintings that had a patriotic flavor. This panel, showing the Battle of Lexington, was one of four patriotic panels that volunteers of Lexington Engine Company of New York hung on their pumper during parades. Firefighters often paid hundreds of dollars for each panel.

Adams and Paul Revere—were loose organizations of radicals. Preparing for the worst, the British took command of the town's engines and posted guards around the fire stations.

On May 17, flames were discovered in a building used as barracks by British troops on the south side of the Town Dock. "Soon as I observed the fire," said a Bostonian, "the bells not ringing, I cried 'Fire,' but was stopped by a soldier who said it was against orders and who threatened to knock my brains out if I did not keep still. When I arrived at the fire there was no engine. I asked the reason of such extraordinary delay, and was told by an engine man that he had been to his engine, but the bayonets were too thick.

"After the fire had been long raging the engines arrived with their new captains and military firewards, and not being used to such an enemy, they, indeed, cut a miserable figure. Upon the whole, it appears to me as plain as the meridian sun that, if the engines had been on the old footing, the fire would have been quenched and twenty-thousand pounds saved." Thirty buildings were destroyed, including one of Hancock's.

The Battle of Bunker Hill erupted exactly one month later, to the day. Preparatory to attacking a thousand colonials who were fortified on Breed's Hill, June 17, 1775, General William Howe landed at Charlestown. Around 2:00 P.M., he ordered troops to burn the town. It was an inexcusable act and helped to solidify public opinion against the Crown. From hills, housetops, and windows, Bostonians watched the battle through the boiling clouds of smoke and flame. Three hundred eighty-seven buildings burned far into the night. Charlestown was a foretaste of conflagrations to come.

On New Year's Day, 1776, a British Royal Navy flotilla bombarded and burned Norfolk, Virginia. Three months later, the Navy took eleven rice-laden ships in the Savannah River. Colonial militiamen set fire to the ship *Inverness* and sent it drifting across the river. The *Inverness* smashed into the rice ships, destroying seven and severely damaging three others. The whaling town of New Bedford, Massachusetts, was wiped out on September 4, 1778, by British troops who also set fire to twenty-eight ships.

On July 4, 1776, the Declaration of Independence was signed. A number of the signers were firefighting volunteers, including John Hancock; Ben Franklin; James Wilson, jurist; Dr. Benjamin Rush, later surgeon general of the Continental Army; George Clymer, a prosperous merchant; Francis Hopkinson, lawyer, writer, and composer; and Robert Morris, a banker who was to become known as the financier of the Revolution. All except Hancock and Franklin were members of Philadelphia's Hibernia Fire Company. So, too, was Continental Congressman Thomas Willing, a merchant-banker who cast his vote against the Declaration of Independence but raised much money for the Continental Army. The Declaration of Independence was read to the assembled people by another Hibernian, John Nixon.

In New York, meanwhile, the 134-member Volunteer Fire Department formed two battalions of home guards under Jacob Stoutenburgh, who reported to General Washington. Stoutenburgh had succeeded fellow gunsmith Turck five years earlier as head of the department. The volunteers armed themselves with muskets and bullets made by Stoutenburgh, Turck, and other fire department gunsmiths. Stoutenburgh's title of overseer quickly evolved into chief engineer and, later, chief. He became the first American firefighter to be officially known by that title. When the British occupied New York on September 15, 1776, Stoutenburgh and his men abandoned their fire apparatus and fell back with Washington's troops to Harlem.

Perhaps, as some authorities say, General Washington considered burning New York as he abandoned it but was overruled by Congress. In any event, incendiaries did what Washington most likely thought of as he gave up the city to the British.

Between one and two o'clock in the morning of September 21, six days after the occupation, flames burst through the roof of the Fighting Cocks Tavern. The saloon was a notorious brothel on a wharf at the southeasterly tip of Manhattan Island.

The weather had been unusually dry, and a vigorous offshore wind quickly jammed the flames into six nearby buildings. There was no way to sound a general alarm, for Washington and his retreating army had carried off all the bells to melt them into munitions. Captain Joseph Henry, a patriot recently returned from the Quebec campaign, was watching from the deck of a ship about four miles out. As he recorded shortly thereafter in his memoirs, *Campaign Against Quebeck:* "A most luminous and beautiful, but baleful, sight occurred to us—that is, the city of New York on fire."

Henry said the fire first appeared to be "the size

Below: *Flames sweeping through brick buildings in New York are fought by volunteers using the city's two Newsham engines.* Bottom: *An early Newsham pumper. Built in England, Newshams were the first significantly improved fire engines since the Great London Fire of 1666. They were widely used in the United States and Europe for nearly a century.*

Below left: *Fire buckets such as this one were frequently decorated with patriotic motifs during and after the Revolution.* Opposite: *Burning of Charlestown, Mass., ordered by British General William Howe on June 17, 1775, just before the Battle of Bunker Hill. No fire during the war had greater impact upon public opinion than this one.*

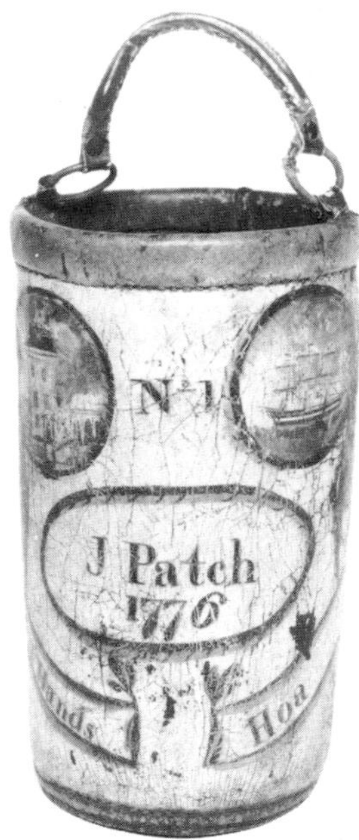

of the flame of a candle." The freshening wind quickly spread the flames. Henry and watchers aboard other ships noticed another spiraling flame off to the west of the first; then another, and still another. To some there appeared to be six fires.

It could be argued that perhaps the wind, encouraging the original fire, was sowing firebrands and starting new blazes ahead of the rapidly advancing one at the Fighting Cocks. Unlike most of New York, which was of two-story brick construction, the Whitehall area was a rat's nest of wooden buildings with shingled roofs. While historians cannot agree who started the fires, the evidence is overwhelming that it was not the British—for days later, cartloads of pine sticks dipped in sulfur were found hidden in the basements of buildings abandoned by patriots who had fled with Washington.

When the townspeople, patriot and Tory, who had remained behind went for the fire engines, they discovered that the engines had been sabotaged. Holes were sliced in the bottoms of fire buckets. British officers sent troops to find blacksmiths, shoemakers, and machinists to make repairs as the fire spread in a northwesterly direction.

Soon dozens of buildings between Whitehall and Broad Streets and as far inland as Bowling Green were in flames, which boiled hundreds of feet into the early morning sky. Troops managed to get some of the engines working, but their inexperience quickly showed in their ignorance of the best positions in which to place the pumpers. The lack of organized firefighting was marked by much shouting of orders. Everybody was a chief; nobody was a firefighter. The flames poured across Broadway and lit up still more buildings. Like a string of up-ended dominoes, block upon block of buildings caught fire from the heat.

"When the fire reached the spire of Trinity Church, the effect upon the eye was astonishingly grand," said Captain Henry. "If we could have divested ourselves of the knowledge that it was the property of our fellow-citizens which was consuming, the view might have been esteemed sublime, if not pleasing. The deck of our ship, for many hours, was lighted as if by noonday."

Boatloads of sailors rowed ashore to help fight the fire. There they saw the bayoneted body of an American hanging by his heels and were told he had been caught in the act of firing houses. They saw another suspected incendiary tossed into the fire. Several people caught stealing and others accused as arsonists were bayoneted. The sailors had seen enough. They returned to their ships.

At dawn, lower Manhattan was shrouded in ugly clouds of thick black and gray smoke while, toward the east, white smoke oozed from the dozens of burned-out buildings. Throughout the day the flames chewed northward as the smoke-grimed troops and a few citizens did their best with the faltering fire engines and whatever buckets could be fixed. Slashing across Manhattan, from the East River almost to the Hudson, the flames veered north with the changing wind.

About the only thing that was not halted by the conflagration was the trial of schoolteacher Nathan Hale, accused of spying on British forces on Long Island. Quickly found guilty, he was taken to the smoky gallows that day and hung.

Flames raged through dozens more buildings during the day and finally stopped when they reached the open grounds of King's (later Columbia) College, near where Barclay Street, City Hall, and Park Street are today. New York's first Great Conflagration destroyed nearly five hundred buildings, about one-fourth of the city. The British seized about two hundred people, many of whom were hanged or bayoneted for carrying matches.

Two years later, on August 3, 1778, another early morning fire started in a ship chandlery on Crugar's Wharf, not far from where the Great Conflagration had begun. Again the military pumped the engines, and again the fire got out of hand. Nearly seventy homes and stores were destroyed.

New Yorkers would have been happy to see the volunteer firefighters return—but few did. Throughout the long war, men who had once fought blazes side by side fought together against another common enemy. Cannonballs and muskets made no distinction between silk-stockinged Philadelphia and blue-collared New York firefighters. It is not known where most of these firefighters fell, but records indicate there was hardly an action in which they did not participate.

New York's volunteers were at Valley Forge, at Trenton, and at Princeton. Although nearly all were killed in these various engagements, at least a few were on hand to taste victory at Yorktown. Boston firefighters also fell by the dozens, including Captain Shubael Hews of Marlborough Engine, No. 5, the company that first got water onto Mrs. Mary Jackson's burning house in Cornhill Street at the start of the Great Boston Fire of 1760.

Many Hibernians formed the First Troop of Philadelphia cavalry and rode off to war. One of them, George Fullerton, was killed when a pistol accidentally discharged while General Washington was reviewing troops near Trenton. Walter Shee was taken prisoner at the Battle of Long Island. John Mease was with Washington during the crossing of the Delaware River the night before the Battle of Trenton. Colonel Nixon fought in the Battle of Long Island and was at Valley Forge. Many achieved high military rank, including Walter Stewart, at twenty-one the "boy colonel" who went on to become a brigadier general.

Hibernian Nicholas Biddle captained the thirty-two-gun frigate *Randolph,* which raided British shipping. The *Randolph* exploded and sank on March 17, 1778, while in action against His British Majesty's *Yarmouth,* which had twice as many guns. Only four men survived when the *Randolph* went down off Barbados, British West Indies. Captain Biddle was not one of them.

FIRE FEVER

When they returned from the Revolution, the volunteers found their apparatus gone or broken. New York's situation was typical. Only two of the city's seven prewar engines remained; only one worked. New York created a department of thirteen engines, two hook and ladders, and three hundred firefighters, and the call went out for volunteers. There was no lack of recruits, especially among veterans.

Why would war-weary men with a bellyful of regimentation volunteer for a dangerous job that paid nothing and required regular, militarylike training drills and mandatory attendance at company meetings? Why would they volunteer to get out of bed in the dead of night, often during a blizzard, to fight fires in somebody else's house or shop?

One influence was a holdover from pre-Revolutionary years, when all able-bodied men were expected to take an active part in community affairs—a concept at least as old as the Massachusetts Town Meeting. The newly won independence strengthened that resolve, for now the men were protecting cities they could truly call their own. Second, male citizens had the choice of either becoming volunteers or serving in the militia and on juries. With all its perils, firefighting was more exciting than close order drill or sitting in a courtroom, and it had an added plus: plenty of young ladies to watch the men in action. But the most compelling reason was best given by Theodore Keeler, a New York volunteer: "If a

This Hunneman-built engine (below) *sported a painting of a woman on its water box. Firefighters often decorated their apparatus with nudes, as did New York's Mazeppa Hose No. 42* (opposite bottom) *and Americus Engine No. 6* (right) *with its "Translation of Psyche." America's first hose wagon* (bottom right) *was built in Philadelphia in 1803.*

Opposite: Top: *Gooseneck pumper, named for swiveling nozzle on top of the engine.* Bottom left: *Pat Lyon engine from about 1810 (left), hydraulion built by James Sellers in 1820, and two wooden hydrants, in front of a Philadelphia firehouse.* Bottom right: *Engine built by Pat Lyon in 1812 for the Washington Fire Company of Philadelphia, organized in 1796.*

fellow took a fancy to going to fires, you might as well kill him as try to stop him."

From every city neighborhood came applications for a company charter. Members were given certificates, which became more and more elaborate in style as years went on—highly ornamented documents depicting the American flag, crossed axes, ladders, helmets, trumpets, the firehouse, and the fearless firefighters battling a blaze and rescuing women and children. A certificate became as highly prized as a sheepskin from Harvard or Yale and for similar elitist reasons, however blue-collar the volunteers may have been.

Companies were run with paramilitary discipline. Officers, including the foreman—a rank similar to today's fire captain—were annually elected by members. A system of fines helped to ensure discipline and to provide additional funds for upkeep of the company and annual dinners. Accused members were tried during company meetings, where guilt or innocence was voted and fines assessed according to bylaws. The worst punishments were for failure to answer alarms, failure to return to the firehouse to wash the rig and hose after a fire, and failure to attend drills. The result of such transgressions could be expulsion.

A volunteer could be fined twenty-five cents for failing to wear his helmet or badge to fires, fifty cents for missing a meeting, and, in the case of New York's Engine Company No. 42, "Introducing politics at meetings, improper behavior, using indecent language, swearing or being intoxicated at any meeting: $1.00." Members of Engine Company No. 13 were fined twenty-five cents for "smoking a segar or chewing tobacco in the Engine House." By today's values, the fines were trifling, but they were substantial in those times.

Company journals in which handwritten entries recorded all activities—a tradition that remains in today's fire stations—began at least as early as 1791, at New York's Engine Company 13. The journal showed: "January 15, 1807. (Fire at 1 A.M., in Fair Street.) Harris Sage's excuse for absence is received. He says at the time of the above Fire he was lock'd in some one's Arms and could not hear the Alarm." The journal does not record his fine.

Fines for failing to answer alarms were rare, however. Volunteers developed a compulsion to drop whatever it was they were doing, whenever and wherever they were doing it, to rush to fires. For years New York volunteers told the story of John H. Waydell, who, having just said his marriage vows, left his bride when the alarm sounded. He did not return until the fire was out the next morning.

Although companies were officially designated by number—Engine Company No. 1, Hook & Ladder Company No. 2—the members disliked the anonymity of numbers as much as people do today. Distinctive names gave the members a greater sense of identity. You were somebody in the community when you could show you were a member of the Knickerbockers, the Excelsiors, Good Will, or Mutual Hook & Ladder.

Names often reflected the patriotic motive for becoming a volunteer. Many companies honored their former commander in chief, as did New York's Washington Engine Company No. 20. Martha Washington was the inspiration for Lady Washington Engine Company No. 40. Other names signified independence: Bunker Hill, Jefferson, Franklin, Lafayette, Union, Eagle, America, and United States. There was hardly a community that did not have at least one of these names in its volunteer roster.

Sometimes companies found themselves saddled with other names. On December 9, 1796, an early morning wharf fire on New York's Coffee House Slip spread to as many as seventy waterfront buildings. Flames forced Union Engine Company No. 18 firefighters to save themselves and their rig by pushing it into the East River and jumping in after it. Forever after, Union Engine's men were known as the Shad Bellies.

Eagle volunteers were in a Madison Avenue alehouse celebrating the election of new officers when an alarm sounded. Stuffing their hot mutton pies in their mouths, they were seen rushing from the saloon to their rig. Eagles they were, but other companies ever after called them Mutton Hose. Lady Washington turned into the White Ghost, not because the pumper was painted white—which it was—but because its members boasted they were so fast on their feet that they could race past any other company going to a fire. Other volunteers could not seem to recall any such feats, and said if Lady Washington passed anybody it must have been while they were white ghosts.

Amid this hoopla, the volunteers looked for better apparatus than bucket brigades, Newsham-type pumpers, and other engines from Europe. There was, first of all, a critical need for more effective

VIGILANT

This is to Certify

That Richard T. Wellington is Elected

MEMBER OF THE Vigilant FIRE COMPANY

Philadelphia Decr. 11th 1827

Attest Davd. P. Auston Secretary Geo. W. Ryan President

machines. Also, there was an intense desire to be able to do a better job of firefighting than neighboring companies.

After the Revolution, America began burning as it never had before. Although fires were relatively infrequent, they were severe. Boston lost 100 buildings on April 20, 1787. In March, a year later, more than 800 buildings were destroyed in New Orleans. Twelve Philadelphia volunteers were killed on May 9, 1791, when walls from a burning block of buildings came crashing down upon them. Savannah lost 229 buildings on November 26, 1796, and the village of Detroit was almost completely wiped out by fire on June 11, 1806.

A New Yorker wrote that the rash of severe fires had reached epidemic proportions. The city was suffering from "fire fever." Boston's Mayor Josiah Quincy said fire was the worst problem challenging American cities.

There were many reasons. Cities were growing, and industrial development was adding new hazards. Building construction was flammable. Clustered as they were along narrow streets, entire blocks of buildings became breeders of conflagration. Wood shingle roofs posed fire hazards of the worst sort, especially when fires coincided with strong winds. America's largest cities were at least a century old after the Revolution, and their aging buildings were ripe for burning. As America built upward, fires in taller buildings required better water supplies at higher pressures and longer ladders. But ladders were short, and water supplies and pressure were poor at the start of the nineteenth century.

Furthermore, cities could not afford paid firefighters, and often only the largest of them could afford any kind of adequate fire protection. Communities often went without fire protection until a major fire forced the issue. In Norfolk, Virginia, and other cities, wealthy residents bought apparatus when the city failed to do so.

Eager and dedicated as the volunteers were, they were disadvantaged from the start. The critical moments of a fire occur during the first few minutes after it starts—for there are no instant conflagrations; they all sprout from small fires. Delayed alarms and slowness in getting apparatus and firefighters into action have always been factors contributing to conflagrations. And at the start of the nineteenth century, alarm systems were haphazard and would continue to be so for another forty years.

When someone managed to alert the volunteers, they had to rush to the firehouse and wait for others to arrive to help them haul the rig to the fire. Much time was lost, and the exhausting effect upon the firefighters of dragging and carrying heavy equipment to fires can be imagined. There followed an

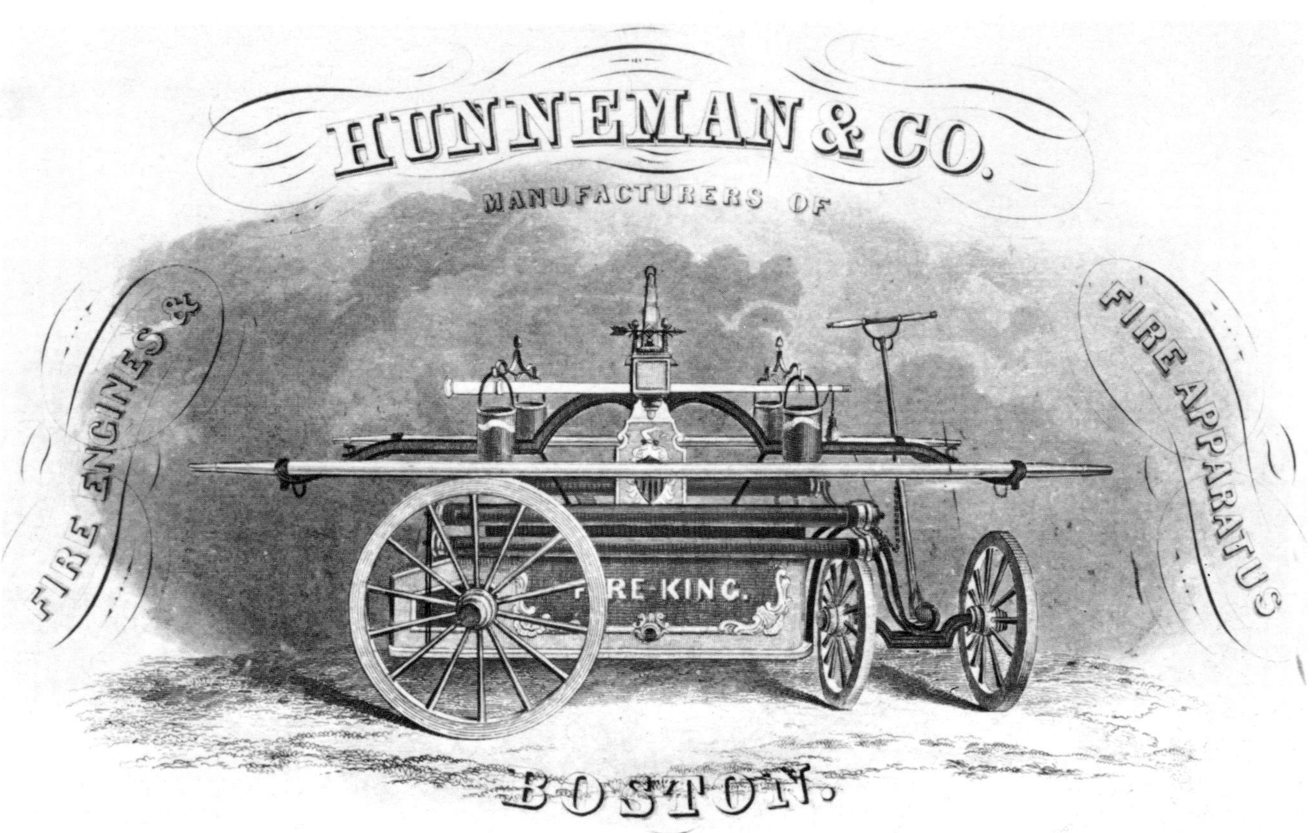

Danvers Fire Department.

THIS CERTIFIES,

That *Jacob C. Peasley* is a Member of **Engine Company** No. *3* and is entitled to all the privileges and exemptions of Enginemen, for and during one year, unless this Certificate shall be sooner revoked.

John W. Proctor President.

Fitch Poole Jr Secretary.

DANVERS, *April 9.* 183*2*

Opposite: *Patent diagram depicting New England-style engines, which were mostly built in Boston. Figure 1 shows the engine in its pumping position. Figure 2 illustrates the air chamber and the two pistons mounted at a 45-degree angle. The three other figures explain the pumping mechanism.* Top: *Engraving advertising Hunneman & Company's Fire King engine. Starting in 1792, the Boston company built 716 hand-operated engines, more than any other firm. They were popular because of their light weight and their mobility, made possible by the crane-neck frame.* Above: *Volunteer's membership certificate from Danvers, Mass., showing that town's gooseneck engine.*

even greater exertion while they fought flames and saved lives.

Nor could the situation improve while firefighting tactics continued to be defensive. For more than a century, a basic firefighting premise was to write off the involved building—pull it down or blow it up if necessary—and concentrate efforts on saving adjacent buildings. If the American firefighter had any hope of reversing the situation, he would have to go on the offensive by carrying the attack to the fire. Somehow he would have to get inside the building with equipment to put out the flames before they spread beyond control. Even under the best of circumstances, this approach was both dangerous and difficult.

But the main reason why American cities burned as fiercely as they did was that apparatus was lacking in quality and quantity. This problem, combined with a competitive spirit and an increasing emphasis upon home industry, spurred the development of the American fire apparatus industry, although many engines continued to be imported. By 1812, there were around a dozen manufacturers, most of them in New York, Philadelphia, and Boston, of which four—James Smith, William C. Hunneman, Ephraim Thayer, and Patrick Lyon—achieved lasting success.

Nobody knows who came up with the gooseneck, the first improved version of the Newsham, but the man who became famous for it was James Smith. He built five hundred such engines starting in New York in 1812.

Goosenecks had first appeared in that city around 1785. Their name resulted from the curved water pipe that led from the air-chamber dome through the roof of the wooden housing that enclosed the condenser case. A swiveling connection at the end of the pipe permitted attachment of a long nozzle. Instead of turning the entire apparatus to point the stream, as with the Newshams, volunteers could easily turn just the nozzle in the desired direction. This was the origin of today's apparatus-mounted nozzles—sometimes called turret pipes, deck or deluge guns, Big Berthas, or wagon batteries—which are capable of delivering huge quantities of water.

Another shortcoming of the Newsham engine was its lack of maneuverability. To round corners, the volunteers had to lift the entire rig and turn it. The front axle of goosenecks, on the other hand, pivoted on a fifth wheel. Goosenecks followed the Newsham pumping principle but were more powerful. In addition, they carried as much as two hundred feet of leather hose, on a covered reel just ahead of the air chamber housing, whereas Newshams carried none. Additional rolls of hose often were carried to fires on volunteers' shoulders. Still another innovation was the attachment of a keg to the front of the rig. Volunteers elected a company steward—he had to be a thoroughly reliable man—to keep the keg filled with gin, brandy, or other spirits. Pumping in winter always seemed to go better with an occasional nip from the keg.

Boston volunteers got their early apparatus from William C. Hunneman and Ephraim Thayer, former apprentices of Paul Revere. Hunneman made pots, kettles, and other hardware before producing his first engine in 1792. Its brakes—or pump handles—were mounted along the sides as in Newsham's design, and were swiveled into a front and rear position for fighting fires. Hunneman pumpers were famous for their light weight and mobility, and were soon in demand in the United States and throughout the world. Edward Tufts, foremost Hunneman authority, has calculated that in the firm's ninety-one years of production, the company built 716 hand engines, more than any other American builder.

Ephraim Thayer and his son, Stephen, began building engines two years after Hunneman. Their firm followed a similar design and continued in business up to 1860, making about a hundred engines.

A Philadelphia blacksmith, Patrick Lyon, began his fire engine company in 1792. His pumpers had front-and-rear mounted brakes, similar to those of the earliest Philadelphia makers, Richard Mason and his son, Philip, who built the first successful American engine in 1769. Lyon's larger and more powerful pumpers were exceeded only by his claims of their superiority. Lyon offered an eternal guarantee, stating that if anybody ever built a better engine than his, he would rise from his grave, make a better one, and give it to the volunteers free. He is not known to have made good on his promise, but while he was still alive he sold around 150 rigs, one of which is said to have been the first horse-drawn apparatus in the United States. Because of muddy roads, Good Will Fire Company of Philadelphia, established in 1802, used a horse to haul their Lyon, while other companies continued to pull theirs by hand.

The arrival of a volunteer company's new rig was always cause for a celebration. City-supplied apparatus usually was drab gray to begin with, and it was up to the volunteers to make their rigs outshine any other. Few women have had more affection lavished upon them than the volunteers lavished upon their apparatus. They appointed committees, and chose her wardrobe often only after considerable debate.

Was the "enjine" of the nearest company painted red? Then the volunteers were sure to vote theirs green, white, blue, vermilion, orange, lilac, yellow, plum, maroon, black, or any distinctive combination of colors that struck their collective fancy—as long as the rig was, in their eyes, prettier than any in the district. With the color chosen, the volunteers anted up more funds to deck her out in silver-, gold-, brass-, and copperplate; solid silver and gold inlays; gold scrollwork; hand-painted lettering and numbering; mirrors; leather insets; silver lanterns; and jeweled signal lights with red, blue, and crystal lenses.

No pumper was complete without at least one painting, and many had more than four. The four-sided condenser boxes and the leather-covered hose reels provided excellent showcases for the paintings, which were usually done on mahogany panels. Some of America's foremost artists were hired for the job. The first panel painting was probably commissioned in 1796 by New York's Peterson Engine Company No. 15, which chose a wreath of roses as decorative motif. Engine 15 subsequently took the name Old Wreath of Roses. Black Joke Engine Company No. 33—named after a famous privateer in the War of 1812—hired an artist to paint Black Joke capturing two British merchantmen. If the volunteers could not agree on a subject for their painting, they left the choice to the artists, who dreamed up such impressions as "The Translation of Psyche" and "Othello's Courtship." Panels were rarely carried to fires, but were hung from the rigs during parades.

The gooseneck of New York's Knickerbocker Engine Company No. 12 was green and yellow with hand-carved dolphins decorating her sides. From her case hung a painting of Diedrich Knickerbocker smoking his pipe. Oceanus Engine Company No. 11 was a rich crimson, heavily gilded. The panel committee could not decide upon a single theme so it compromised on four portraits: Helen of Troy, Udora, Neptune, and Commerce.

Quaker merchants and clerks painted their gooseneck, Eagle Engine Company No. 13, a shiny black with gold striping. Their rig was the first in New York to feature silver-plated brasswork. Her panel showed Jupiter hurling thunderbolts. Jefferson Engine Company No. 26 was royal blue with gold trim. Its members called themselves the Blue Boys.

The men of Brooklyn's Engine Company No. 7 decked out their rig in varnished mahogany, rosewood, polished steel brake arms, and blue wheels with gilt stripes. A white "Seven" was inlaid on the shiny black patent leather hose jacket. One of her panels showed a full-sized eagle perched on a rock with wings outstretched and a claw clenching an American flag; in the distance was depicted the USS *Constitution,* Old Ironsides, in command of the sea. Above the painting was the company motto, Union Forever. An oval panel showed a firefighter saving a woman by carrying her across burning rafters. Another panel depicted a beautiful lady crowning a heroic firefighter with a wreath.

St. Louis volunteers of Engine 2, the Emperor, painted their pumper blue with vermilion rails and gilt striping. The gleaming brasswork was finely engraved with the motto, In Union There Is Strength. A panel showed an Indian on horseback spearing a buffalo. Surrounding the hose connections was a carved American eagle holding arrows in its talons. The Emperors bought parade uniforms to match their rig: blue shirts, white trousers, red patent leather belts, round-topped and low-crowned blue hats, and red silk scarves that fastened at the neck with gold "2" emblems.

New York shipbuilders who formed Engine Company No. 44 took the name Live Oak after the wood used for frigate hulls. Following a trip they made to Constantinople to build a ship, they affected Turkish beards and long hair and took on a new name, Old Turks. They outfitted their maroon and blue gooseneck with carvings of two costumed and sabre-carrying Turkish figurines. On the engine box hung a painting of a woman with outstretched arms. The company's motto: We Extinguish One Flame and Cherish Another.

The volunteers' grab bag of gewgaws and attention grabbers stretched as long as their imaginations and their funds. Zophar Mills, foreman of Eagle Engine Company No. 13, who later had a New York fireboat named after him, said, "I kept an account of my expenses in connection with the Fire Department, and I found that in seven years I had paid three thousand dollars." The saying is nearly forgotten today, but "All dressed up like a fire engine" was once common in America. It is easy to understand why.

HOOSE, HOASE, HAUSE

What the volunteers gained by their distinctive names, colors, and decorations was not matched by their firefighting effectiveness. For this they could hardly be faulted. They did the best they could with their small pumpers, poor water supplies, leaky hose, and ladders too short to reach upper floors. That there were not more conflagrations and greater loss of life was testimony to their efforts.

The volunteers were a determined lot, and their ingenuity brought many improvements. That some of their ideas worked and many did not never dulled their enthusiasm. For example, they encouraged manufacturers to develop imitations of the coffee-mill type of engines imported around the time of the Revolution. In these, side-mounted cranks turned an axle that rotated a gear, while the teeth of the gear scooped water from the box and sent it through the nozzle. Coffee mills were the first rotary-type fire engines in America.

A variation of the rotary was the cider mill or windlass engine. With this engine, long poles extending from the rotary pump were pushed by men or horses running in a circle around the rig. None of these pumps enjoyed great success. Rotary firefighting engines would not become practical until steam- and gasoline-driven pumps provided the greater power required for effectiveness.

Rotaries appealed, however, to a group of New York volunteers who formed a distinctively new type of fire company. In 1800 they built America's first fireboat. Stationed on the East River at the foot of Roosevelt Street, this Floating Engine or Floater was a scow with a sharp bow and a square stern, and the coffee mill mounted amidships. The Floating Engine was rowed to fires by twelve volunteers. Wintry weather often made for rough rowing around the tip of Manhattan to reach fires along the Hudson River. But despite these extraordinary demands upon the firefighters, the fireboat remained in use for twenty-four years.

A group of merchants and accountants hit upon an easier and warmer way to fight fires. Taking the abandoned Floating Engine's coffee mill, they mounted it inside a wooden firehouse built over one of the deepest wells in the city. Supply Engine volunteers stayed comfortably warm while they cranked out water through hose connected to as many as three pumpers fighting neighborhood fires. Many companies resented the Supply Engine company, but none refused the water. The company enjoyed the distinction of having the only engine in the United States that never left its firehouse.

Until around 1800, American communities drew drinking and firefighting water from wells, cisterns, and natural bodies. There were less than twenty waterworks throughout the Republic. On January 27, 1801, however, Philadelphia began to operate its water main system, which was supplied by the Schuylkill River. It was the best in the country. In the same year, Chief Engineer Frederick Graff of the Philadelphia Water Works designed the first post-type hydrant, in the shape of a T with a fire hose connection on one side and a spigot for drinking water on the other. The leg of the T was a pipe 4½ inches in diameter, which fitted into a wooden main consisting of hollowed logs snugged end to end. The hydrants were successful, and on December 6, 1802, more were ordered from Foxall & Richards, a local ironworks that had cast cannon barrels for the Revolutionary armies.

With water in good supply, Reuben Haines, a member of Philadelphia's Fellowship Engine, came up with an idea for a new type of fire apparatus—a hose wagon, which could work either from supply engines or directly from hydrants. Hose wagons had another advantage—they enabled volunteers to run to fires with around three times more hose than could be carried by engines, whose hose capacity was limited by the weight of the pumps. On December

Philadelphia's Masonic Hall burning on the evening of March 9, 1819. Firefighters were hampered by the lack of ladders long enough to fight the flames more effectively. The painting shows the volunteers in parade capes, although it is unlikely that they wore them while at work.

15, 1803, Haines and twenty other youthful Quakers formed America's first hose company, Philadelphia Hose No. 1.

Patrick Lyon was hired to build the rig, a four-wheeled rectangular box about seven feet long with a twenty-four-inch-deep hose bed. The wagon was painted olive green on the outside and red on the inside, where short lengths of hose, 600 feet in all, were folded. A nozzle was hooked to the side. Lyon charged ninety-eight dollars for the rig, and the volunteers bought hose—spelled in contemporary advertisements variously as "Hoose," "Hoase," and "Hause"—for forty-three cents a foot. Philadelphia Hose turned out to its first fire on March 3, 1804, when the Israel stables burned in Whalebone Alley.

The novelty of the hose wagon caught the fancy of other young Philadelphians, and more companies were formed, including Good Intent Hoase. No doubt a strong part of the appeal was the glamour that went with being up front at a fire and squirting water on the flames. Certainly, the firefighter who held the nozzle was more in the limelight—as any young lady could plainly see—than those behind him who laboriously stroked the pumps. Hose companies proliferated, and by 1823 there were nineteen of them in the city. The hydrants were opened with a

Above: *Philadelphia's waterworks, opened in 1801, the best in the nation.* Below: *The system supplied water to wooden mains that fed hydrants similar to these.* Opposite top: *Baltimore volunteers run out hose to fight a theater fire.* Opposite bottom: *Hose carriage built by Jeffers & Nuttall for Southwark volunteers, Philadelphia, with spring-suspended bells, delicate wood carvings, and silver and nickel plating.*

special wrench called a spanner—today among the most frequently used firefighting tools—and a spanner insignia became the badge of authority for Philadelphia fire officers.

In contrast, New York volunteers were slow to form hose companies, mainly because of the city's poor water supply. In 1799, Aaron Burr and Alexander Hamilton had helped to form the Manhattan Company and built the first waterworks. (The company's excess income was used for investments that formed the Bank of Manhattan, later Chase Manhattan Bank.) Because Manhattan slopes from north to south, water flowed by gravity from streams and springs north of City Hall to a 132,600-gallon reservoir that fed a slightly underground system of hollowed pine logs.

To obtain water, firefighters dug down to a log, cut a hole, and filled their engines from the bubbling water fountain. Afterward, they stopped the hole with a wood plug, from which the word fireplug originated. Some of these wooden mains are occasionally unearthed by excavators in New York and other cities.

Manhattan's sporadic supplies and low pressures disappointed the volunteers, who fell back upon using the forty cisterns dotting the city. They knew they could always get water from these wells—which had a capacity of one hundred barrels—because they were filled daily by jail prisoners using old fire engines. Otherwise, the firefighters had to draw from the Hudson or the East River. They calculated that it would require twenty-six engines to relay water from either river to reach a fire in the middle of Manhattan Island. It was only a matter of time before New York paid dearly for its poor water supply system.

Hoseman Haines was not the only Philadelphia Hose volunteer brimming with ideas. Two members of his company, James Sellers and Abraham L. Pennock, came up in 1807 with a method for improving leather hose by using metal rivets to bind the seams. Up to that time, seams were stitched the way shoemakers made boots. But stitched leather hose leaked badly and could not withstand the higher water pressures that the newer pumps could deliver.

Before this innovation, hose had changed little since around 1672, when Jan and Nicholaas van de Heide (or Heijden) first made leather hose in Amsterdam, Holland. Some historians claim an earlier hose was used around 400 B.C. That hose consisted of ox gut. According to the Athenian painter Apollodorus, firefighters filled bags with water and forced it into the ox gut. Water was jetted onto the flames by sitting or stomping on the bag and gut.

Sellers and Pennock made their hose from the

thickest and best rear-quarter cowhides. The hides were cut into pieces three feet long, which were then folded over to form a tube; the ends and joints were riveted together. Hose lengths ran from forty to fifty feet and weighed more than eighty-four pounds, including the metal couplings. But despite its weight, the hose was immediately popular. Sellers & Pennock were able to form a manufacturing company that sold hose throughout the United States. Western makers who copied their design used buffalo hides. In 1816, Sellers & Pennock began to make fire apparatus, too, and for eleven years built hose carriages and engines.

Riveted hose was not the ultimate answer. It lacked the flexibility of rubber hose; but rubber hose would not be developed for at least another quarter of a century, when, in 1839, Charles Goodyear discovered the vulcanization process that led to the growth of the rubber industry.

Leather hose, moreover, required great care to prevent rot or cracking. Every company had its favorite method of washing, drying, and preserving it. Philadelphia's Diligent Hose washed theirs in a coffin. That city's Humane Hose stored it in a dill-pickle barrel—but the hose rotted anyway. Some companies used codfish and whale oil or other preservatives. Probably the most accepted method was to mix warm beef tallow with neat's-foot oil made from cattle bones and massage the mess into the hose. The heat of a fire brought out the full aroma of this goo, and made the hose sticky. Hose was often stored in horizontal racks. Much later would come the traditional firehouse towers where hose was hung vertically to drip dry.

The significance of Sellers & Pennock hose for American firefighting cannot be overemphasized. Sturdier hose spurred development of suction, the ability to draw large quantities of water quickly and directly into the engine, rather than the slow method of dumping it in by buckets. The suction principle was known as early as 1698, and New York had, in 1793, stationed a suction engine at the rear of City Hall. Practical development of the idea was delayed because suction required a stronger hose than the old leather type. Sellers & Pennock hose met that requirement.

By 1819, all New York engines were retrofitted with suction capabilities. The city repealed its law requiring all householders to provide and maintain fire buckets. The first apparatus manufactured with suction hose and fittings was produced in 1822 by Sellers & Pennock. The rig went to Providence, Rhode Island, where it was named Hydraulion No. 1. A hydraulion, sometimes called hydraution, was an

Opposite: *Members of Philadelphia's Hibernia Hose Company gathered around their hose carriage, in front of their brick firehouse.* Above: *A hook and ladder truck bought by the Philadelphia Fire Company in 1799. Its equipment included three ladders and eight buckets.*

end-stroke pumper with a single piston and a reel of hose. Because of the engine's weak stream, and the combined weight of the pump and hose, the rigs were unwieldy and were never popular.

The new hose made it more practical for pumpers to relay water to the fire from distant sources. The pumper at the source suctioned water into its apparatus, and the men at the brakes then pumped the water through a discharge hose leading to the next pumper in line, which relayed the water to others until the pumper nearest the fire sent the water surging through the nozzle and onto the flames. Boston's Mayor Josiah Quincy noted in 1825 that one hundred feet of hose did the job that formerly required sixty men with buckets. A few years later, Chief Harry Howard of the New York Fire Department counted thirty engines pumping in a line a mile and a half long between the water and the fire. The era of fire engine tubs filled by leather buckets was nearing an end.

Better hose and hose wagons touched off a scramble among volunteers to acquire rigs that could give them a jump over other companies in getting into action faster. Four-wheel hose reels that spun out precoupled hose gave the edge to Philadelphia Hose's competitors. In 1819, David J. Hubbs, ex-foreman of Eagle Engine Company No. 13 in New York, built a fast cart with only two wheels. These "Hubbs' Babies" were pulled by two firefighters or were attached to the rear of the engines.

The hose reel craze set off new waves of ornamentation, especially when it hit New York. Oceana Hose Company No. 36 decorated their rig with paintings of Oceana surrounded by nymphets rising from the sea, a group of Indians near the Harlem Bridge, a small girl washing her feet at a hydrant, and a boy squirting a hose.

A rich plum color along with carmine wheels and blue panels set off Forrest Hose Company No. 30. The paintings showed Diana, the Goddess of the Chase, and a nymph beside a waterfall. Another painting showed a girl putting a fish into a basket. The company motto, Fearless of Danger, was hand-lettered in gilt across the front. Above it was an ornate signal lamp with red and blue lenses.

The rig of First Ward Hose Company No. 8 was tan with exquisite gold striping. Her silver-plated reel was set off by solid silver castings, including eagles with the number "8" in their bills. Red glass lamps, silver-engraved with the seal of the city, were topped by solid silver cedar trees calling attention to the company's Cedar Street location.

The black of Independence Hose Company No. 3 was highlighted by gold striping, polished silver, and gold fittings. A painting of the Boston Tea Party was on one side of her reel and the Battle of Bunker Hill on the other. Other paintings depicted the signing of the Declaration of Independence and Colonel Ethan Allen demanding the surrender of Fort Ticonderoga.

The most expensive rig in the United States was that of Amity Hose Company No. 38. Its members, wealthy New York businessmen, commissioned Pine & Hartshorn, a local carriage and fire equipment builder, to make a hose reel of the finest hard wood, painted snow-white with blue stripes. The rig was heavily silver-plated, including the two large trumpets mounted up front. The trumpets were set off by twin gold lamps with red lenses. The lamps were pineapple shaped. Exquisite paintings of two cupids and a mermaid rising from the sea completed her attire. The outfit cost eight thousand dollars.

Opposite: *Signers of the Declaration of Independence are shown in this banner carried by Philadelphia's Independence Hose Company 3.* Below: *Hose reel built by Charles Hartshorn in 1837 for New York volunteers. Two-wheel rigs, the idea of Firefighter David J. Hubbs, were called Hubbs' Babies and were pulled by hand or attached to fire engines.*

In comparison, hook and ladder companies did not proliferate and were not able to come up with better apparatus, although the volunteers tried. Development of ladders that could reach upper floors was hampered by length and weight factors. Ladders were necessarily short so the trucks could turn corners. Volunteers partially solved that problem by building rigs with rear wheels that turned by means of a wooden tongue, or tiller, extending from the rear axle. Later, they mounted a steering wheel and seat over it. The volunteer who rode up there became the tillerman.

Weight problems were more difficult. Extension ladders around seventy-five feet long were the longest the volunteers could raise by hand. Effective ladders that could be mechanically extended to greater heights would not be developed until after the Great Chicago Fire of 1871, when a San Francisco firefighter, Daniel D. Hayes, figured out a solution.

Despite these drawbacks, the hook and ladder volunteers competed with the other companies in decorating their rigs and winning acclaim for their rescues. The Mutual Hook and Ladder No. 1 volunteers of New York painted their truck jet black with gold stripes. Over the front they hung a signal lamp with brass scrollwork and the company number ground into crystal. Mutual's exploits inspired a Hoboken baseball team to name themselves after the company, which in turn then became known as Mutual Ball Club Hook and Ladder Company No. 1.

RIVALRY AND ROWDYISM

While they gussied up their rigs and polished the brasswork, the volunteers discussed ways to shave seconds off the time it took them to get to fires. Company pride and prestige were built by being able to outshine others in the district.

There also were the cash bonuses cities and insurance companies awarded the first companies to reach a fire. Engine Company No. 5, the Old Honey Bees, boasted they could buzz out of their fire station so fast and be the first to sting fires that they had won twenty first prizes of thirty dollars each in five years, more than any other New York outfit. Asked how they did it, the Honey Bees would say only that they threw their boots out of the upstairs windows of the firehouse and got down to the street before the boots did. Surprisingly, nobody thought of the sliding pole. That would not come until after the Great Chicago Fire of 1871.

In 1819, a Boston volunteer company came up with a novel idea. They loaded their rig with water so they could begin pumping as soon as they reached the fire. The idea was so good that there is hardly a fire department today that does not have apparatus that carries water. But in 1819, Boston officials cried foul play. They said carrying water to fires gave the company an unfair advantage over others in competing for first-water bonuses. So the volunteers dumped their water, and one of the best ideas to hit the American fire service fell into limbo for years.

Anguished mother (right center) *watches as a firefighter saves her child, in a lithograph from "The Life of a Fireman" series by Nathaniel Currier. Volunteers stroked their hand pumps in time to the cadence called by their foreman. The best was about sixty strokes per minute.*

A basic weakness of the volunteer system was the delay in getting to the fire. Firefighters were not often at the station when the alarm sounded. The problem was especially acute at night, when most of the serious fires occurred. The volunteers solved the problem by renting rooms above their stations or in nearby stores, hotels, and churches. They bought bunk beds to begin what firefighters today call bunking in.

Old Turk Engine volunteers turned out fast to night alarms by tucking their trouser legs into their boots and keeping their bunkers, as they called the assembled outfit, beside their beds. When an alarm hit, they shoved their feet into their boots and pulled up their trousers. Early one morning, the Old Turks were astonished to find Frank Clark arriving at the rig before them. Then they saw how he did it. Clark was wearing neither boots nor trousers.

Black Joke volunteers, of New York, slept on the floor beside their rig to insure a fast pushoff. The members of New York's Mechanics Engine Company No. 47 said they got to fires faster by greasing their wheels with butter. Somebody came up with the wintertime idea of clamping skis or sleds to the engine's wheels. The company beat its competitors whose wheels mired in snowdrifts. Soon everybody was copying the idea.

New York's Bolivar Engine Company No. 9 was determined to beat their rival, the Honey Bees. A Saturday night rarely went by without an alarm. Several Bolivars positioned themselves in a line between

Opposite: *A torch boy lights the way as Eagle Company No. 2 of New York turns out to an early morning fire, in a Currier & Ives lithograph by Louis Maurer.* Below: *Philadelphia volunteers, pumping their end-stroke engines made by John Agnew, display their capabilities in an 1850 demonstration. Capes were worn to shed water and identify the company.*

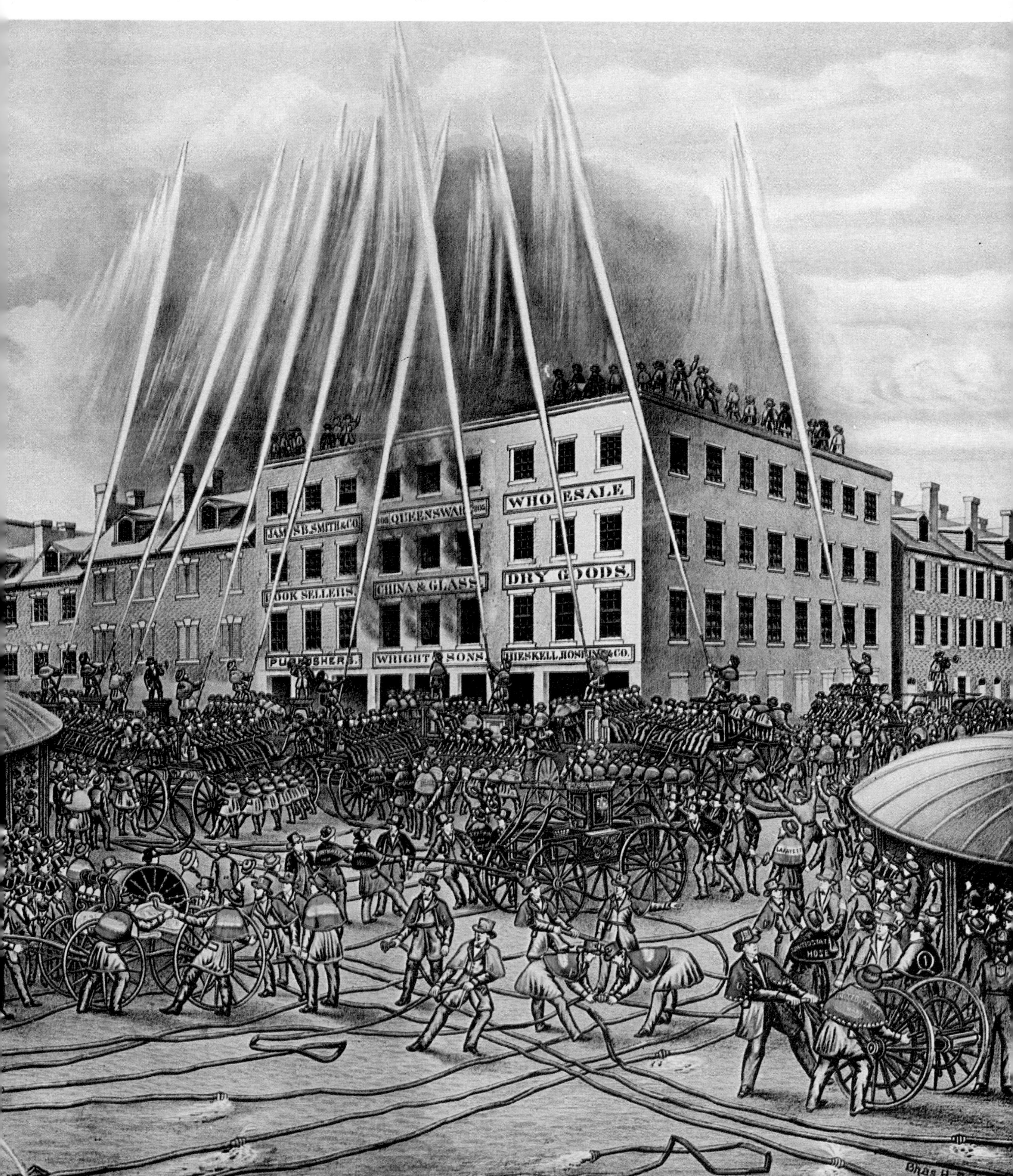

Middle Dutch Church, where alarms were received, and their Beaver Street station. Clapping hands three times would be the signal to the rest of the company, standing by in the firehouse, that an alarm was about to be struck. However, the idea backfired when someone chased a barking dog by clapping his hands. A few minutes later, the Bolivars came running up Broadway with nowhere to go.

Although cities prohibited it, the volunteers raced each other to fires, sometimes bowling over pedestrians and anything else that got in their way. The volunteers went up sidewalks if that was the only way around zigzagging companies that were determined not to let them pass. Some streets were so muddy or poorly paved that there was no alternative.

To be passed by a rival company was an insult that could only be erased by returning it. When a foreman realized his company was certain to be passed, he might save face by ordering the rig stopped on the pretext of needed repairs. "The carriage was new and the wheels were tight" was used as an alibi. Collisions and injuries were frequent, and when they occurred the result often was a brawl.

Answering alarms was dangerous business. The engines weighed more than a ton, and when they got rolling it was difficult to stop them. Many volunteers were killed or maimed when they tripped and fell under the wheels. Night alarms were especially hazardous, because few cities had street lights. To alleviate such dangers as colliding at intersections or crashing into piles of building materials, the volunteers sent young runners ahead with torches to light the way.

To clear the way, Philadelphia Hose No. 1, around 1803, mounted a large bell with a spring-operated clapper that clanged as the wheels turned. This bell is believed to be America's first apparatus bell, and the members patented the idea. Rival Good Intent Hose ignored the patent and put two bells on their rig. The outraged Philadelphia hosemen took their case to court and got an injunction. Good Intent quit the official volunteer department and ran as an independent outfit clanging its bell whenever and wherever it pleased. Philadelphia Hose then acquired an eighteen-inch Chinese copper gong. The members also hooked up a blacksmith's bellows, which was actuated by the up-and-down jiggling of the wagon's springs. The bellows forced air through a whistle—resulting in America's first fire siren.

While running to fires, members of New York's Clinton Engine imitated the cry of a stag deer at bay. The company became known as Old Stag and the volunteers painted a deer on their waterbox and topped the pump with a head of a buck cast in brass.

When water systems were built and hydrants installed, the volunteers sent their fastest runners ahead to make first claim on the fireplugs. An alarm in the early 1850s called Detroit volunteers to Michigan Avenue and Cass Street. Engine 8 was closest to the fire, but Volunteer William Woods of Engine 5 ran ahead with an empty barrel, put it over the nearest hydrant, and sat on it with what was described as "a look of angelic innocence." Engine 8 pulled up, looked for a hydrant, and continued another block before they found one. Engine 5 arrived, hooked up, and got first water on the fire.

Pittsburgh volunteer companies enlisted prize-fighters, whose job was to race to the fire and stand guard over the fireplug until the rest of the company arrived. The practice resulted in many fights and an American idiom, plug-uglies. New York's Knickerbocker Engine Company No. 11 signed up Bill Burke, who had lost an arm in the War of 1812. Burke tied a stone in his armless sleeve and used it with telling effect whenever anybody challenged Knickerbocker for a hydrant. New York's Atlantic Hose Company No. 14 got into a fight in the dark with a rival outfit claiming the same hydrant. After some minutes and some bloodied noses, the volunteers discovered there was no hydrant—they were fighting over a cannon barrel stuck in the ground as a hitching post!

One of the first actions of James Gulick when he was elected chief of the Fire Department of New York was to try to put an end to rowdyism and hydrant fights. He formed three hydrant companies whose duty was to take charge of and supervise the use of hydrants. Their apparatus consisted of one wrench per member.

Neighborhood companies often formed pacts to help each other. Hose companies supplied water to their favorite engines. Hook and ladder outfits worked closely with friendly engine and hose companies. Any other companies running into their turf to fight fires would have to fend for themselves and could probably expect a fight. A clique of seven Brooklyn gooseneck companies working closely together was called the Holy Alliance.

The foreman of the first company at the fire was in command until the arrival of the chief or an assis-

Above: *Racing to fires was forbidden, but volunteers often ignored the rules. Here the foreman of Philadelphia's White Turtle hose reel of the Northern Liberty Company urges his men on as they race the Lafayette Hose Company's Red Crab in the 1840s.* Below: *Engine believed to have been made by John Agnew about 1830 for the Franklin Company of Philadelphia. Decorative panels showed Ben Franklin assisting at a fire and, for some reason, holding a loaf of bread.*

tant. Pumping demanded great stamina. Half a dozen or more volunteers stroked the brakes in time to the foreman's beat, which he called out in cadence through his trumpet while standing on top of the engine. The Blue Boys of Jefferson Engine stroked in time to the chanting of their motto, True Blue Never Fades. The beat was usually sixty up-and-down strokes a minute.

During the March 10, 1828, fire that destroyed a blacksmith shop, two livery stables, and a house, New York's Fulton Engine Company No. 21 pumped 128 strokes, a record that remained unbroken for many years until another company hit 170. At these faster speeds, men had to be relieved every few minutes. Many firefighters suffered crushed fingers and broken arms when they jumped in to take their turn and were struck by the pump handle.

When one engine pumped water faster than the next company in line could relay it, the water spilling over the sides resulted in a washing. There was no greater disgrace than a washing, and firefighters sometimes draped their rigs with black bunting until they could wash the offending company in return. A New York gooseneck, Chatham Engine Company No. 15, was known as the Old Maid. She did not suffer a washing until ripe old age.

Washings often provoked fistfights. Oceanus 11 was supplying Black Joke 33 during an all-night fire, in 1832, on Pearl Street near Maiden Lane, in New York. While Black Joke's members were being relieved by company runners, Oceanus seized the opportunity to wash. Toughs from both companies were squaring off when Chief Gulick waded into the melee. With an uppercut, he laid out the ringleaders and ended the fight. Said one firefighter: "A blow from his fist was like a kick from a horse."

When Eagle 13 of New York got the latest model gooseneck, Foreman David T. Williams issued a challenge. Eagle was so powerful, he said, that nobody in the city could wash them. The Eagles were so certain of this that they would buy a suit for the foreman of whatever company managed to do the impossible. At a fire on Dutch Street near Fulton, Eagle was being supplied by Oceanus under Foreman Abraham B.

Opposite: *William C. Hunneman of Boston, America's foremost manufacturer of hand pumpers, produced this piece of apparatus for delivery to the Exeter, N.H., Fire Department on April 12, 1852.* Below: *Oil lanterns carried by officers flank a speaking trumpet, used for calling orders.*

Purdy. Oceanus decided to accept the challenge. Purdy bawled a cadence that quickly grew from 60 strokes to 130 and then 150. In less than five minutes Eagle overflowed. Williams burst into tears, and Purdy got a new suit.

Many volunteers hooted in November, 1832, when Foreman Gabriel P. Disosway of Mutual Hook and Ladder Company No. 1 bought a black horse to pull their black truck and stabled the horse near the firehouse. It was the first horse in the New York Fire Department. A horse, said other volunteers, had no place in the department. Were the Mutuals not men enough to pull their own rig to fires? The facts are obscure, but apparently part of the explanation was that Mutual was shorthanded after a yellow fever epidemic had reduced its numbers. A horse was needed to help pull the rig. One night the anti-horse element stole into the stable, shaved the horse's mane and tail, and painted a white stripe down its back, allowing rival companies to proclaim that Mutual's rig was now being pulled by a horse-sized skunk. More embarrassment followed when Oceanus beat the horse-drawn Mutuals to a fire.

When an infrequency of fires in Philadelphia caused interest to lag, the volunteers took to turning in false alarms. Racing through the streets became an almost nightly nuisance. Citizens protested, but the volunteers replied that they were only answering calls to duty. A newspaper noted that alarms never seemed to be sounded on rainy nights or when it was snowing. Soon irate citizens were complaining that gangs of young men hanging around firehouses were insulting every female who passed. Early records indicate that many fires were set intentionally, and some people wondered whether the volunteers might not be kindling a bit of action during slow periods.

For the most part, however, rivalry among companies was limited to practical joking. New York's Eagle Hook and Ladder Company No. 4 taunted its rival Peterson Engine Company No. 31:

The silver hook and ladder
The pretty, golden Four.
To make Thirty-one the madder,
Wash the paint from off her door.

When Engine Company No. 6 created the position of assistant secretary, an office no other outfit had, Lady Washington volunteers poked fun:

Number Six has come on deck
With a new assistant sec.,
Do ye mind?
He's as dirty as its water,
Tho' he thinks himself a snorter,
But he really hadn't oughter,
Do ye mind?

POMP AND POWER

The volunteers loved parades and pageantry and needed little excuse to set up a ceremonious display. We must remember that theirs was a day when there were no weekend baseball or football games, no movies or television or radio, no automobiles or camper vans to take people to weekend resorts.

The biggest and best shows in town were put on by the flamboyant volunteers. And the best thing about it was that the shows were free. Fires were few—New York had only about one hundred a year; had they been more frequent, the volunteers' energies might have been otherwise directed.

It took little coaxing to get up a parade. Fourth of July parades became traditional, and the volunteers strutted on May Days, when their rigs were covered with flowers, or whenever the occasion suggested: the building of the Erie Canal in 1825, the celebration of the French Revolution in 1830, the laying of the cornerstone for the Washington Monument on July 4, 1848, and the laying of the Atlantic Cable in 1858. A torchlight parade of 6,000 volunteers greeted the visiting Prince of Wales, who paid a visit to New York on October 13, 1860. A truck company raised a ladder to the prince's reviewing balcony at the Fifth Avenue Hotel, brought him down the ladder, and invited him to join the firefighters at an all-night party—which he did.

Philadelphia volunteers, many wearing distinctive capes, paraded on the birthday of another volun-

New York's Niagara Engine volunteers strutting in a torchlight parade on January 23, 1858. Niagara's engine, one of the city's prettiest, was white with gold trim. Lanterns lit her panels, which depicted Niagara Falls, The Maid of the Mist, *and the motto, Ever Ready, Ever Willing.*

Opposite: *Hotchkiss Fire Company No. 1 of Derby, Conn., paraded with this hose carriage about 1870. The reel has etched glass side panels that reflected the lights of the lanterns as the rig moved.* Below, top to bottom: *Motto of company, mounted up front; one of the glass lamps; reel hub with names of the company and the builder, Buckley & Merritt.*

teer firefighter, George Washington, and in 1832 the thirty-seven companies were applauded by a crowd of 100,000. The volunteers' headgear varied from stovepipe to porkpie hats, but many were wearing the new leather helmets designed four years earlier by Henry T. Gratacap of New York's Columbia Engine Company No. 14.

Gratacap's helmet had an extended rear brim and side edges curving upward. An elaborate frontpiece showing the name of the company was held in place by a brass eagle's head. The rakish helmet was ideal for firefighting. It protected the firefighter from falling debris and hot water, since curved sides and rear brim caused water to spill off behind him. Worn backwards, the brim deflected heat from his face. The helmet also was useful for breaking windows to ventilate smoke and heat. A firefighter who found himself trapped in a building needed only to get to a window or roof and throw his helmet to the street. It was then and is now the signal for help.

Supplying helmets to firefighters throughout the United States became a fulltime business for Gratacap. In Sacramento, California, volunteers bought one for their chief—for $2,100. It sparkled with precious stones mounted in gold and silver. The plainer Gratacap helmet has changed little and its basic design is still the one worn by most of today's firefighters.

Companies were known by their distinctive parade uniforms. Jefferson Engine's Blue Boys wore snappy royal blue uniforms to match the color of their pumper, and other companies strutted in white duck suits with black leather belts. The Old Honey Bees were the first, in 1840, to wear the now-traditional firefighters' red flannel shirts, black pants, and fancy suspenders. As the *New York Times* wrote, "Young women consider their shirts and black inexpressibles the finest uniforms in the world."

Volunteers spent days polishing and preparing their rigs and uniforms for parades. The apparatus frequently was draped with floral wreaths and red, white, and blue bunting. Some companies called attention to their outfit by decking it out with live or stuffed animals—foxes, porcupines, or eagles. Oceanus Engine paraded with a bronze statue of Daniel Boone, which eventually was sent to the Capitol Building in Washington, where it is today.

Phoenix Hook and Ladder Company No. 3 paraded with a black bear chained to the top of the six orange ladders on their light claret, gold-striped

Left: *Naiad Hose Company, organized on January 21, 1852. Its firehouse, on Church Street in New York, was one of the city's handsomest.* Opposite: *Parade of the New York volunteers before the mayor and the city council at City Hall.*

truck. A lovely Indian maiden in native paint and feathers posed on the rig of New York's Mohawk Hose Company No. 39. Bunker Hill Engine Company No. 32's dog carried their signal lantern.

Parades could be nearly four miles long, including marching bands from local saloons and sometimes from out of town. The Sing Sing prison band often came down to New York to tootle "Yankee Doodle" for the volunteers. On October 17, 1859, a Manhattan parade down Fifth Avenue began before noon and did not finish passing the reviewing stand until twilight. Stores and businesses closed that day, flags fluttered from windows, and the *New York Herald* reported, "Banners and floral decorations were suspended across Fifth Avenue while bevies of blooming maidens swarmed on every stoop."

Sunday afternoons were marked by company races down major thoroughfares. Sidewalks were thick with cheering crowds. Musters called out firefighters who competed for the trophies and ribbons awarded to companies who could shoot water the fastest, highest, and farthest. The most popular New York water carnivals were on Thanksgiving Days, at the 137-foot-high Liberty Pole put up by Democrats at the corner of Franklin Street and West Broadway. Judges sat on the roof of Tom Riley's Fifth Ward Hotel across the street and quaffed beer from their steins while they picked the winners.

When General Lafayette visited New York in September, 1824, the entire department of forty-six engines, several hook and ladders, and two Brooklyn pumpers passed in review in City Hall Park. Then the hook and ladder boys raised their ladders to form a pyramid. A small wooden house was put on top, filled with flammables, and touched off.

"Simultaneously the engines turned their streams upon the burning object and to the delight of the spectators each hit the object with wonderful accuracy. The spray from the water was remarkably pretty, and as the sunlight shone through the white cloud the brilliancy of the prismatic colors drew forth repeated exclamations of admiration from 30,000 spectators," said one account. When Lafayette died five years later, the volunteers turned out in mournful parade, as they would upon the deaths of other patriots, including Presidents John Adams and Andrew Jackson.

Easier transportation, beginning with the opening of the Baltimore & Ohio Railroad in 1830, encouraged the volunteers to solicit invitations from departments in other cities. They rarely were turned down. Loading their rigs on flatcars, they would set out for a weekend of wining, dining, toasting, parading, and swapping stories of their individual exploits. Did a truck company know a faster way to ladder a building? Did a hose company have a faster system for laying a line? The volunteers wanted to know about it so they could copy the idea.

Visitations became a volunteer tradition. In December, 1834, as a result of one visitation, New York and Philadelphia firefighters debated which department could pump more water and faster. The Philadelphians, some two hundred strong, were set to leave for New York to prove themselves, when city officials convinced them of the dangers of leaving Philadelphia unprotected.

Before anybody realized it, the volunteer firefighter had become a uniquely American institution. Nowhere in the world was there anything like him. The firehouse was his private club. Firefighters carpeted their bunkrooms and meeting rooms, planted gardens, put in libraries, and hung pictures—all the

better if these showed the men at their flamboyant best. There were more amenities at the local firehouse than in their drab homes, and the volunteers had all the more reason to congregate there for camaraderie, a few songs, and reminiscences of fires fought.

One that would never be forgotten was the alarm at 2:45 A.M. on July 1, 1834, for a fire at 273 Pearl Street, New York. Smoke and flames were boiling from the brick warehouse of Haydock, Clay & Company, wholesale druggists. The firefighters pumped for three hours and took an awful beating from the heat and smoke, and from the fumes from the burning drugs. At dawn came an ominous rumbling—a sound every firefighter learns to recognize and dread—the warning that walls are about to come crashing down.

Dropping their hoselines, the firefighters fled as the brick building collapsed. Foreman Zophar Mills of Eagle Engine Company No. 13 was driven into the cellar and escaped with minor injuries. William E. Crooker of Eagle was buried up to his neck. Eagle nozzlemen Eugene Underhill, twenty years old, and Frederick A. Ward, twenty-two years old, were lost somewhere under the mound of bricks.

Disregarding the danger that a remaining wall could come crashing down upon them, the firefighters plunged into the smoking rubble and began pulling away debris. Chief Gulick ordered one engine to play water on the bricks to cool them and another to pump air through its hose to the trapped men. Digging and pumping continued all day. Crooker was at last freed, with some of his toes burned off and a searing brand, the size of a brick, on the calf of his leg. He was crippled for life. Underhill and Ward were found dead. The entire department paraded at their funeral, and they were buried the way they died, side by side.

Despite these dangers, joining the volunteers was something young men aspired to for years until they came of legal age or a company opening occurred. Young men unofficially attached themselves to their favorite companies and became known as aides. They ran with their companies to fires and stood ready to help if the need arose, which it often did, or merely to stay on the sidelines and cheer.

Sometimes their enthusiasm got the best of them, and much of the rowdyism blamed upon the volunteers was the fault of their boosters.

Being accepted as a volunteer went beyond the official certificate. A man first had to prove himself by taking a bellyful of smoke in some murky basement or attic, by holding the nozzle while icicles dripped from his helmet and chin, and by hard and tedious hours spent cleaning the rig and hose after fires. Once accepted, he became a member of what would later be called the establishment. Friendships forged at fires were stepping stones to better jobs, higher social standing, and political office. No longer was a man an anonymous benchworker doing humdrum work in some dingy shop. Clerks who proved themselves at fires made company allegiances that could even lead to bank presidencies. From the ranks of volunteers came seven New York mayors, eighteen St. Louis mayors, and at least two United States presidents—James Buchanan of the Union Company, Lancaster, Pennsylvania, and Millard Fillmore of Buffalo's Eagle Hose.

An English visitor to Philadelphia wrote home in 1819: "You have no idea of the consequence of a fire company. It is the summit of the hopes and wishes of one-half the clerks, counterhoppers and quill drivers in the city. A trumpet in one hand, a spanner wrench in the other and a lantern affixed to his leather belt and he is in the zenith of his glory, more especially if the night be dark when the effect of the various lights is more striking."

Lucky was the lady invited to Saturday night chowder parties at the firehouse. Every company had its favorite seafood recipe. The rest of the week woman's place was in the home and man's at the firehouse. Fire department balls became the social event of the season, although the women could not always expect to be escorted home. During a dance at Detroit's Protection Engine Company No. 1, fire was discovered in a store next door. The women got home as best they could, while their escorts spent the rest of the night fighting the fire.

Many a girl longed to marry the young man who displayed his masculinity with his handling of a nozzle, hauling hose up a ladder, or vigorously stroking the handles of his fire engine—which he sometimes referred to as "the Old Gal." Marrying the company foreman was prestigious, but the real prize was the bridegroom who had saved a life or rescued a fellow firefighter trapped under the rubble of a fallen wall.

Starting in 1818, a few women managed to break the sex barrier that excluded them from active firefighting. The earliest known was Molly Williams, a black slave of New York merchant Benjamin Aymar of Oceanus Engine 11. Firefighter Adam P. Penz said, "Molly was a very distinguished volunteer of No. 11 Engine. She used to be called 'Volunteer No. 11.' I can see her now, with her nice calico dress and checked apron, a clean bandanna handkerchief neatly folded over her breast and another wound about her head and rising up like a baby pyramid. Once, during a blinding snowstorm in 1818, there was a fire in William Street and it was hard work to draw the engine; but among the few who had hold of the dragrope was Molly, pulling away for dear life. When asked what engine she belonged to, she always replied, 'I belongs to ole 'Leven; I allers runs wid dat ole bull-gine.'" It is interesting to note that Molly apparently referred to the engine in the male gender, while the men spoke of the pumper as feminine.

In Pittsburgh, two years later, Marina Betts, a five-foot, ten-inch woman of French-Indian ancestry, became a volunteer and later claimed she never missed an alarm. Betts became famous for dumping buckets of water over male bystanders who refused to help fight fires. She remained a firefighter for ten years, until she married a farmer.

America's most famous female firefighter was Lillie Hitchcock of San Francisco's Knickerbocker Engine Company No. 5. Around 1851, when she was a teenage socialite, Lillie began running to fires with the Knickerbockers. They voted her honorary membership and gave her a diamond-studded gold badge, which she rarely removed from her dress, even while attending Nob Hill social functions. Lillie retained her firefighting interest following her marriage to financier Howard Coit, and when she died, she bequeathed funds for a monument honoring the volunteers.

No community service grew faster than did fire protection, though before 1850 no city seriously considered fully paid, full-time firefighters. The volunteers saw to that. For concurrent with this growth, the local volunteer company was emerging as a political cell dedicated to preserving the status quo—the continuation of the volunteer system. The Democrats took control of New York Engine Company No. 12, and the Whigs controlled Engine Company No. 7. When all community fire companies united upon an issue they became powerful blocs. No state or local politician undertook a position, especially if it concerned fire protection, without consulting the volunteers. The gradual entrenchment of the volunteers

Opposite: *Baltimore's Mechanical Fire Company volunteers in parade hats and uniforms.* Top: *Pumper made in 1822 by John Rodgers of Baltimore for the city's Patapsco Company No. 14. It saw service until 1888, when it was rebuilt for parade use only.* Above: *Parade hat of Philadelphia's Decatur Company showing the company's namesake, naval hero Stephen Decatur.*

10
NEW YORK: "ONE BRIGHT, BURNING, HORRIBLE FLAME"

The devil could not have picked a better night than Wednesday, December 16, 1835, to turn New York into a flaming hell. A piercing gale from out of the northwest sent thermometers plunging to seventeen degrees below zero in the city of 270,000 people.

A rash of fires had exhausted New York's volunteers. On Monday night the entire department of forty-nine engines, five hose companies, and six hook and ladders had turned out to Chrystie and Delancey Streets to fight a fire raging through six buildings. Later that night they had run with their rigs to Water Street, where flames destroyed seven more buildings and two carpenter's shops. Tuesday's alarm had called them to an all-night blaze that burned several stores in Burling Slip.

At least one of the gooseneck pumpers, Knickerbocker Engine Company No. 12, was out of service after breaking a king bolt on its way to the Tuesday fire. Four Knickerbocker members were warming themselves in the Rose Street fire station after stealing coal from a nearby coal yard to fuel their small sugarloaf stove. (The city did not provide enough fuel to heat the stations, nor oil to light them, so firefighters either bought their own or cadged it.) One of the Knickerbockers was a twelve-year-old company runner who planned to become a certified volunteer when he turned twenty-one—William Marcy Tweed, later to be known as Boss Tweed of Tammany Hall.

The Great Fire of New York, December 16–17, 1835, the worst conflagration in the modern world since the London fire of 1666. The blaze destroyed the center of the Wall Street business district and burned a seventeen-block area. Losses were more than $20 million.

Nor was department strength what James Gulick, the six-foot, two-inch fire chief, would have liked. Recent yellow fever epidemics had killed many New Yorkers, including volunteers. The department was down to 1,500 men, many of them relatively new.

At the time of the fire, the narrow, winding streets of the Wall Street district in lower Manhattan had been deserted for hours after businesses had closed for the night. The area had been the mercantile and financial hub of the United States since the early 1820s, when New York moved ahead of Philadelphia to become America's largest city. The most prominent building on Wall Street was the Merchants' Exchange, one of the city's largest in square footage, and only eight years old. Architects boasted of its fireproof design. The elegant building, a testimonial to the finest Ionic-style architecture, was over three stories tall, with a colonnaded entrance and a high dome. In the rotunda stood a fifteen-foot statue of the city's most prominent lawyer and banker, Alexander Hamilton.

The Merchants' Exchange was the heartbeat not only of New York's commerce but of much of that of the United States. The Exchange housed the Chamber of Commerce and Board of Brokers, the Post Office, the Ship Letter Office and News Room, the Ship Telegraph Office, and several newspapers. Almost as important in the economic life of the city was the large Tontine Coffee House nearby. Except for the district's Dutch Reformed Church—as much famous as a city historical landmark as it was for its huge organ—the Wall Street district was a conglomeration of business establishments, banks, exchanges, and other commercial ventures. New York's residential area lay to the north.

Dominating the district were five- and seven-story brick stores and warehouses, the hub of New York's wholesale dry goods and hardware district, which supplied not only local retailers but stores throughout the United States. Here, too, were merchants dealing in every imaginable type of goods: teas, coffees, wines, brandies, and champagnes, saltpeter for gunpowder, and lead for hardware.

Many of these buildings were new in prospering

Opposite: *The rig of Eagle Engine No. 13, whose volunteers and foreman, Zophar Mills, braved the blistering heat from burning buildings to save the gigantic Tontine building in the Wall Street district.* Right: *This Staffordshire plate shows the Merchants' Exchange burning during the Great Fire.*

New York. Owners believed them to be fireproof, having roofed them with copper sheathing after previous fires had proved the hazards of wood shingles. The fact of the matter was that no more fertile breeding ground for a conflagration existed anywhere in the United States. Given the value of the buildings, their contents, and the area's significance to local and national economy, here was a potential for disaster greater than any known in the New World.

Chief Gulick and his men feared fires in the Wall Street district. Water supplies and pressures maintained by the Manhattan Company were poor. Automatic sprinkler and alarm systems were yet to be invented. Nor did the fire department have ladders that reached beyond the fourth floor. When higher fires occurred, the firefighters could expect to wait for the flames to burn down to where their hoselines could reach. Tuesday night's fire in Water Street was a case in point.

Many buildings had been fitted with iron window and door shutters after the anti-slavery riots and looting of the previous year. The shutters kept burglars out, but they also made it impossible for firefighters to get in to attack fires quickly. Tonight New York would discover what happens when flames become bottled up in burning buildings that do not permit quick venting of heat and gases.

Firefighters considered themselves lucky when they were able to confine the fire to the building of origin. In their firehouse speculations, they often wondered about the disaster that could result if coincidence should forge a different chain of circumstances. Their scenario might have run this way: Suppose a fire started in one of those warehouses after everyone had left for the day, and, with streets deserted, the flames gained tremendous headway before being discovered. And suppose the fire occurred when, for some reason or other, the fire department was not at its best. And suppose the wind happened to be unusually strong and able to send the flames leapfrogging across the district's narrow streets and alleys into other blocks.

Given the delay that inevitably occurred between the sounding of the alarm and the arrival of the firefighters at their firehouses and then at the fire—only to find they had to batter through iron doors and shuttered windows to get to the flames—the situation could be disastrous. And to add another horrifying factor: Suppose subzero weather froze cisterns, wells, and hydrants, so that no water was available to fight the flames. Altogether, the result could become a holocaust worse than the New York conflagration during the Revolution.

Shortly after 9:00 P.M. on Wednesday, city watchmen—known as leatherheads because of their caps—were patrolling lower Manhattan. One of them, William B. Hays, was nearing Exchange and Pearl Streets when he smelled smoke. He summoned other leatherheads, including Peter A. Holmes, who found smoke seeping from a five-story brick building at 25 Merchant Street. The first floor was occupied by the dry goods purveyors Comstock & Andrews, and the upper floors by the French importing firm of Henry Barbaud.

"We managed to force open the door," Hays said later. "We found the whole interior of the building in flames from cellar to roof and I can tell you we shut that door mighty quick. Almost immediately the flames broke through the roof. It was the most awful night I ever saw." Later investigation determined that the probable cause of the blaze was a broken gas pipe, whose leaking fumes had been ignited by a heating stove. The fire probably had been burning for several hours prior to discovery.

The alarm was relayed to the City Hall bellringer, who began a continuous tolling, the signal that notified volunteers the fire was in the Fifth District. He indicated the location by hanging a lantern on a stick from a window and pointing it toward Merchant Street. But the bellringer need not have bothered, for the glow was visible throughout lower Manhattan. The City Hall bell was quickly joined by the jailhouse bell and others in watchtowers and churches.

At the sound of the alarm, groggy volunteers stumbled from bed, dressed, and hurried to their firehouses. Tweed and his friends left their broken gooseneck and ran to help other companies. Fulton Engine Company No. 21, Excelsior Engine 2, Old Honey Bee, Lady Suffolk, Mutton Hose, and the Ball Club Hook and Ladder were among the first rigs to turn into Merchant Street.

True to their firehouse speculations, firefighters found that cisterns and wells were frozen. They tried a hydrant. It was frozen. They tried another. Frozen, too. By now the gale was slanting the Comstock & Andrews flames in a southerly direction toward other tall stores and warehouses along Exchange Place and Water Street.

More pumpers arrived, and a line of engines was formed to the nearby East River. Again the firefighters were frustrated by the thick river ice, which prevented the use of suction hoses. Hook and ladder companies were redirected from the fire to hack holes in the ice. Pumpers were lowered onto the ice and their suctions dipped into the water. "Will you take our water?" was bawled up and down the lines. A chorus of yeses came in reply. Other gooseneck companies reeled out all 200 feet of hose that each carried and coupled it to other pumpers to form lines to Merchant Street. "Play away!" shouted Gulick, who had arrived and taken command. The volunteers stroked their brakes to the singsong cadences of their foremen.

The men of Black Joke Engine Company No. 33 lowered their rig onto the deck of a brig and took suction. The company stroked their water into the box of Chatham Engine Company No. 2, some 200 feet up the line. Chatham relayed the water to Eagle Engine Company No. 13 another 200 feet ahead.

The Eagle firefighters pumped the water surging through the leather hose to their nozzlemen. But the stream lacked both quantity and pressure, for the subzero temperature was turning the water to slush before it could spurt from the nozzles. Firefighters stomped on the hose to keep the water from freezing solid, but at best only ineffective streams gushed from the clogged lines. In ten minutes, many hoses were frozen as rigid as iron bars.

Within the hour, the flames along Merchant Street had spread to at least fifty buildings, and many more were smoldering in blocks downwind. Foremen bellowed to make their orders heard over the roaring flames. "It is impossible to imagine the fervent heat created by the increasing flames," said Gabriel O. Disosway, a Wall Street businessman and volunteer who rushed to the area when he heard the alarm. "Many of the stores were new, with iron shutters, doors and copper roofs and gutters. One after another building ignited under the roof from the next edifice.

"Downward from floor to floor went the devouring element. As the different stories caught, the iron-closed shutters shone with glowing redness, until at last forced open by the uncontrollable enemy. Within, they represented the appearance of an immense iron furnace in full blast. The tin and copper-bound roofs often seemed struggling to maintain their fast hold, gently rising and falling and moving until, their rafters giving way, they mingled in the blazing crater of goods, beams, floors, and walls." In the streets below, volunteers dodged the molten copper goo that ran down sides of buildings, dripped from roofs, and puddled in the streets.

Manhattan, surrounded by water, could not get enough of it to fight the flames. In desperation,

Opposite: *The Wall Street financial district is engulfed, in this view of the fire from the top of the Bank of America at Wall and William Streets.* Above: *This print probably shows Fire Chief James Gulick discussing the progress of the fire with a group of worried businessmen.*

someone remembered that barrels of vinegar were stored at Downing's Oyster House on Broad Street. Firefighters tapped the barrels, formed a bucket brigade, and filled their pumpers. Spouting vinegar from their hoses, they managed to save the restaurant and the nearby New York Journal of Commerce Building.

Water or not, the firefighters found they must keep on pumping or their rigs would freeze. Foreman Zophar Mills of Eagle Engine Company No. 13 poured a pipe of brandy into the pumping mechanism and his men kept stroking. (He poured another into his boots to avoid frostbite.) Many other rigs did freeze, and the discouraged firefighters hauled them back to their stations until the apparatus thawed and they could return to the battle.

To remain in any battle position and attempt to make a stand against the onslaught was to risk death under the constantly falling brick walls. But stand the firefighters did, and Chief Gulick kept them at their pumps, only to fall back to new positions with his men as the overwhelming heat and suffocating smoke drove them backwards.

Realizing the futility of the battle, many volunteers left their rigs and joined merchants in carrying goods from threatened buildings to safety. Surely, they thought, the marbled Merchants' Exchange could not burn; the flames would never turn back upon themselves to strike the Dutch Reformed Church. By midnight, the Exchange and the church were piled high with salvaged dry goods. Nobody realized they were creating a fuel dump that would doom both structures.

Hanover Square, a large open area, also seemed to be a safe area to stack salvaged merchandise. Soon there was a sixty-foot-long, twenty-five-foot high mound of French silks, satins, lace, cartons of dresses, capes, and cashmere shawls. Augustine E. Costello, author of *Our Firemen: A History of the New York Fire Departments* (1887), wrote, "Just as the goods were stacked, a gust of flame, like a streak of lightning, came from the large East India warehouse of Peter Remsen & Company, and shooting across the square, blown by the strong wind, set fire to the entire mass. In minutes the costly pile was reduced to cinders."

Despite the fearsome cold, the spectators grew into a mob of thousands. Nobody knows who picked up the first bolt of cloth and ran with it, but others soon were grabbing what the firefighters and merchants had worked so hard to save. Cases of cham-

Opposite: *Merchants examine the contents of their safes, which were hauled to Hanover Square before the fire reached their buildings. James Gordon Bennett, editor of the New York* Herald, *interviewed a businessman who said, "New York is bankrupt."* Below: *Portrait of a volunteer during the Great Fire, by the artist Nicholas Calyo.*

pagne, ports, and barrels of liquor were broken into. The perimeter of the fire quickly became a vast arena of looting, brawling, and boozing as the mob went wild. The leatherheads were outnumbered.

Oblivious to the pandemonium, the falling walls, and the blazing firestorm of debris raining down upon them, the mob surged from one street into another in its lust for more loot. The only injuries this night would be those suffered by rioters fighting over baskets of champagne, French hats, and Manchester woolens. Mass insanity infected the city. In front of dozens of witnesses, a man torched a house at Stone and Broad Streets. He was immediately seized by the crowd and lynched from a tree. In the Dutch Church-turned-warehouse, somebody began to play the organ. Outside, frenzied merchants, pleading with passersby for help in saving their stocks, were mostly ignored. One merchant, stopping the driver of a horse cart, paid him $500, loaded the wagon with his goods, and had the driver haul them to safety.

The gale, with a determination that seemed lifelike, spared virtually nothing. In a few hours an ugly blanket of smoke and flame silhouetted lower Manhattan's skyline. "Street after street caught the terrible torrent, until acre after acre was booming an ocean of flame," said Costello. A reporter for the *New York Courier & Enquirer,* one of the few newspapers to survive the fire, wrote, "The whole city seemed in one awful sheet of flame."

Capriciously reversing itself around 2:00 A.M., the heat from the blazing block of buildings near Wall Street shattered the rear windows of the Merchants' Exchange. Within minutes, the interior was glowing. Feeding upon the salvaged dry goods, sheets of flame swept up to the dome. Spectators tried to drag the statue of Hamilton to safety, but the smoke and heat drove them from the building. Within two hours the Exchange was engulfed, and around 4:00 A.M., the dome came crashing down into the flames, demolishing the statue.

Among the firefighters was twenty-two-year-old Nathaniel Currier, who had recently started a print business. Immediately after the fire he struck a lithograph, "The Burning of the Merchants' Exchange." It was the first of many lithographs of noteworthy American fires and other disasters made in that era before newspaper and magazine photojournalism and television. (Two decades later, Currier was to form a partnership with James Merritt Ives and produce with him a lithograph series, "The Life of a Fireman," generally considered to be the most authentic portrayals of volunteer firefighters.)

While the mob gawked in disbelief at the flaming Merchants' Exchange, the gale took another unexpected turn and sent flames spilling into the Dutch Reformed Church, two blocks south. The organ fell silent as the church became a torch. Flames roared up to gorge upon the spire with its landmark gold ball. Steeple and ball came crashing down into the flaming mass of pews and salvaged merchandise.

The Tontine Coffee House was now seriously threatened. If it went, nothing short of a miracle would stop the flames from spreading into the city's residential area to the north. Suddenly, a firebrand landed on the building's wood shingle roof. The Tontine was burning!

Foreman Mills bawled an order to his men to drag their rig to the front of the building. They managed to find water, but they knew they could not pump hard enough to drive a stream to the roof. Then a spectator, Oliver Hull, offered Mills a one-hundred-dollar donation to the Firemen's Charitable Fund if he could save the Tontine.

Mills and his men lugged a showcase from a nearby store and fastened their nozzle to a long pole. William H. Macey, age thirty, climbed onto the showcase and, standing on a barrel, held the pole high. As the blistering heat scorched his hair and his firecoat and roasted his leather helmet to a crisp, Macey's fellow Eagles played a stream on him to keep him alive. With Mills exhorting the men to pump harder, the stream gradually intensified, finally splashing onto the roof and boring into the flames. The Tontine was saved—and with it the residential area of the city. (Macey later became president of the Seamen's Savings Bank, but historians better remember him as the nozzleman who saved the Tontine and the rest of the city to the north.)

Meanwhile, the situation was worsening on the east, as flames swept like a tidal wave into blocks of buildings along the East River. In a flash, stocks of turpentine ignited, spilling onto a wharf and into the harbor to create a blazing sea many hundreds of square yards wide. The burning turpentine, coupled with the towering flames from the tall stores and warehouses, lit the harbor. "The water looked like a sea of blood," said Costello. "Every spar and every rope in the ships was distinctly visible. Clouds of smoke, like dark mountains suddenly rising in the air, were succeeded by long banners of flame, reaching to the zenith and roaring for their prey." Fiery debris was blown over Brooklyn and set fire to at least one roof. Days later, charred business records of many New York merchants were found scattered in New Jersey cranberry bogs.

Indeed, the burning city could be seen for hundreds of miles. Brooklyn volunteers—including the Holy Alliance, seven gooseneck companies that always worked together at fires—loaded their rigs on barges and rowed across the East River to join the battle. Newark volunteers also set out with their apparatus. When news of the city's agony reached Philadelphia, 400 volunteers, including Franklin Fire Company and Northern Liberty, loaded their end-

The Great New York Fire seen from Brooklyn on the night of December 16, 1835. New York firefighters were assisted by Brooklyn's Holy Alliance, seven gooseneck companies that worked together at big fires. When news of the disaster reached Philadelphia, 400 volunteers put their pumpers on flat cars and left for New York City aboard a special train.

strokers on flatcars and left on a special train. The tracks ended somewhere in New Jersey, and ahead lay a long stretch of open country, including sand dunes. Undaunted, the Philadelphians unloaded their rigs and pulled them the rest of the way to New York. They did not arrive until Saturday.

New York burned throughout the night. On Front Street, flames surged into a warehouse loaded with sacks of saltpeter. An enormous explosion shook Manhattan, then more explosions, which Disosway likened to cannonfire. "Shock after shock followed in rapid succession, accompanied with the darkest, thickest clouds of smoke imaginable. Suddenly the whole ignited and out leaped the flaming streams in peculiar colors from every door and window." It looked like a mammoth fireworks display.

"One of the most grand and frightful scenes of the whole night was the burning of a large oil store at the corner of Old Slip and South Street. It was four or more stories high and filled with windows on both sides without any shutters," said Disosway. Stored in the building were hundreds of barrels of sperm whale oil and other oils. The exploding barrels soared high into the churning smoke and flames and rocketed across the sky.

Toward dawn, the decision was made to create a firebreak at Coenties Slip by blowing up buildings. Eighty marines and sailors brought powder from the magazine at Red Hook. They wrapped blankets and their jackets around the kegs and dashed through the blizzard of sparks. They planted the powder in the large brick warehouse of Wyncoop & Company, wholesale grocers. When they touched it off, the enormous building "heaved up as if by magic and losing its fastenings from the cellar to the roof, tottered, shook and fell," according to Disosway. But the flames remained unchecked. The blast only broke windows of buildings downwind and invited the gale to sow fire inside them.

New York was still burning at daybreak, but the gale was subsiding. Lower Manhattan was shrouded with ugly clouds of gray and black smoke. James Gordon Bennett, editor of the *New York Herald,* wrote: "On reaching the corner of Front and Coenties Slip the most awful scenes burst upon my eyes. I beheld the several blocks of seven-story stores, full of rich merchandise, in one bright, burning, horrible flame. About forty buildings were on fire."

That afternoon the flames ran out of fuel, although the burning hulks would cough up suffocating smoke for days and forbid entry into the fire zone. So complete was the incineration that when merchants finally picked their way through the rubble, many of them could not even find where their stores had stood. A Philadelphian who owned 800,000 pounds of lead bars stored in a warehouse found them melted into a 400-ton blob.

Around 674 buildings were destroyed in a seventeen-block area of fifty acres. Losses were put in excess of $20 million, which by today's values translates into several hundreds of millions. As many as ten thousand people were left jobless. Most of the twenty-six insurance companies doing business in New York did not have resources to meet claims, and failed. The conflagration was the worst in the modern world since the Great London Fire 169 years earlier.

America's largest city was numb. "The heart of the city seemed to have ceased to exist," said Costello. "Of business there was none. New York was stricken as with paralysis." Bennett interviewed a prominent businessman who said, "New York is bankrupt."

Alexander Hamilton put forward his plan for rescuing New York: "Application should be made . . . to Congress to put at the disposal of the state government whatever amount of money it may judge proper to employ in order to administer to the urgent wants of this crisis. The necessity of some legislative interference cannot be questioned and, if promptly given when the legislature meets in January, the benignant influence of confidence will generally be felt.

"In order to extend assistance the state treasury should be authorized to loan on all the good securities, bonds and mortgages. It is necessary that promptness of action should be pursued; every delay but increases the embarrassment and renders the palliative more difficult of application. In short, a discreet forebearance on the part of the banks and the prompt action of the government will relieve the community from further distress and eventually give new vigor to our commercial enterprise, the vital spirit of our national prosperity."

History records that Congress did not bail out New York. The bankruptcies multiplied, and New York banks suspended interest payments for a year. Some authorities believe the fire contributed to the national economic depression two years later.

pump manufacturing, and it was a simple matter to convert to fire engines. First to locate there was Paine and Caldwell in 1839, followed by Cowing & Company, and Silsby Manufacturing Company six years later. Rumsey & Company moved there after the Civil War. Located on the New York State barge canal, which provided cheap freight transportation, Seneca Falls became the fire-engine manufacturing capital of the world. The industry flourished there until around 1900.

In the race to build better apparatus and to win fame and financial success, many companies seemed to be groping their way to popularity. In 1847, Dudley L. Farnham and Franklin Ransom patented engines that were rowboats on wheels. Three rows of two men sitting on top of the rig rowed handles connected to horizontal bars that operated the center-mounted pump. The apparatus created little interest among New York volunteers. Farnham moved to Cincinnati, where the rig had some appeal, and sold a number of them throughout the midwest and in St. Louis.

Insurance companies were greatly alarmed by continuing high losses in mercantile districts. These areas were usually deserted at night, and fires therefore went undiscovered until they were beyond control. In November, 1839, the New York Board of Fire Underwriters organized a forty-man Fire Police Force that patrolled the high-value districts from 7:00 P.M. to 5:00 A.M.

Six years later the insurance patrolmen were given a small wagon carrying six buckets, four brooms, and six covers for protecting property threatened by water damage from hoses. The rig was called the Pie Wagon because of its similarity to bakery trucks. The insurance patrolmen's red leather helmets earned them the sobriquet Red Heads. During the day the Pie Wagon was kept in the loft of the Dutch Street headquarters so as to be out of the way of insurance clerks working on the first floor. When patrolmen reported for duty at night they lowered the rig to the first floor. Fire insurance company salvage patrols eventually were formed in most of America's largest cities. Many insurance patrolmen became firefighters and fire chiefs.

Insurance companies also encouraged cities to

build better water supply systems to supply the more powerful engines. On the Fourth of July, 1842, New York officially opened the $11,452,619 aqueduct from the Croton watershed north of the city. The 155-mile system supplied 1,500 hydrants. The event was celebrated with one of the biggest parades in the department's history, with volunteer outfits coming from as far away as Philadelphia to march. L. Maria Child wrote, somewhat optimistically, "Fires are now mere trifles." A song was composed for the occasion and sung in all firehouses:

Water leaps as if delighted
  While her conquered foes retire;
Pale Contagion flies affrighted
  With the baffled demon Fire.

Three years later New Yorkers learned they needed more than a good water system to fight fires, when the city suffered its third conflagration. The fire started at 3:00 A.M. and destroyed three hundred buildings. Explosions killed thirty people, including four firefighters.

Nor did other cities escape disasters. The Great Pittsburgh Conflagration on April 10, 1845,

Opposite bottom: *John Rodgers built this double-decker engine, an 1850 model, for Baltimore volunteers.* Below: *Merrick & Agnew were making double-deckers in this Philadelphia factory in 1834.* Bottom: *James Smith built this side-stroke pumper in 1853 for the Storm Engine Company of Babylon, N.Y.*

destroyed more than 900 buildings. Nantucket's preeminence as the whaling capital of the world ended on July 13, 1846, when flames wiped out most of the waterfront. In 1848, Albany lost 600 structures, and in 1849, St. Louis suffered a riverfront fire that destroyed twenty-three Mississippi steamboats and 430 buildings. Two years later Philadelphia was hit by a conflagration that left 400 buildings in ashes and thirty-nine people dead. On September 25, 1851, a Buffalo conflagration took around 200 buildings. That same year a fire in the Library of Congress in the Capitol Building virtually destroyed the famous Thomas Jefferson collection, but the original Declaration of Independence was saved.

Poor alarm systems were a major contributor to severe fires. Tower watchmen or church sextons rang bells, but they did not give an exact location of the fire. In Philadelphia, when the Liberty Bell clanged, the volunteers first ran to Independence Hall to learn where the fire was. Much time was lost. In Buffalo, in 1837, the number of bells told the direction of the fire. Two strokes signaled an alarm in the northern part of the city, three, in the southern. Systems varied during the 1800s. In colonial Alexandria, Virginia, alarms were sounded by shooting muskets, and in Los Angeles by firing pistols, as late as 1870. Detroit clanged a large iron triangle in 1827, and smaller communities raised alarms by striking iron hoops. In 1808, Cincinnati blew fox horns and beat a gigantic drum. Brooklyn set off a steam whistle on the roof of a glue factory in 1846.

Alarm systems were revolutionized by Dr. William F. Channing of Boston, a young Harvard medical school graduate who tinkered with electricity instead of practicing medicine. In 1839 he invented a system for pinpointing the location of fires by means of alarm boxes containing telegraphic devices that transmitted a signal to a central alarm station. Each firebox was simply a telegraph key that could send only one message: the number of the box that corresponded to a list of locations posted in the alarm office.

An alarm was turned in by opening the box and cranking a handle that caused a notched gear, or character wheel, to turn. The notches transmitted electrical impulses that opened and closed circuits at the central station, where they were received on registers and bell strikers. When the box number was received, the dispatchers relayed the number by telegraph to bells in fire stations and churches.

Dr. Channing's principle was so sound that it has been used for more than a century. The firebox at Independence Hall, Philadelphia, for example, is numbered 1776. An alarm from this box sends a series of electrical taps to the alarm office: a single tap, followed by a pause; then seven taps and another pause; seven more taps and a pause; then six taps, which totals 1–7–7–6. Alarm dispatchers then transmit 1776 to fire stations.

As with many new fire protection ideas, however, years passed before Dr. Channing's invention was tried. In 1851, Boston appropriated $10,000 for a system built by Moses G. Farmer, an electrical engineer. The boxes were mostly mounted on public buildings, such as Faneuil Hall and Old South Church. America's first firebox alarm was turned in at 8:25 P.M., April 29, 1852, when J. H. Goodale cranked the box on the wall of the Cooper Street Church for a fire in a nearby house. The excited Goodale cranked faster than the instruments could record the alarm. When nothing happened he ran to the alarm headquarters and reported the fire. The *Boston Transcript* nevertheless said, "So successful did the new system work in quickly summoning the department that little damage was done by the fire." Dr. Channing sold his patents seven years later to John N. Gamewell of Camden, South Carolina. The name Gamewell became synonymous with alarm systems throughout the United States.

A new breed of volunteer began to emerge shortly after New York's Great Fire of 1835. Those who had earlier joined out of a sense of civic duty were growing older—some had put in more than twenty-five years—and they were no longer up to the rigors of firefighting. Too, business obligations gave them less time. Their better financial situation enabled them to move to outer areas of cities. No longer were they as eager to spend their nights in downtown fire stations. Many of the old guard remained, but they were infiltrated by young men with seemingly little more motivation in life than to turn fire stations into dens of drinking and gambling.

The transition to this new breed accelerated as political machines corrupted the volunteers. Irony of ironies, the political power that the volunteers had themselves created was slowly turning to feed upon them. Fire chiefs often were picked not because of ability but because of political connections. Tammany Democrats controlling the Common Council voted in 1836 to put in their own chief and fire Gulick on phoney charges of incompetency in the Great Fire.

Chief Gulick learned he was through while he was fighting the May 4, 1836, Union Market blaze on Houston Street. When the firefighters saw him walking away and learned why, they turned their helmets around in protest and stopped pumping. The mayor was unable to change their minds and the fire worsened. Gulick hurried back to take command for the last time.

Brawling was nothing new, but now it became more vicious and more frequent. The newer volunteers seemed more interested in fighting other companies than in fighting fires. Fighting was official cause to order a company to "turn tongue in"—that is, to return the apparatus to the city storage yard and leave it with the front tongue turned under the rig. But the city needed the protection and companies were reinstated, often with a worse bunch of men than before. The revolving-door system of political clout put the brawling and drunken firefighters back on the streets soon after they were arrested.

New York's Bowery Boys, the Rock Boys, the Bloods, the Fly-by-Nights, and similar gangs that began to infest the volunteers in other American cities were at first mostly in the minority. But their behavior was smearing company and department reputations earned over years of proud service. You could not fight City Hall, said the old guard, and many of them quit. The love of firefighting and the need to protect their uptown homes caused many to form new companies. But downtown, what had started as a case of healthy, competitive rivalry was about to turn into mayhem and murder.

Firefighting tools became lethal weapons. Nozzles, trumpets, spanners, helmets, and axes were as effective as clubs, bricks, and cobblestones. New York's Knickerbockers became the Arsenal Engine because revolvers were hidden in the rig. Two companies of Washington, D.C., volunteers, the Franklins and the Anacostias, were returning from a Georgetown fire when one company passed through the other's turf. The resulting fight in front of the White House was said to have lasted five hours and was watched by President John Tyler. When Philadelphia's Weccacoe Engine visited Washington its members got into a gunfight in the dining room of the Willard Hotel. Seven were shot.

A rash of fights among Baltimore volunteers caused the creation of a special investigating committee, which reported on February 14, 1837: "Riots, turbulence, disgraceful conduct and personal violence have repeatedly occurred. The name of a fireman has almost ceased to be respectable, and the badge which once was a badge of honor has almost become a badge of obloquy and an emblem of disorder. Public opinion has been loudly expressed in strong disapprobation of the violation of order which has been caused by the fire companies, and the public press of the city have teemed with charges which materially affect the honor and reputation of the department."

Irish immigration sparked prejudices among firefighters who saw themselves as superpatriots. On Sunday afternoon, June 10, 1837, a scuffle in Broad Street between a Boston volunteer and an Irishman attending a funeral touched off a riot that brought out the entire department. Rigs were smashed, Irish homes were sacked, and the firefighters took as bad a beating as they gave. Captain Charles Sears of Ladder Company No. 2 was nearly stomped to death by ten Irishmen who waylaid him on a wharf. The mayor called out the troops and order was restored only after the volunteers were ordered to go to Faneuil Hall to cool off.

An even worse riot occurred in Philadelphia in 1844. It started during a meeting in the Nanny Goat Market. This time it was the Irish volunteers of Hibernia Hose who started it against the Native Americans, a group opposed to immigration and Catholics. Before the battle ended, three days later, two churches, two rectories, a school, and a convent were burned. Eight people were killed. The Hibernia Hose House was pockmarked with bullet holes.

In the 1840s, women's temperance societies crusaded to persuade firefighters to give up booze, which the women said was the root of all the evil among the volunteers. The Lady Lafayette Temperance Benevolent Society gave the pledge to New York's Engine Company No. 10. After a prayer, "Temperance Millennium," and some songs—"Drunkard's Resolve" and "The Old Oaken Bucket"—a silk banner was presented to the volunteers and Engine 10 became known as the Water Witch.

Union Engine Company No. 18, wearing their parade uniforms, sat soberly in the front pews of the Bedford Street Methodist Episcopal Church during their teetotalling ceremony. Accepting the silk temperance banner, Foreman Henry Wilson said, "Are we not of all men the most steadfast believers in the efficacy of water? We could not get along without

New York's Southwark Company volunteers use their double-decker engine to battle a fire at Broadway and Cedar Street in 1840. Greatly favored over the old goosenecks, double-deckers were among the most powerful hand pumpers. With two sets of handles at each end, they could be worked by four rows of men and threw water higher than any other engine.

water. It is our native element, and may we always have enough of it." The New Yorkers' Union name was dropped and Engine 18 became Dry Bones. "Dress a fireman up and he would do anything his buddies did, all the way from a riot to a revival," wrote a skeptical Philadelphian, Andrew H. Neilly. The temperance women had some success, possibly because many were firefighters' wives and girl friends, but for the most part the drinking and brawling continued.

Thugs controlling New York's once-proud North River Engine Company No. 27 frequently fought with Red Rover Engine Company No. 34. Feuding boiled over one July night in 1842 when Red Rover washed North River during a Greenwich Village furniture store fire. Arming themselves with bricks, table legs, and other rubble, North River hid along a dark street that Red Rover would travel while returning to their station.

When Red Rover was surrounded, Ely Hazleton, North River's best fighter when he was sober, cried "Boots!"—the signal to attack. Caught by surprise, the Red Rovers were badly clobbered. Foreman David C. Broderick was knocked unconscious by a brick. North Rivers were defacing Red Rover's engine paintings and ripping off her polished silver fittings when the battered Rovers rallied. During the half-hour free-for-all a Red Rover laid open John Mount's stomach with a barrel stave. The Battle of the Boots went down as one of New York's bloodiest, but every city could tell a similar story.

North River hung Broderick's cap from the flagstaff of their firehouse until he negotiated for its return. The battle was followed up two years later when the drunken Hazleton committed suicide by putting an awl to his head and punching it into his brain with a mallet.

On the afternoon of Christmas Eve, 1843, some six hundred members of three engine companies—Neptune Bean Soup, Peterson Old Wreath of Roses, and the Old Turks of Live Oak—were in saloons sharing Yuletide cheer as well as their mutual hatred of Tammany-Hall-dominated Black Joke Engine. Arming themselves with bricks and clubs, the three companies marched on Black Joke's Gouverneur Street station intending to steal the carved golden eagle decorating the front of the firehouse. The station looked deserted. This was going to be easy.

As they approached the firehouse, the doors suddenly swung open. The assault force stopped dead. Black Jokers were massed around a cannon. The invaders were warned that the gun was loaded with iron slugs, chains, and bolts. The invaders then turned to attack Black Joke's favorite saloon, the Ten-to-One Tavern. A Black Joke sniper on the roof of the tavern tried to repulse them by firing his musket. The shot went wild, and he was preparing to get off another as police riot squads arrived. Constables confiscated the cannon, thirteen muskets, six pistols, and a wagon load of cobblestones. Several Black Jokers were arrested, but not for long—for their foreman, Malachi Fallon, was a Tammany leader and warden of the Tombs prison.

Similar rioting was reported in every city. "They defy the law, terrify the magistrates and newspapers, have constantly violent affrays and consider themselves with peculiar rights and privileges," wrote a Philadelphian, Sydney G. Fisher. A Philadelphia newspaper offered the opinion that firefighters "of low class" were jeopardizing homes and businesses of "capitalists who seek comfort and ease." The editor of the *Philadelphia Gazette* thundered, "Is there no one to stop this?" Editors raged and capitalists complained, but many citizens seemed to enjoy every minute of it. In Buffalo and other cities, newspapers reviewed fires much as music and drama critics today do the arts. Henry Ward Beecher, the Congregational preacher, asked, "Would you have a company of French dancing masters to extinguish fires?"

Hundreds of songs and dances were written to glorify their exploits: "The Empire Hook & Ladder Polka" and "The Diligent Hose Company Quick Step." The volunteers were lionized in Samuel D. Johnson's play, *The Fireman,* which opened in 1849 in Boston and enjoyed a successful road trip.

Mose Humphreys, the King of the Bowery Boys and foreman of Lady Washington Engine Company No. 40, became a national hero when portrayed by Frank Chanfrau in the successful Broadway play, *A Glance at New York.* Old Mose was depicted as a swashbuckling hero more than six feet tall, with flaming red hair—an apt description of him. Old Mose was a typesetter by trade who lost only one fight, and that to Chanfrau's younger brother.

Old Mose was described as "a coarse creature with an abominable dialect and . . . other habits of speech and conduct unfitting him for refined society. But he would plunge into a burning house and bring out in his arms helpless women and children and stand on top of a ladder with flames all around him,

SMITH & SHERMAN.
ENGRAVERS & PRINTERS.
COLTON & DISTURN

Explosions and flames in St. Louis on the night of May 17, 1849, destroyed twenty-three Mississippi riverboats and 430 buildings. Volunteer Fire Captain Thomas Targee was killed by a dynamite explosion as he tried to blast a firebreak. The fire, seen in this Currier lithograph, caused $5 million in damages.

enacting exploits of the most prodigious peril and valor and the people loved him." When last heard of, Old Mose had gone to Honolulu, married a native, fathered a large family, operated a billiards saloon, and so impressed the king with his tales that he was named chief of police.

While every city had its share of toughs, none compared to Philadelphia's notorious Moyamensing Hose Company, led by Bill "Bull" MacMullin. This gang called themselves the Killers, and they spoiled for a fight with any company that rolled into their turf. Before Bull was elected foreman, his chief claim to fame was his arrest record: pulling a knife on an alderman who tried to stop a fight, and stabbing a police officer and injuring another while resisting arrest. Both charges were dropped. Bull was the worst of the bunch, but there were others, including the Moya who murdered Policeman Neil Mooney when he put out a bonfire set by the gang to decoy a rival company into their territory.

But the Killers topped all that on election night, October 9, 1849, when they decided to torch the four-story California House, a tavern and hotel owned by blacks. Around 8:00 P.M., the Killers rammed into the hotel with a wagon containing barrels of blazing tar. The blacks opened fire and the Killers shot back. Police came, but the Moyas chased them away.

The clanging Liberty Bell called out the volunteers. Hope Engine, one of the first to arrive, was chopped into kindling by the Moyas and the white mob that had joined them. There was more gunfire when Good Will Hose pulled in. When the smoke cleared, three Good Will firefighters lay dead—Thomas Westerhood, Charles Himmelwright, and Thomas Marshall. Good Willer John G. Hallick was shot through the eye.

The volunteers retreated until the militia arrived. At daybreak the Moyas and the mob attacked again. The Robert Morris Hose carriage was smashed. The hose of Diligent Hose Company was cut. As more troops arrived, Phoenix Hose rallied with Good Will and stopped the spreading flames.

After the riot, authorities searched Moyamensing's station. No guns—no ammunition—no arrests. Philadelphia finally hit upon a clever way to stop the Moyas. The city formed a special police force to put a stop to the fighting. One of the first deputized was Bull MacMullin. The Killers became law-abiding and MacMullin ran for alderman. He won.

UNCLE JOE ROSS

It took a fire in a Cincinnati wood planing mill to set in motion the chain of events that eventually toppled the volunteer system in large American cities. On an autumn night in 1851, Western Fire and Hose Company No. 3 and Washington Company No. 1 began fighting and ten more companies joined in. The flames were sighted by volunteers across the Ohio River in Covington, Kentucky. Crossing the state line to help their friends the Washingtons, they saw that the best help they could give was with their fists. While thirteen volunteer companies rioted, the mill burned to the ground.

The city was outraged. There had been 123 fires and many riots during the past year. Losses came to $600,000, a 200 percent rise in one year. Insurance companies had hiked their rates, and now the citizens were demanding action. But the 1,800 volunteers were confident the scandal would blow over. They knew as well as anyone that Cincinnati could not afford to pay them. A paid department would become feasible only if somebody came up with a fire engine that could be operated by only a few men instead of the as many as fifty needed for hand pumpers. In the unlikely event that occurred, they were prepared to do whatever was necessary to crush the idea into oblivion, just as New York volunteers had.

The idea of steam fire engines had long intrigued a number of Cincinnatians, including Abel Shawk, maker of door locks and hand-operated engines, and Alexander Bonner Latta, who built the first railroad locomotive west of the Allegheny Mountains. Two problems needed solving before steamers could become practical: a method for generating steam quickly, and a lightweight apparatus that could be taken to fires speedily.

Shawk solved the first problem by adapting Joseph Buchanan's invention of a copper coil that increased in size from the opening where water was injected to the point where it became steam. The larger surface resulted in a rapid expansion of the heated water into steam. Shawk got a second-hand Farnham rowboat engine, stripped everything from it except the pump and running gear, acquired a boiler from Latta, and mounted it on the frame.

A large crowd, including councilmen—their

The first successful steam-driven fire engine in America was built in Cincinnati by Latta & Shawk in 1852. It was so successful that a public subscription raised $13,400 for this second steamer, which was named Citizens' Gift.

pocket watches in hand—gathered on March 1, 1852, for the first public demonstration. The rowboat sagged from the weight and the axles sprang. But three to five minutes after smoke puffed from the boiler stack, a solid stream of water spurted 130 feet. Nine days later, Councilman Joseph S. Ross introduced a resolution to appropriate $5,000 to hire the newly formed partnership, Latta & Shawk, to build the city a steamer that could shoot six streams.

When the motion carried, the volunteers jeered at what they charged was a waste of taxpayers' money on a "sham squirt." Shawk and Latta lived in constant terror. They built the steamer behind locked doors in the city shops.

"I sometimes fear that I shall never live to see this grand idea brought into the service of the world," said Latta. "The recent riots here show what a mob can do in our city. My steps are dogged. Spies are continually on my track. I am worried with all sorts of anonymous communications threatening me with all sorts of ills and evils unless I drop work on this engine and pronounce it a failure. I'll never give up! I'll build it, and there are men enough in this city to see that it has a fair trial. When it is finished, it will be heard from at the first fire, and woe to those who stand in its way!"

Latta and Shawk were not the only targets of the volunteers' hostility. Councilman Jacob Wykoff Piatt introduced legislation to create a salaried fire department, but the volunteers' lobbying succeeded in killing the resolution each time it came up. Piatt's thirteenth-district constituency was mainly Irish, and he was escorted everywhere by shillelagh-carrying bodyguards. When a mob of firefighters demonstrated outside his home, the Cincinnati police force—only 130 strong—fled as the mob burned Piatt in effigy.

Many ideas went into the steamer, including those of Miles Greenwood, one of the city's best mechanical engineers and a volunteer firefighter for twenty-four years. Cincinnati was not lacking in steam technology talent. The city was a steamboat- and locomotive-building center. Shawk and Latta, however, frequently argued during construction, mostly over Latta's ideas that resulted in an engine heavier and costlier than Shawk's plans. The partnership lasted only until the steamer was done. The engine was intended to be self-propelled, but when finished it was so heavy it required four horses to help pull it. The cost was double what the city appropriated. The engine was named Uncle Joe Ross, after the councilman who led the floor fight to provide money to build it. On the strength of this fame, Ross later ran for mayor, but lost when the volunteers campaigned for his opponent.

A public demonstration of the new steamer was set for New Year's Day, 1853. It was a bitterly cold day. The volunteers of Union Fire Company showed up with the city's most powerful Hunneman, Ocean No. 9. Their foreman promised, "We'll prove who's better, us or the sham squirt." With growing excitement the crowd awaited the steamer, which took nineteen minutes to arrive. It could be heard before it was seen.

"Pulled by four big horses, the engine rumbled

Above: *Fire insurance companies hired Paul Hodge, an engineer, to build this steam fire engine, the first in America, but volunteers refused to use it.* Opposite top: *Advertisement for Latta's line of fire engines.* Opposite bottom: *Curving hose gave this rig the name "squirrel tail."*

A.B. & E. LATTA

LIGHTNING

Ehrgott, Forbriger & Co. Lith

Carlisles Block S.W. Cor. 4th & Walnut Sts. Cin.

The original and only successful

STEAM FIRE ENGINE BUILDERS.

BUCKEYE WORKS, CINCINNATI, O.

down Fourth Street, shaking the buildings on either side. Belching smoke and sparks, the clanging engine drowned out the cheers of the crowd," said Kathleen J. Kiefer. The ponderous thing had only three wheels, one up front and two in the rear. It weighed 22,000 pounds, and the wheels ground the cobblestones into powder.

While the apparatus was building a head of steam preparatory to taking suction from a cistern, the Ocean volunteers seized their chance to show how much faster they could go into action. The brawniest members stroked the Hunneman and a stream jetted 200 feet. Now it was the steamer's turn. Water surged through the hose and shot 225 feet. Pressure was so strong it took two men to hold the nozzle as the water spewed over a five-story building. The volunteers pumped harder, but 200 feet was the best they could do, and in half an hour they fell back exhausted as the steamer continued to pound out its steady 225-foot stream.

"Let's show them what we could do in case of a fire," said Greenwood. Two, four, and finally six streams shot from the steamer. A fire engine that did the work of six hand pumpers and needed only three men to operate it—a driver, a stoker to fuel the boiler, and an engineer to work the pump! This prompted Piatt to reenter his resolution for a paid department. The volunteers fought it, but at 1:30 in the morning of March 10, 1853, the council voted for a salaried department effective April 1. Greenwood was named chief. The *Cincinnati Daily Commercial* stated in an editorial that the volunteers were "archangels ruined" and hoped that their good deeds would be remembered and their faults forgiven.

However, nobody believed that the volunteers would give up easily. They would challenge the paid men and the Uncle Joe Ross at the first fire, which was not long in breaking out at a warehouse. The volunteers arrived first. Chief Greenwood drove the Uncle Joe Ross. Close behind ran Councilman Piatt and 250 Irishmen. The Uncle Joe was hooked up, and the volunteers slashed its hose. But the thirteenth-district shillelaghs settled the issue. "The fight was fierce, bloody and brief," said Piatt's brother, Donn.

The next day many volunteers applied for jobs with the paid department, and those whose records were clean were hired as part-time firefighters. (In 1873, the department became full-time paid.) In the spring of 1854, a public subscription raised $13,400 for a second steamer, which was named Citizens' Gift. The Latta & Shawk partnership was by then dissolved and Latta won the contract. While the new engine was being built, the boiler of the Uncle Joe Ross exploded and the engineer, John Winterbottom, was killed.

The Cincinnati success story sparked agitation for paid departments in many American cities, demands that were fueled by the volunteers' continuing outrages. Philadelphia had sixty-nine riots in one year and as many as seventeen firefighters were jailed in a single day. New York's Tompkins Engine Company No. 30 was ordered to turn tongue-in after a firefighter punched Chief Alfred Carson. A false alarm by Baltimore's New Market and United Fire companies decoyed Mount Vernon Hook and Ladder into a trap. Shots were fired, bricks flew, and the volunteers hacked at each other with axes, iron picks, and firehooks. Two were killed and many were severely injured.

Smaller cities were the first to reorganize into paid departments. The volunteer Lafayette Hook and Ladder Company No. 1 of St. Louis disparaged salaried firefighters with its company motto, Public Servants, Not Hirelings, but it was a losing battle. St. Louis started a paid department in 1857. Chicago, Boston, and Baltimore quickly followed.

The ranks were at first filled with paid drivers, engineers, and stokers during the transition to fully paid departments. Some were immigrants, especially from the 1,600,000 Irish who came to the United States from 1847 to 1854 following the potato blight and famine in their homeland. Farming was all most of them knew, an occupation that ill equipped them for city life. But they were strong, accustomed to hard work and long hours. They eagerly took to

Opposite: *Mark of the United Firemen's Insurance Company depicts a steam fire engine built by Reaney & Neafie of Philadelphia.* Below: *James Smith, New York, is believed to have built this hand-drawn hook and ladder in 1854. The truck could be steered from both ends. The signal lantern was removed before the ladders were taken off the rig.*

battling flames, a job that offered steady pay and in every way ideally suited them. The Irish tradition in the American fire service has continued for generations, as firefighters' sons became firefighters and their sons followed them.

The volunteers clung to their system in the two major cities. New York volunteers represented a voting bloc of more than 3,000 in the city of 814,000, and Philadelphia volunteers mustered more than 2,100 votes. There were some who saw significance in the release, starting in 1854, of a series of colorful lithographs, "The Life of a Fireman," by Nathaniel Currier, and by James Merritt Ives, who became his partner in 1857. Currier himself is portrayed in the lithograph "The American Fireman—Always Ready," in which he is shown turning out to an alarm as a member of New York's Volunteer Excelsior Engine. The series did as much as anything to perpetuate New York's romantic attachment to the glorious era of the volunteers. New York would not go paid until 1865, Philadelphia not until 1871.

The big city volunteers had come full circle. Originally dedicated to providing the best fire protection and to searching out better ways to fight fires, they were now offering their firefighting expertise in an effort to disparage the obviously superior steamers. Chief Harry Howard of the New York volunteers said that water from the steamers caused more property damage than fires did. John Decker, the last chief of the Volunteer Fire Department of New York, said steamers would never replace hand pumpers: "Eight fires out of ten are brought under con-

A steamer, probably built by Latta, fighting flames at a Cincinnati theater. Volunteers at first disparaged the obviously superior steam engines, for steam power signaled the end of volunteer fire departments in large cities. Steamers could be operated by only a few men and thus made full-time paid fire departments feasible.

trol by the quickness of operation of hand-engines, so there is no need to use steamers." Decker conceded that perhaps one steamer might be used as a standby in each district to be used only at big fires. To which Chief Greenwood replied, "Steamers never get drunk. They never throw brickbats. Their only drawback is that they can't vote."

Despite the gradual changeover to steam in smaller cities, the New York and Philadelphia volunteers could not divorce themselves from their Old Gal hand engines, and the apparatus industry continued to turn them out. They came in five sizes. First-size engines, operated by as many as fifty firefighters, delivered about 150 gallons a minute at forty to sixty strokes per minute. These engines were chiefly used in large cities. The smallest engines were the fifth sizes, which put out around 30 gallons a minute. A minimum of four men was needed to pump these engines, which were usually bought by villages that could not afford bigger engines.

Lysander Button came up with a new model, which firefighters nicknamed squirrel tail, because the suction hose was permanently coupled to the water intake and curved back over the rig when not in use. Squirrel tails handled easier than double-deckers and the fixed coupling expedited suctioning. Around 1858, Smith began to build Shanghais, which had pagoda-shaped decking. Shanghais, only used in New York, were among the most powerful hand pumps ever built and usually were placed first in line when relaying water. They were, however, heavy, cumbersome, and consequently not popular. Hand pumpers continued to be made in the United States until after 1910. During the manual era there were around one hundred manufacturers, although many built only one or two rigs.

Realizing that steamers and paid departments were inevitable, and disgusted with the notoriety that was smearing their reputations, many volunteers looked for adventure elsewhere. But their love of firefighting never faltered and they never forgot company loyalties. When Dr. Elisha Kent Kane led his 1853–55 Arctic expedition to the northernmost point, he planted a flag on the glacier. The banner said Not for One But for All, the motto of his old Philadelphia Hose No. 1.

Some volunteers headed for the California gold fields and ended up in tinderbox San Francisco, where they joined volunteer companies or formed new ones. Among the members were Claus Spreckels, the Sugar King, and Mathew Brady, who formed Washington Hose Company No. 1, but is best remembered for his Civil War photography. Former New York Honey Bee David Scannell became fire chief and Malachi Fallon of Black Joke was named police chief. Tom Sawyer left New York's Columbian Engine Company No. 14 and became foreman of Liberty Hose Company No. 2. *The History of the San Francisco Fire Department,* published by Harry C. Pendleton, says Sawyer became a close friend of a local newspaper reporter, Samuel Clemens, and that *Tom Sawyer* was named after him. Mark Twain, however, said he modeled Tom after three friends.

Foreman David C. Broderick, the Red Rover who lost his cap during the Battle of the Boots, went to California, joined Empire Engine Company No. 1, and was elected to the United States Senate. In 1859 he fought a duel with Southerner David S. Terry, a former chief justice of the California Supreme Court, in which he was mortally wounded. His last words were, "They have killed me for opposing the extension of slavery." In his honor, Empire Engine changed its name to Broderick.

Boston volunteers emigrating to San Francisco formed Howard Engine Company No. 3 and ordered a Hunneman hand pumper from Boston. Former Philadelphia volunteers organized Pennsylvania Engine Company No. 12 and sent back for an Agnew double-decker. There was plenty of action to keep them busy. San Francisco burned often and burned big, including five conflagrations in three years. Running with their hand pumpers made it seem like the best of old times to the relocated firefighters.

In the East, meanwhile, the rioting of a minority of firefighters, many of them not official volunteers but company hangers-on, overshadowed the continuing feats of courage and dedication of the majority. What is recognized as the most courageous act in the annals of the Volunteer Fire Department of New York occurred shortly after 1:00 A.M. on St. Patrick's Day, 1852, when bells rang out an alarm for a fire in a three-story building at 89½ Bowery Street.

Among the first companies in was Atlantic Hose No. 14 under Foreman James R. Mount, recovered from the slashed stomach he suffered during the Battle of the Boots. Smoke and flames were boiling from a paint and wallpaper store on the ground floor and spreading to upstairs apartments. Six people trapped on the third floor were ready to jump.

MID SUMMER
NIGHTS DREAM

"Wait!" yelled Mount, "I'll get you." Wrapping his coat around his head, Mount dashed into the building. At the first floor landing he found a semiconscious girl. Scooping her up, he threw her down to Atlantic Hoseman Joe Skillman. Mount groped through the thick smoke and searing heat to the second floor landing where he found a dead man. Mount continued to the third floor and discovered another body.

Crawling along the third floor hallway, he found the room where the six were trapped. They were too terrified to follow him down the stairs. Mount ran to the street, where firefighters had raised a ladder. It reached only to the second floor. They found a barrel, put the ladder on it, and Mount climbed to the highest rung. He was still four feet away from the third floor windows. The first victim eased himself off the window ledge and dropped onto Mount's shoulders. Mount brought him down and went up after the others. The last down was a 245-pound woman. Mount then collapsed in the street.

For saving seven lives—two children, three women, and two men—the members of Atlantic Hose presented Mount with a $260 gold watch and chain. The Association of Exempt Firemen gave him a silver-engraved trumpet, and the Common Council

Opposite: *Steam power and manpower combine forces to battle a fire that destroyed seven buildings at Murray and Church Streets, New York, on the night of September 9, 1861. This lithograph is a Currier & Ives print from the famous series "The Life of a Fireman."* Below: *Many songs were composed to glorify volunteer firefighters. This is the sheet music cover for a song called "The Fireman's Heart is Bold and Free."*

voted him $300 and a silver pitcher and tray. Accepting the honors, Mount said that he had only done what was expected of him.

The wonder was that so many firefighters of Mount's dedication stayed as the dangers increased with ever-larger buildings and heavier concentrations of flammables, and as editorials chipped at the volunteer system. Firefighting must have seemed like a thankless service as much of the public came to lump both the good and the bad firefighters into what they considered a bunch of bums who sat around playing checkers and spoiling for fights.

Andy Schenck of New York's Mutual Ball Club Hook & Ladder Company No. 1 was visiting his fiancée on Tuesday evening, April 25, 1854, when alarm bells rang. She begged him not to go. "My duty is to the Mutuals," he said. "I'll go to this fire and it will be my last."

Arriving on Broadway across from City Hall, Schenck found the four-story brick clothing store of William T. Jennings & Company fully involved. Companies were racing in from up and down Broadway. Ladders went up and hoses were lifted to the roofs of adjoining buildings. Firefighters crawled through the thick smoke and heat while dragging their hoselines to get in close and bore into the flames.

Half an hour after the fire started, the rear wall came thundering down in a torrent of stout rafters, thick iron beams, and bricks. A huge safe crashed from the fourth floor into the basement and crushed two firefighters. Chief Harry Howard had no idea how many were trapped—certainly at least a dozen. The firefighters began pulling apart debris, lifting timbers, and throwing aside bricks.

A stream from an adjoining building was shooting onto a burning flap of roof. Scalding water poured off it and onto the rescuers. "Shut down that line! Shut it down!" they screamed. But it could not be done. The rooftop firefighters had to keep the line going or the flaming supports would burn through and drop the roof onto the rescuers.

The digging continued all night. Coroner O'Donnell arrived and learned that his twenty-two-year-old son, John, of Haywagon-Mankiller Engine Company No. 42, was one of those trapped. He talked to his son during the eight hours he was held fast by redhot bricks and showered by water and steam. Soon after they dug him out, Coroner

Early hook and ladder company firefighters had an especially perilous job, because their ladders lacked strength and often slipped. This child is lucky, however, as the firefighter makes a successful rescue. But it is not likely that he would have burdened himself with a trumpet.

O'Donnell would take his son's body to the morgue along with the others.

The last victim was recovered after dawn. Twenty firefighters went to hospitals. Eleven firefighters went to the morgue, including the McKay brothers of Fulton Engine Company No. 21 and Mutual's Andy Schenck, whose fiancée was there when they carried out his body.

Steamer experience in other cities gradually proved their worth, and the volunteers' bloc began to crumble, especially after the four-round competition on February 9, 1855, between a Latta steamer and New York's most powerful hand pumper, the Mankiller, held before a large crowd in City Hall Park. Mankiller quickly produced a stream while the Latta took over eight minutes. Round one went to the volunteers. Round two was a contest for the best horizontal distance. The steamer did 182 feet, but Mankiller won with 189. Round three was a repeat of round two.

With the score 3–0 in favor of Mankiller, the final round consisted of shooting a perpendicular stream over the statue of Justice on the City Hall cupola. Mankiller's stream went higher, but after thirty minutes the men were exhausted and had to quit. The Latta continued to chuff its steam, and showed it could do so for as long as the boiler was fired. "That settles it," said Zophar Mills, a prominent New York fire officer for more than thirty years. "The steamer is the engine of the future."

Many makers of hand pumpers rushed to convert to steamers, but most lacked the know-how or facilities. Agnew, for example, built only four, Smith built fourteen, and Cowing turned his attention to other types of apparatus. Agnew lost out to half a dozen Philadelphia steam fire engine builders who sprang up almost simultaneously. Of these, only Reaney and Neafie produced any number of steamers: thirty-three. In Boston, Hunneman & Company built around thirty steam fire engines but could not compete with the Amoskeag Company of Manchester, New Hampshire. In Rhode Island, William Jeffers converted from a lucrative hand engine business to steamers, with moderate success. He turned out more than sixty engines before quitting. The only one of the old hand engine builders to achieve substantial success was the Button Company, which sold more than two hundred steamers.

One of the early steam fire engine builders was the Silsby Company, of Seneca Falls, New York. The Silsby engine was of the rotary design as opposed to the piston or reciprocating-type pumps used by other manufacturers. This simpler construction was thought to make the engines more trouble-free and produce less friction loss in the hose. The Silsby firm and its successor, the American Fire Engine Company, sold more than eight hundred engines.

Others quickly entered the field, most of them producing less than fifty engines in all. But several firms prospered and produced a considerable number of engines. Among them were the Ahrens Manufacturing Company of Cincinnati (successor to Latta and Lane & Bodley), 300 engines; the Clapp & Jones Fire Engine Company, Hudson, New York, 400 engines; and the LaFrance Fire Engine Company, Elmira, New York, 430 engines. Early LaFrance engines were rotaries, like the Silsbys.

In Manchester, New Hampshire, the Amoskeag Company, builders of textile machinery and locomotives, entered the steam fire engine field in 1859. The name Amoskeag became to steam fire engines what General Motors is to automobiles today. Some 854 engines were sold to fire departments everywhere by Amoskeag and its successors, the Manchester Locomotive Works, the American Locomotive Works, and the International Power Company, of Providence, Rhode Island.

After 1891, three companies dominated the steam fire engine market: the American Fire Engine Company, a merger of Ahrens, Button, Clapp & Jones, and Silsby; the Amoskeag complex; and the LaFrance Fire Engine Company. The American Fire Engine Company developed the "American" from the Ahrens engine and from that came, in 1896, the famous Metropolitan. When American LaFrance was formed by the merger of American Fire Engine Company and the LaFrance Fire Engine Company, the Metropolitan became its principal product. Probably a better fire engine was never built.

By 1860, there were twenty-one steamers in the Philadelphia Fire Department and Boston had entirely converted to steam pumpers. The city's fire chief reported that the switchover saved Boston twenty percent a year in fire protection costs. And then, on April 12, 1861, Fort Sumter was bombarded. The firefighters' battles against fires, rival companies, paid departments, and steamers were quickly put aside. There was a war to be fought.

13 RALLY 'ROUND THE FLAG, BOYS!

Volunteers who had fought fires together now marched off to fight a war and die together. Eight days after President Lincoln appealed for troops, some 1,100 New York volunteers enlisted at their firehouses; 11,000 would sign up in Philadelphia by the end of the war. In the South, members of Atlanta's Mechanic Fire Company No. 2 joined as a body and kept their name as they marched off to war and a fatal rendezvous with New York and Philadelphia firefighters at Gettysburg. Norfolk volunteers formed a heavy artillery company and left their Agnew double-decker with black firefighters.

President Lincoln appointed his friend Elmer E. Ellsworth to lead the New York firefighters. Except for his choice of General Grant and a few others, Lincoln was a poor judge of military talent. Colonel Ellsworth was a twenty-four-year-old Chicago patent attorney who liked to play soldier. He had impressed the president with his precision marching teams, which wore flashy military uniforms similar to the French Zouaves: short blue jackets, baggy, bloomer-like red trousers, reddish brown boots, and red fezzes. That summed up Ellsworth's combat credentials.

The patriotic fervor of the New York volunteers flamed higher when they learned they would wear Zouave uniforms, and they vowed to follow Ellsworth anywhere. Nobody realized that the brilliant colors would make them stand out like peacocks in the woods of Virginia and Pennsylvania. On April 20,

A Currier & Ives lithograph shows the burning of Richmond, Va., on the night of April 2, 1865. The Rebels torched the city before abandoning it to General Grant's troops. As the flames rage, the city is evacuated by residents and Confederate cavalry crossing the James River bridge.

Opposite top: *Civil war regiments of volunteer firefighters enlisted in New York and Philadelphia. They called themselves Zouaves because their uniforms were patterned after those worn by French Algerian troops of the same name.* Opposite bottom *and* below right: *New York Zouaves, bivouacked in Washington, fight a fire next to the Willard Hotel in 1861.*

1861, the volunteers were officially sworn in as the Eleventh New York Volunteers, but nobody called them that. They were better known as the First New York Zouaves.

Wearing their outlandish uniforms, the Zouaves were cheered by thousands as they marched down Broadway to the East River, boarded a steamship for Washington, and set up barracks in the House of Representatives. The feisty volunteers were as rowdy in the capital as they had been at home, and Ellsworth took out advertisements in the local press in which he apologized for their conduct, and invited citizens to make their complaints to him at 10 o'clock each morning in his office.

Military training consisted mostly of close order drill, and the volunteers looked for more action. They got it, early May 9, when a fire in a liquor store spread to the Willard Hotel next door. The Zouaves joined the Washington firefighters. Contemporary illustrations show the Zouaves hanging by their heels and, for want of ladders, standing on each other's shoulders as they fight the fire. In two hours the fire was out, the Willard was saved, and the manager treated the Zouaves to breakfast.

On May 24, Lincoln ordered eight regiments, including the Zouaves, to invade Virginia. Crossing the Potomac into Alexandria, Colonel Ellsworth saw a Rebel flag on the staff above the Marshall House. He ran into the hotel, cut down the flag, and was returning to the street when the manager, James T. Jackson, appeared and blew his chest open with a shotgun blast. Seconds later, a Zouave killed Jackson. Lincoln ordered Ellsworth's body brought to the White House, where it lay in state in the East Room. The Union had its first war hero, and the Zouaves had a new leader, Colonel Noah L. Farnham of Mutual Ball Club Hook & Ladder Company No. 1, who knew even less about war than Ellsworth.

The Zouaves got their first taste of combat during the First Battle of Bull Run, July 21, when Jeb Stuart's Virginia cavalry slashed into the center of the firefighters' line. Lieutenant Daniel Divver of Eagle Engine Company No. 13 led a charge while shouting Eagle's call to fires, "Get down, Old Hague!" Six bullets killed Divver. Another shot hit Farnham behind the left ear and he fell mortally wounded. First Bull Run cost the Zouaves between 75 and 100 dead and 200 wounded. In their rout, they left 125 behind. They lost the battle, but in their retreat they took a prize—the double-decker of Valley Forge Engine Company No. 1 of Alexandria—which they later lugged back to New York.

When the Philadelphia volunteers learned of the Zouave uniforms, they got similar ones and changed their name from the Seventy-Second Infantry Regiment to Baxter's Philadelphia Fire Zouaves and Birney's Zouaves of the Twenty-Third Regiment. The first Philadelphians into the field were the Rangers, captained by Moyamensing Hose Company Foreman Bill "Bull" MacMullin. During the war a total of 210 Philadelphia volunteers would be killed; another 120 died from diseases, 558 were wounded, and 165 were

captured or declared missing in action. Among the battles they fought were Yorktown, the Peach Orchard at Shiloh, Malvern Hill, Antietam, Fredericksburg, Chancellorsville, Gettysburg, the Wilderness, and Spotsylvania.

Comparatively little is known of the firefighters who fought for the Confederacy, other than the Norfolk volunteers who largely formed the crew of the ironclad *Merrimack* in its battle with the *Monitor.*

The Second New York Fire Zouaves had meanwhile been organized and bivouacked on Staten Island until they joined the Army of the Potomac. Around 150 Second Zouaves fell at Williamsburg. More died at Second Bull Run and Chancellorsville. At Gettysburg, the Second Zouaves suffered 51 killed, 103 wounded, and 8 taken prisoner. The Philadelphia Zouaves and Atlanta's Mechanic Fire Company No. 2 fared little better. A monument on the battlefield at Gettysburg honors the fallen volunteers.

As the wounded streamed north aboard trains and steamships, Philadelphia volunteer firefighters who had remained behind to protect the city formed an ambulance corps of thirty-five horse-drawn wagons. The ambulances were purchased by the volunteers and their friends and were decorated as lavishly as the Old Gal fire engines. When bells in fire towers struck nine times, then six more times, the men raced with their ambulances to meet arriving hospital trains and ships. In the five days before Christmas, 1862, the ambulance corps carried 2,500 patients. During the war, the ambulances transported a total of 120,000. When the hospitals became overloaded, the volunteers turned their firehouses into medical stations. Philadelphia's was the first fire-department-operated ambulance service in the United States.

As southern jails filled with Union prisoners, War Secretary Edwin M. Stanton looked for a spy who could freely cross Confederate lines to report prison conditions and other intelligence. Bill Post of New York's Columbian Engine Company No. 14 was an ideal choice. Post, forty-one years old, was too old to look like a spy and yet, as one of the Bowery Boys, intrigue was his forte. Few knew that his true name was Adolphus Borst and that he was a native of Strasbourg, France, and spoke fluent French and German.

Post was a New York policeman when he came to Secretary Stanton's attention. Post's sleuthing had led to the seizure of Confederate bank note plates and $300 million in Southern currency. Stanton quietly contacted the friendly Prussian government and arranged for Post to be commissioned as Adolphus Borst, a Prussian agent serving as a neutral observer of the welfare of Union prisoners. Affecting a Prussian accent and wearing a Teutonic uniform, Post-Borst crossed Confederate lines time and again while spying for Stanton.

While being escorted by the warden through the stockade of the notorious Andersonville Prison in Georgia, Post-Borst was recognized by an inmate who was a volunteer with Columbian Engine. "Hey, Posty!" the volunteer called. "Got you, too, have they? You'll have a jolly time here, old man!" Post-Borst adjusted his monocle, ignored his friend, and managed to retain his masquerade until the war ended.

With Union losses running high, President Lincoln signed a conscription act making all men

Opposite: *Col. Elmer Ellsworth, who knew more about flashy uniforms than about war. He was appointed by President Lincoln to lead the First New York Zouaves, who were formed from the ranks of the Volunteer Fire Department of New York.* Below: *The Zouaves' uniforms made them stand out like peacocks, easy marks for Rebel forces, who slaughtered them.*

between age thirty and forty-five eligible to be drafted. The only exemptions were for those who provided an acceptable substitute or paid $300. It was as unwise a piece of legislation as Lincoln could have signed. Poor people charged that they were being forced to fight the war for the wealthy, who could afford to stay home. Disturbances broke out in many cities, but none approached the New York draft riots that erupted less than two weeks after Gettysburg.

They started at 11:05 A.M., Monday, July 13, 1863, when a mob, mostly foreign-born laborers and Southern sympathizers, attacked and burned the draft office on Third Avenue near Forty-sixth Street. The rioters tried to stop Chief John Decker and his volunteers from hooking up to hydrants. Ducking a barrage of brickbats and constantly replacing their slashed hoses, the firefighters were not able to prevent flames from spreading to three other buildings.

Next to be fire-bombed were two brownstone buildings on Lexington Avenue between Forty-fourth and Forty-fifth Streets, followed later that same day by the Bull's Head Hotel at Forty-fourth Street and Fifth Avenue. As soon as firefighters brought one blaze under control they hurried off to another. At 4:50 P.M., the mob looted and burned the five-story brick Marston & Company gun factory on Twenty-first Street and Second Avenue. Firefighters were busy there when they learned the entire block of Broadway from Twenty-eighth to Twenty-ninth Streets was blazing.

Shortly before 7 o'clock the mob, swelling to thousands, stormed up Fifth Avenue and attacked the Colored Orphan Asylum, a huge three-story building occupying nearly an entire block between Forty-third and Forty-fourth Streets. Rioters were chopping through the doors when Chief Decker arrived. They clubbed Decker, dragged him to a tree, and prepared to lynch him. It is said that Decker told

Right: *Two houses burn in New York City in 1863 during riots opposing Lincoln's conscription act. The rioters set fire to many buildings and attacked firefighters who tried to put out the flames. Chief John Decker was nearly lynched before troops quelled the riots.* Below: *The burning of Columbia, S.C., set by Union troops on the night of February 17, 1865, after General William Sherman took the city. When the war was over, New York firefighters donated a new hose carriage and other apparatus to Columbia.*

them, "What good will it do to hang me? You will only stop my draft, not the government's." The pun saved Decker's life, but by then the orphanage was flaming and the mob was chasing and pummeling the terrified black children who were fleeing up Fifth Avenue.

Rioting, burning, and looting continued throughout the night and the next day. Homes and tenements occupied by blacks were torched. Abolitionists were beaten. Blacks were hidden in fire stations, and the volunteers patrolled the streets looking for new outbreaks. Washington Irving Hose Company No. 44 was attacked shortly after noon on Tuesday, while fighting a hotel fire on Eighth Avenue and Forty-first Street. At 3:04 P.M., the Weehawken Ferry Terminal at Forty-second Street and the Hudson River was set afire, and soon after, two Roosevelt Street tenements of black families were torched. Tuesday night a burning building on East Twenty-second Street set fire to the Eighteenth Police Precinct Station, which was destroyed along with the fire alarm bell tower and the firehouse of Mutual Engine Company No. 51.

At 2:40 A.M., Wednesday morning, a huge lumber yard was torched on Fourteenth Street. The glow was seen throughout lower Manhattan and the firefighters' strength was further sapped as they turned out to battle the flames. The fire was being brought under control when the volunteers were called at 10:50 A.M. to West Thirty-second Street, where three more tenements were burning. Black families fled through rear doors and found themselves trapped by a fence around the yard.

Answering the alarm was Mohawk Hose Company No. 39. Their faces grimy with soot from other fires, they came down the alley and yanked down the fence. Then, as the inhabitants escaped, the mob attacked Mohawkers Dan Rooney, Joe Twombly, and John F. McGovern, who flayed at them with their helmets and spanner wrenches. McGovern picked up a child who had been overlooked and ran. The crowd chased him. He leaped a fence and waited until the mob passed. McGovern hid the boy in a large bread box and took him to a police station, where his mother finally found him.

New York's Seventh Regiment was recalled from Gettysburg and put down the riots with the help of West Point cadets. Nobody knows how many were killed or injured, but estimates say as many as a thousand. Damage came to around $2 million. Praising the volunteers' work under conditions experienced for the first time by American firefighters, the *New York Herald* said: "No class of men are more entitled to praise for heroism and self-sacrifice . . . than the firemen of New York in extinguishing fires and saving valuable property." The riots were largely responsible for an amendment to the conscription act, in which only conscientious objectors were excused from service.

As Union troops pushed deeper into the South, they destroyed volunteer fire apparatus. During General William T. Sherman's siege of Atlanta, the firehouse of Tallulah Fire Company No. 3 took a direct hit. When Sherman's army took Atlanta they smashed Blue Dick Engine and confiscated Tallulah's rig, sending it to Chattanooga to protect Union supplies. As Southern towns and cities fell, Union troops shoved dead horses and garbage into cisterns. These acts left communities virtually without drinking water and defenseless against fire and helped to kindle deeper Southern hatred of their conquerors.

As the end of the war neared, volunteers began returning home to reorganize their departments. When members of Independence Hose Company No. 1 returned to Columbia, South Carolina, they found their apparatus and all other equipment destroyed. They appealed to New York volunteers for old fire hose and a cast-off carriage. In less than a week the New York Firemen's Association raised $5,000, bought Independence a silver-plated hose carriage, 500 feet of new hose, 100 helmets, red shirts, belts, trumpets, and a white hat for the chief. The gifts were shipped aboard the steamer *Andalusia,* and the volunteers left by train to make the presentation. Arriving in Columbia, they learned that the *Andalusia* had burned and sunk at sea. The volunteers returned to New York, raised another $5,000, and Independence Hose was back in service.

As fire protection was restored, burned-out areas of cities were rebuilt. In Atlanta, Hook and Ladder Company No. 1 volunteers helped pull down "Sherman's Monuments"—smoke-blackened walls and chimneys. Washington, D.C., had many fires during the war, including a building at 511 Tenth Street, Northwest. Unfortunately, the burned-out hulk was rebuilt, else the course of American history might have been different. The building was Ford's Theater.

14
SAGA OF THE STEAMERS

If the New York volunteers could have picked the time and place to fight their last major fire and literally go out in a blaze of glory, Phineas T. Barnum's American Museum would have been their first choice. Barnum's Museum, at the busy intersection of Broadway and Ann Street, near City Hall Park, was the city's major attraction in the days before the Statue of Liberty and the Empire State Building.

Plastered on the sides of the five-story brick theater were enormous color posters hinting at the sideshow marvels inside: the bushy-haired Albino Lady from Darkest Africa; the Cherry-Colored Cat from Long Island; the 400-pound Fat Lady of the Circus; General Tom Thumb and his midget bride, Lavinia Warren; Admiral Dot, smaller than Tom Thumb, and Dot's paramour, Anna Swan, eight feet tall and 413 pounds; Moby-Dick, the Great White Whale, and a menagerie of animals and reptiles, including a python Barnum claimed was thirty-six feet long, although nobody was allowed to uncoil the snake to measure it. Whether you actually saw all these things was something you found out only after you paid admission. If New Yorkers and tourists wanted to be flimflammed, Barnum's was the place for it.

Lunch-hour crowds were surging along Broadway at 12:30 P.M., Thursday, July 13, 1865, when smoke and flames were seen pouring from Barnum's basement. Billowing black smoke attracted thousands of noontime spectators as the volunteers, many with the new steam fire engines, raced to the scene. Fortunately, few people were in the building, or the fast-spreading fire would have been disastrous.

Volunteer companies stroked their double-decker, squirrel tails, and a Shanghai, while the steamer engineers of the three Amoskeags and two Silsbys watched boiler pressure gauges. Streams bored into the flames as other volunteers ran into the thick smoke to save performers and as many animals as they could. Hundreds of birds were released from cages to flutter over Broadway, their exotic plumage adding to the spectacle of the flames stabbing through the smoke.

The crowd cheered as volunteers led flippering seals to safety. Inside the steaming murk, the axe-swinging firefighters mercifully killed Moby-Dick, crocodiles, lions, zebras, and a baby elephant. Coming upon the smoldering python, Firefighter George W. Collier, of Engine Company No. 29, smashed its glass cage and slew the snake. More hand pumpers, steamers, hose reels, and ladder companies came clanging up to join the battle. Hoselines twined like spaghetti along Broadway as the volunteers labored at their brakes and the steamers spewed smoke and sparks.

Suddenly the crowd screamed. A glaring Bengal tiger appeared at a second-floor window and leaped onto Broadway. Policemen emptied their pistols, but Barnum's Bengal only shrugged. The tiger crouched as if to pounce and the panicky crowd began to stampede, when Johnny Dedham of Atlantic Hose Company No. 15 killed the snarling tiger with one whack of his axe. The mob cheered and Dedham later said he "felt a flow of feeling," as he ran into Barnum's, rescued the 400-pound Fat Lady of the Circus, went back in again and saved two midgets, and returned a third time to bring out the Albino Lady from Darkest Africa.

That anything was left of Barnum's was credited to the steamers. Losses came to $500,000, but Philip W. Engs, president of the Exempt Firemen's Association, said the steamers saved a quarter of a million dollars. At day's end, the weary volunteers rolled up their hoses and trudged back to their fire stations. It was their last hurrah, a spectacular ending to a spectacular era in New York.

Fire Chief John Decker made one last attempt to save the volunteers. In his final report to the Common Council he asked it to reconsider the decision to replace the volunteers with a paid department. "The

A matched team of horses galloping to a fire and pulling the shiny engine was a thrilling sight in America after the Civil War. The finely trained horses responded instantly to the reins as the engines, smoke streaming from the boilers, came rumbling down the street.

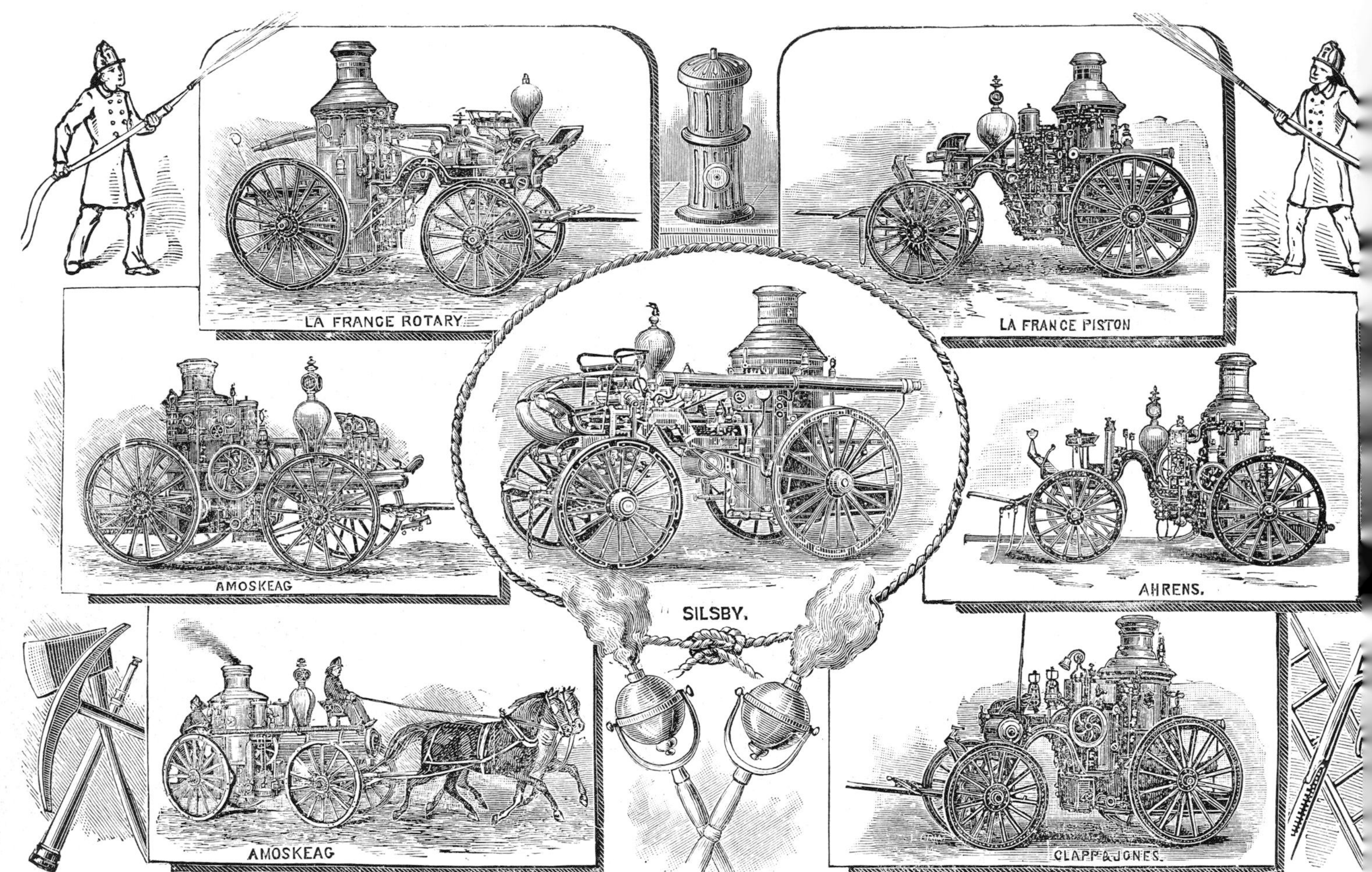

firemen of this city are as intelligent, honest, sober, and industrious as any body of nearly four thousand men in the world. Some of our best merchants, bankers, mechanics, and tradesmen have been or are at present members of the fire department and are proud to have it known in their social and business circles, and will always be pleased to remember that they belonged to the Volunteer Fire Department of the City of New York."

But it was not to be. On July 31, 1865, eighteen days after Barnum's fire, the paid Fire Department of the City of New York became a reality. Eighty-nine steamers, eleven hook and ladders, and fifty-four hose companies soon were formed. The department included about five hundred firefighters, whose annual salaries ranged from $700 for Ordinary Fireman to $3,000 for Chief Engineer Elisha Kingsland. They got one twenty-four-hour day off each month. Even today, more than one hundred years later, the forty-hour work week is just beginning to be enjoyed by a few fire departments, and that mostly through the efforts of the AFL–CIO International Association of Fire Fighters, founded in 1918.

Recalling the excesses of some of the volunteers, paid departments were organized on paramilitary lines, a system that continues today. Officer titles consequently took on military connotations soon after the Civil War. The head of a company of firefighters no longer was called a foreman, but a captain or lieutenant. Over him was a battalion chief, who commanded several companies. When the fire became larger than a battalion chief's companies could handle, more would be called and a division commander would take charge. Above division commanders in rank and authority were deputy chiefs. The highest of all was the fire commissioner, fire

Opposite: *Types of steam fire engines used in New York City around 1887. At one time the city owned more than 300 steamers.* Right: *In January, 1898, Engine Company 35 of Boston got this self-propelled steamer, which was built by the Manchester Locomotive Works.* Below right: *An American LaFrance steam pumper drafts from a hydrant at a New York fire.*

chief, or chief engineer (the name varies from city to city), who was, in effect, the commanding general of the entire fire department.

One of the first rules of the Fire Department of New York required the officer in command to lead his apparatus going to or returning from fires. Only the driver, engineer, and stoker could ride the engine; the other firefighters ran ahead to clear the way for the apparatus.

Considering the long hours in their stations, it was little wonder that firefighters sometimes dawdled while returning from alarms. But New York Fire Commissioners, in General Order Number 11, May 18, 1868, said: "The habit of loitering home . . . must be discontinued. Hereafter when a Company is ready to return . . . the men will be formed and marched on the street ahead of the apparatus in two ranks, with the officers ahead, or on the sidewalks abreast of the Engine or Truck. . . . The files will be not more than one pace apart."

With the passing of the nation's stronghold of volunteers, other cities quickly went paid or partly paid. On the day of the changeover, the volunteers would gather around their Old Gals for a final farewell and a toast of auld lang syne. Members of Buffalo's Hook and Ladder Company No. 2, the Red Birds, sang in chorus the company's traditional song, written by Firefighter Arthur W. Gregory and set to the air of *Champagne Charley:*

Come, gather 'round you citizens,
  A song I'll sing to you
Of the men so brave who a name have made
  For Hook and Ladder 2.
Our truck was built by Hartshorn.
  Who made her tough and strong,
And proud are we of our own "Red Bird"
  That swiftly glides along . . .
Hussah! We sing for Citizen 2.
  May the "Red Bird" run forever;
May no dissensions part us,
  May we all be friends together.
And when the bells are ringing clear
  May our bunkers true
Earn the right to say, "The first thing there
  Was Hook and Ladder 2."

Soon there was a new look in the old firehouse, as the hand-drawn Old Gals were hauled away for scrapping or auctioning off to small communities that could not afford steamers. The engines that

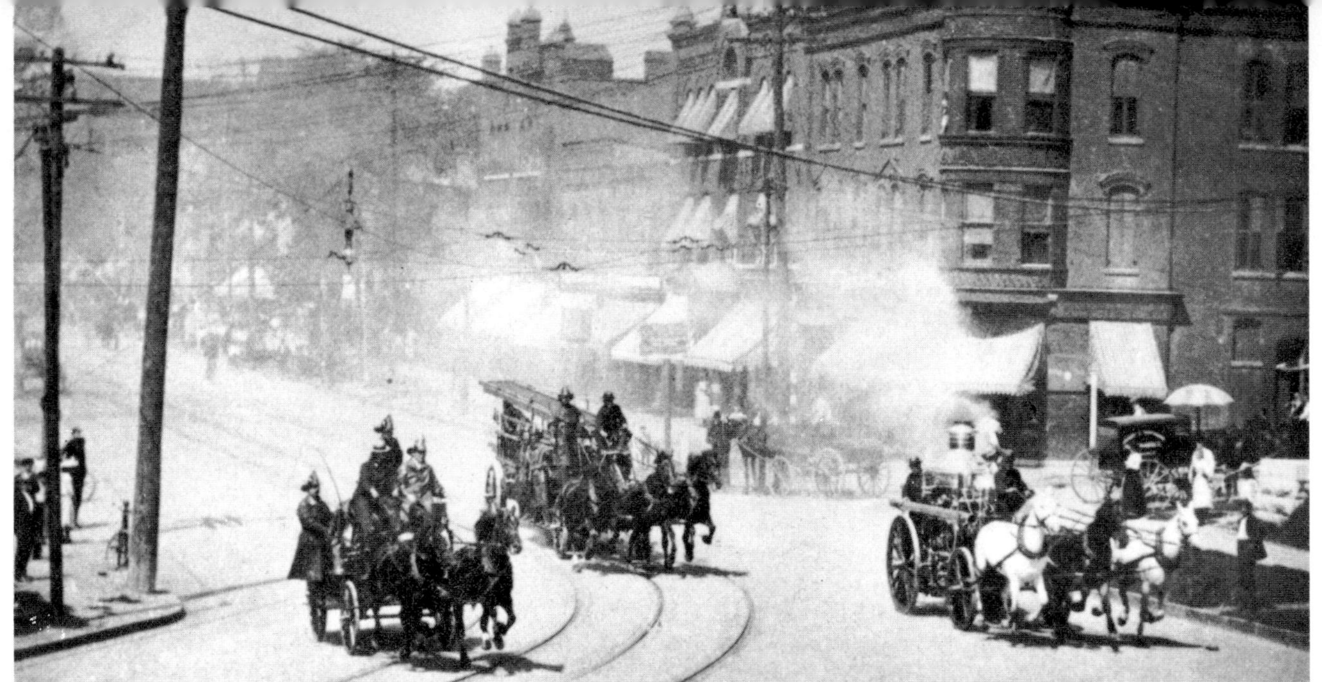

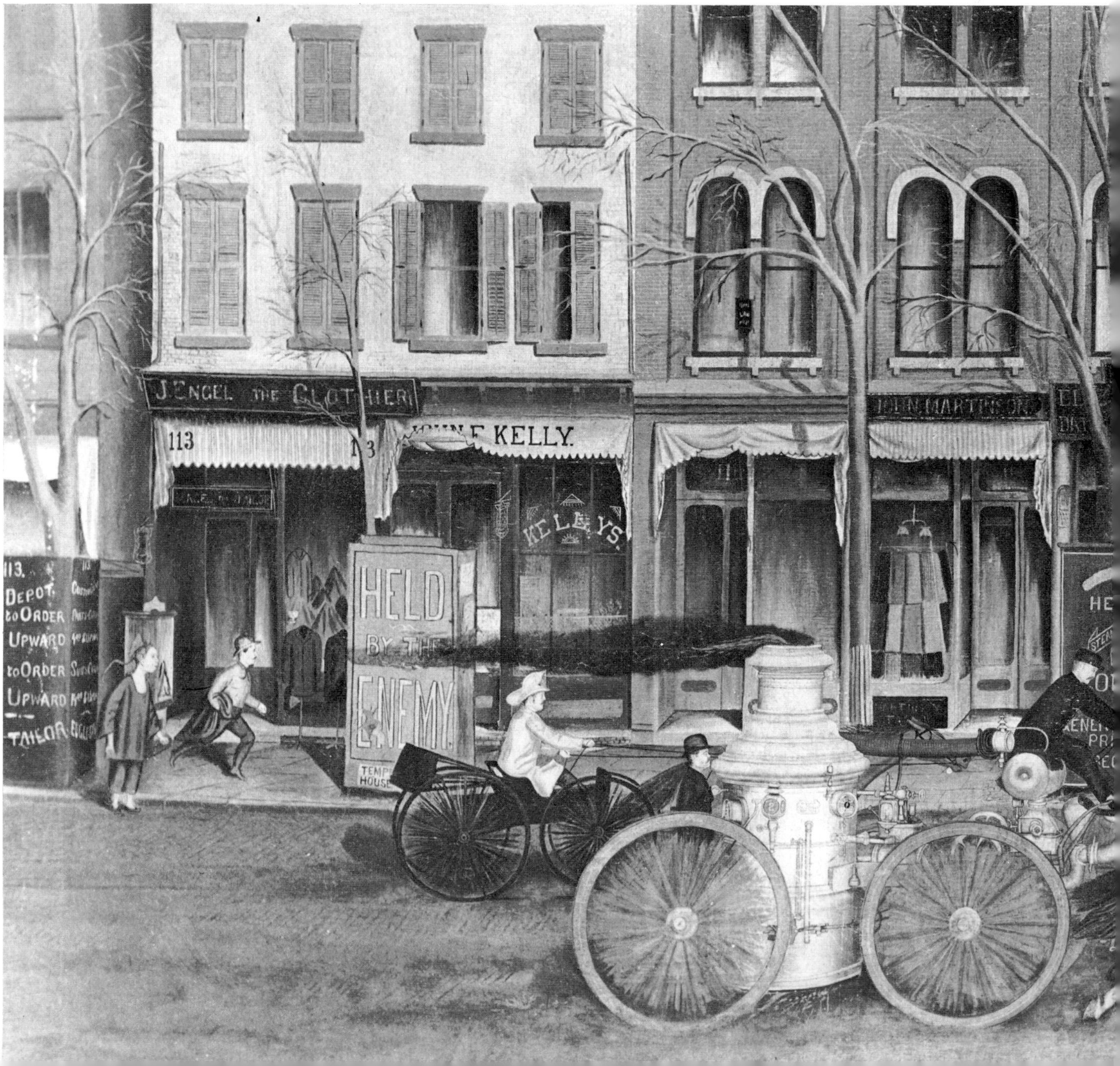
J. ENGEL THE CLOTHIER
113
HELD BY THE ENEMY
113.
DEPOT
to ORDER
UPWARD
to ORDER
UPWARD
TAILOR

Opposite: *In a Syracuse, N.Y., street scene in 1906, a hose wagon, a ladder truck, and a steam fire engine race to the alarm.* Below: *Smoke streams from the boiler of an Elizabeth, N.J., steam fire engine as the driver urges the horses on down Broad Street, in this 1889 painting. The fire chief in his buggy follows close behind.*

replaced them were every bit as colorful: shiny brass, nickel, and black boilers; maroon chassis; gleaming nickel-, copper-, and brasswork; black suction hose; and gold-striped wheels. They looked powerful, and many were. Depending upon size, they could pump from 300 to more than 1,300 gallons a minute.

A chief drawback of the engines was the time it took to generate steam from cold water—an average of five to seven minutes. But the paid firefighters were as ingenious as the volunteers in coming up with new ideas. One of the first was a system for faster steam operation, invented by Firefighter William Gleason of New York's Engine 20.

Gleason's idea was to keep boilers filled with hot water. A heater, usually in the fire station basement, was connected by pipes to the steamers. The heater circulated hot water in the boiler coils of the steamers. A damper fitted over the stack helped to keep the water hot. Firefighters often decorated their stacks with crown-shaped dampers or, in Philadelphia, with covers resembling Indian totem poles. Preheated water enabled the steamers to start pumping in less than three minutes after arriving at a fire, and some companies boasted they could do it in eighty seconds.

Self-propulsion would not become common until the development of gasoline-powered motors. Many steamers were at first hand-drawn, but as they became larger and heavier, horses became necessary. Firefighters did not like that idea one bit—"A firehouse ain't no place for no stinkin' horse!" A compromise was reached for a while by renting or buying horses and stabling them near fire stations or in barns behind firehouses. But too much time was lost in unlocking barns, leading the horses into the station, turning them around, and backing them to the harness. So ultimately the horses came into the houses, and the firefighters grumbled. But not for long. More than half a century of mutual affection, comparable only to the volunteers' love of their Old Gals, was about to begin.

Stalls were located at the rear or sides of the fire apparatus. Doors or chains kept the horses in their stalls, which it became the rookie's job to clean. At first, horses stood harnessed most of the time, until methods were devised for suspending the harness from the ceiling and dropping it onto the horses' backs when an alarm sounded.

Nobody knows who first developed the quick hitch, but evidence suggests it may have been a St. Joseph, Missouri, firefighter in 1871, who hung a single harness. The same year, firefighters in Allegheny, Pennsylvania, worked out a double harness for two-horse hitches. In July, 1873, Charles E. Berry, a Cambridge, Massachusetts, firefighter, came up with a hanging harness with quick-locking hames. When the apparatus driver pulled a cord, the harness dropped onto the horses' backs and the hames were quickly hooked by other firefighters. When the harness dropped, a system of pulleys, counterweights, and springs lifted the holders out of the way.

The famous line of Amoskeag fire apparatus is shown in this advertising broadside of about 1868. The Amoskeag Company of Manchester, N.H., was the nation's major builder of fire apparatus prior to the motorized era. Amoskeag and its successor companies produced about 854 fire engines, which were sold to departments throughout the nation.

Before the quick hitch, harnessing required several minutes. The new system enabled firefighters to shave two to three minutes from the time it took them to roll out of their stations. It has ever been axiomatic that the most time that can be saved in getting to fires is the time saved before leaving the station—for traffic congestion was almost as bad then as today, and in downtown areas sometimes worse.

Berry's system became so popular that he quit the fire department and sold his patented Berry Hames and Collars throughout the United States. In Pittsburgh, meanwhile, Firefighter John J. Freyvogel of Engine Company No. 5 made an improved metal collar which, like handcuffs, quickly adjusted to the size of the horse's neck.

The second floor of the firehouse was now devoted to bunking and recreation rooms. Oats and hay were stored above the stable area. With the new look, the day when the firehouse was the neighborhood social center ended. Gone were the chowder parties, and gone, too, were the days of going to the firehouse and sitting around the potbelly stove reminiscing about fires past.

The apparatus floor became austere. Fire stations now were places where the serious business of fire protection was carried on, and, in larger cities, often the only person regularly permitted on the apparatus floor was the man standing his share of the twenty-four-hour watch. He sat at a desk near the alarm gong and regularly checked the hot water gauge on the steamer, looked in on the horses, and scribbled pertinent entries in the company journal. Nearby was the alarm register, a list of the nearest fire alarm box numbers and locations, and a clock. Some stations were equipped with devices that, when an alarm hit, automatically stopped the clock, so that the company officer could record the time of alarm and length of duty until the firefighters returned.

As the alarm sounded, firefighters ran down iron spiral staircases to the apparatus floor. A few stations had sliding chutes. In Chicago, Captain David B. Kenyon of Engine Company No. 21 decided that a pole would be faster than a chute. He constructed a wooden pole three inches in diameter. Sanding and oiling it smooth, he hung it from the hayloft window and brought in the fire chief to have a look. The chief gave permission to cut a hole in the bunkroom floor—if Kenyon promised to fix the hole should the pole fail! The first firefighter slid the pole to an alarm on April 21, 1878—and poles thereafter were quickly installed in Chicago firehouses. The idea rapidly spread to other cities. Two years later, Captain Charles Allen of Engine Company No. 1, in Worcester, Massachusetts, built the first brass pole, which extended from the bunkroom to a platform beside the steamer. Sliding-poles cut still more seconds off the firefighters' time in answering alarms.

Another method was an invention by New York's Fire Insurance Patrol No. 3, although it is doubtful the idea was widely used. Patrolmen built a trapdoor with a four-foot-high brass railing in the bunkroom of their West Thirtieth Street station. Another brass rail was fastened to the ceiling under the trapdoor. When the alarm sounded, the driver held the bunkroom railing and sat on the trapdoor, which sprang open. Dropping through the hole, he caught the second brass rail—like an acrobat swinging from one trapeze to another—and, straightening out, dropped vertically into the seat.

Turnout times became even faster as stations were electrified. At the first clang of the gong the doors opened, lights flashed on, and the stall doors or chains were automatically released. Freyvogel in Pittsburgh even invented an electrically operated flank-slapper to get the horses going! The trained horses then trotted from their stalls and backed under the harness in less time than it took the firefighters to slide the pole. The driver tugged a rope, the harness dropped, and the hames were quickly hitched.

The engineer, meanwhile, lifted the damper and, flipping a match into the boiler furnace, ignited wood shavings or kerosene-soaked cotton waste. Some engineers fired their boilers with a ready-to-light oil-soaked torch. Some firehouses had burning gas jets in the floor ahead of the boiler, which ignited the kindling when the engine passed over them. Finally, as the steamer started ahead, the coupling to the hot water heater snapped apart and a clapper valve automatically shut off the flow. Companies prided themselves on being able to leave their stations within forty-five seconds.

If the fire was only several blocks away, the engineer could turn a petcock and drain some water so that he would have a working head of steam upon arrival. Most downtown companies kept boiler water fairly low to enable them to start pumping within three minutes after an alarm. Furnace kindling and coal often were sufficient to raise steam for fighting small fires. Additional water was fed to the boiler by a

small pump connected to the main one. Cannel coal, which ignites quickly and burns fiercely, was carried in the fuel pan behind the boiler. It was sometimes hauled aboard tenders hooked to steamers. When more was needed for large fires, it was brought in canvas bags aboard fire department coal wagons. Engine operators signaled for more coal by blowing their steam whistles.

Gradually, the single company firehouse, a volunteer tradition, ended. For reasons of economy, cities had, during the volunteer era, tried to station engine, hook and ladder, and hose companies in the same houses, but feuding had forced them to separate stations. Paid departments, however, now could locate several companies together in one house.

As cities spread outward and fire districts grew, chiefs could no longer run to fires. Soon there appeared a new apparatus in fire department fleets: the chief's wagon, buggy, or sleigh. San Francisco and a few other cities often provided an apartment over the fire station for the chief and his family; elsewhere, a buggy and sleigh were kept at the stations closest to his house, where at night his driver would pick him up and drive him to the fire.

It was commonplace in larger cities to station extra horses in the firehouse. When the chief's horse became winded, he stopped at a fire station, hitched up a fresh horse, and continued, perhaps making several Pony-Express-like changes before reaching the fire. About 1920, when there was a major blaze in Hollywood, many miles distant from downtown Los Angeles fire headquarters, the chief's buggy took him out Sunset Boulevard until the horse tired. The chief left his buggy and horse at a firehouse and continued to the fire aboard a Pacific Electric Railway trolley.

Chiefs' buggies became an American fire service tradition that endures. Few firefighters would think of referring to the chief's car as a sedan or station wagon; it was then and is now "the buggy."

There was no more thrilling sight in the America of that era than the shining steamers, pulled by galloping horses, rumbling down the streets—the finely trained horses responding instantly to the tugging of the reins, smoke and sparks streaming from the boil-

er stacks, and the engineer pulling the bell rope and blowing the whistle.

Frequently following the engines were scores of youngsters on foot and on bicycles as they yielded to the irresistible urge to follow the fire and not go home until the last ember was out. Harold S. Walker, a consulting fire protection engineer of Marblehead, Massachusetts, recalled in 1976 that he was thirteen when he hurried to the Chelsea conflagration on the afternoon of Palm Sunday, 1908. "I got home about midnight. In the course of events I ruined an almost new coat that I had been given for Easter. If I recall correctly, my mother said very little about it. Maybe she didn't like the coat any more than I did. I never had to wear it again."

New York firefighter John A. Cregier also told that "At seven years of age I would run block after block after Thirty-four Engine. There was no boy who was whipped more for it, but my father never could whip it out of me."

Opposite top: *Los Angeles Engine 23 firefighters show how fast they can answer a night alarm in May, 1915. As the gong over the watch desk strikes the alarm box number, chains across the horses' stalls drop. The horses quickly take their places in front of the engine before the firefighters slide down the poles. The driver pulls a rope and the quick-hitch harness drops onto the backs of the horses. A system of ropes and counterweights then pulls up the harness holders as the firefighters complete the hitch. The engineer, meanwhile, is kindling the boiler so that he will be ready to start pumping when they get to the fire.* Opposite bottom: *The engineer of this New York steamer has a good head of steam going as the three-horse hitch races to the fire.* Above: *Firefighters were proud of their horses and showed them great affection.*

15 HOODOO AND HORSES

Firefighters' lives were ruled by the striking of gongs. They learned the hazards of each neighborhood by associating them with fire alarm box numbers. Los Angeles' Box 15 was at Berth 90 on the waterfront. That could mean a major fire. Buffalo firefighters recognized the location of Box 1531, Mapleridge Avenue and Deerfield Street, as an area of single-family residences. When that box struck it usually meant a false alarm. Washington, D.C., firefighters knew Box 157 was for 1600 Pennsylvania Avenue—the White House.

Buffalo's most notorious fire alarm box—number 29—was installed on a pedestal at the corner of Seneca and Wells Streets, in 1868, in a downtown district of brick warehouses, factories, cheap hotels, and loft buildings. Firefighters expected disaster whenever Box 29 was pulled. For three-quarters of a century it was sounded for fires causing millions of dollars in damage, killing many firefighters and injuring dozens more. There were other fireboxes in the neighborhood, but none seemed to be sounded for fires that approached the severity of Box 29's. When it was pulled in winter and late at night, firefighters who did not answer the first alarm often hitched the horses anyway and waited for the gongs to strike a second or third alarm that would send them to the fire.

Firefighters named the box Hoodoo Box 29 as early as July 18, 1878, when the volunteers, including

New York Engine 39 and Hook and Ladder 16 pull out of their 67th Street station to answer an alarm in this typical American scene of the early 1900s. The firehorses were well trained, and only the best from the breeding farm were selected for the job.

Opposite: *What's up ahead? Probably a five-alarm fire blazing out of control, judging by the excitement on the faces of the firefighters and the horses in this 1885 painting.* Below right: *With its clanging bell and shrieking whistle clearing the way, Engine 69 is pulled to a New York fire in 1900 by a galloping three-horse matched team.*

the Red Birds of Hook and Ladder Company No. 2—the truck nearest Seneca and Wells Streets—were called to the Red Jacket Hotel fire, in which a falling wall crushed Firefighter John D. Mitchell of Columbia Hose No. 11.

Hoodoo Box 29 hit at 2:41 A.M. on February 2, 1889, a bitterly cold night when a frigid wind was gusting in off Lake Erie. Firefighters could see the glow of the Great Seneca Street Fire as they pulled out of their stations. The steamers pumped all night. Spray turned to ice that coated the buildings. Icicles dripped from the firefighters' helmets and chins. Walls came crashing down; an entire block of tall buildings was destroyed; and Dick Marion of Engine Company No. 10 became the first paid firefighter who did not return alive from a Hoodoo Box 29 alarm.

Three more firefighters were killed and twenty were injured when a wall collapsed during the 5:15 A.M. fire on January 28, 1907, which engulfed the abandoned Columbia Hotel at 101–7 Seneca Street. And so it went, year after year, as Hoodoo Box 29 was pulled time and time again: the Burnberger Popcorn Company; the Eureka Coffee Company; the Broezel House hotel (twice); and the Stoddard Brothers Drug Company, where Firefighter Martin Haley of Hook and Ladder Company No. 2 was killed when a ladder broke, and thirty firefighters were sent to hospitals by smoke and fumes from the burning drugs.

Joseph S. Masterson was a substitute firefighter with steamer Engine Company No. 9 at the Stoddard fire. After he had become fire commissioner, Masterson said he still tensed whenever he heard Box 29 strike. Around 1965, the Hoodoo Box was removed from its pedestal—and the hundred-year-old jinx mysteriously ended.

The drudgery that awaited weary firefighters returning from fires sometimes could last for days. Grooming the horses and readying the apparatus for the next alarm came before rest. At a time when brawn was more important than brains in the making of a professional firefighter, a firefighter was easily replaced, since a new one could be trained in a few weeks. A horse, on the other hand, represented a considerable investment of training time and money.

The firefighters profoundly admired the job these supposedly dumb animals did without hesitation. Consider the horses' job requirements: They had to react as quickly as race horses at the starting gate when the big gongs sent them trotting from their stalls, sometimes out of a sound sleep. Without prodding, they had to back up to a strange and hulking piece of fire apparatus while some weird spiderweb of harness hung over them. Nor could they flinch when the heavy gear dropped onto their backs.

Horses had to be strong, as well as fast and surefooted, to pull apparatus weighing several tons along streets sometimes slickened by rain, sleet, or snow. Galloping at full speed, they had to avoid holes that could send them sprawling to fatal injuries. With single-minded concentration they had to work as a finely tuned team, responding to the reins and orders of their drivers as they veered around corners and avoided other horse-drawn wagons and trolleys that did not hear them coming.

During the long hours at fires, the horses were required to stand patiently—despite the heat and roaring flames, the showers of sparks and glass, and the steamer smoke swirling around them, which was sometimes thicker than the smoke from the burning buildings; despite the din of shouted firefighting orders, the hubbub of more horses galloping in with more apparatus, the sound of crashing walls, and the whistles shrieking for more coal; despite subzero temperatures, and icy spray blowing in their faces; and despite the mobs of milling spectators.

Fire departments selected horses with greater care than they did firefighters. To get a firefighter's job—in those days before the Civil Service—it helped

Below: *Frederick Seagrave was making wooden ladders for use in orchards when he began building fire apparatus in 1886. The Seagrave name became famous for excellence. This 1906 75-foot aerial, a Seagrave, was used by New York's Hook and Ladder Company 28.* Opposite: *Racing to fires was risky. Horses sometimes fell, as here, and had to be destroyed.*

to be a relative of an alderman or a fire chief, or to know or bribe someone in City Hall. Any horse could pull a bakery wagon or a milk truck, true, but a firehorse was a unique animal: young, in excellent health, big—perhaps fifteen hands—strong, agile, obedient, fearless—in short, the cream of the breeding farms.

Cities competed for them and many eastern departments ranged deep into the midwest to buy the very best. After running candidate horses at full speed, fire department veterinarians listened for breathing irregularities and examined the animals from hoof to mouth. There was no sex discrimination between stallions and mares, providing they showed they could do the job. The Detroit Fire Department specified 1,100-pound horses for hose wagon teams, 1,400-pound horses for steamers, and 1,700-pounders for hook and ladders. Teams of two and three horses were matched for size and sometimes color—lucky was the company that could show off a team of matched whites, browns, or blacks! The Fire Department of New York, and probably others, entered teams in horse shows and often won blue ribbons.

While some cities had training stables, the favored system was on-the-job instruction with the help of veteran horses. Training began after a new horse became accustomed to his stall, the clanging of the gong, and watching other horses when the alarm struck. The driver held the trainee's bridle while another firefighter stood beside the horse's flank. When a third firefighter rang the gong, the horse's flank was slapped and he was pulled to the front of the apparatus and pushed under the harness. The process was repeated many times with increasing praise and rewards of apples or sugar as the trainee learned to follow the other horses and became part of the team.

Detroit claimed to be the only fire department that had a horse college. The site was an unused portion of the Russell Street cemetery that had become a garbage dump. Firefighters turned it into a parklike training academy that reminded some people of a small, whitewashed farm in the bluegrass country of Kentucky. There was a fire station with apparatus, training stalls, hanging quick hitches, a feed room, a horse hospital, and a 700-foot racetrack. Progress reports and final report cards were meticu-

lously kept, and educated horses went on to post-graduate work in fire stations.

The horses never lacked extra care. Firefighters exercised them at least once a day, an occasion eagerly anticipated by neighborhood children, who brought treats for their favorites and were rewarded with the horses' tricks. One of New York's Engine Company No. 8's horses had a bag of them. He could open a water faucet with his mouth, take a drink, and turn it off. He could catch a handkerchief tossed in the air and stuff it in the firefighter's pocket. He could lift whatever leg he was asked. His grand finale was to kneel and appear to pray.

Strong bonds of affection developed between firefighters and firehorses. The men often brought the horses apples and sugar cubes. The horses' names were painted in gold above stalls; but unlike those of thoroughbred racers, the names were purposely kept simple: Jim, Bill, Molly, Flash. In the rush of going to a fire, there was no time for such tongue twisters as the racehorse Jerry Everts.

Horses took to the fire service as if they had been bred for it. One of the horses at New York Engine 17 learned to recognize the box numbers as they struck. If the strikes totaled six, he knew it was a run for him, and whinnied. When the stall chains dropped he trotted up to the rig and stood whinnying some more as if to say, "Hurry it up, boys!" while the firefighters came sliding down the pole.

Pittsburgh's Engine Company No. 3 had a matched pair of browns, who broke their halters one day in their excitement to get out of their stalls. Billy, of Pittsburgh Engine Company No. 9, needed no urging to go faster; when he saw smoke and flames ahead, his hooves would barely touch the pavement. Some idea of the power that drove those flying hooves may be had from an incident in Rochester, New York. A horse of Hook and Ladder Company No. 2 threw a shoe while galloping to a fire. The shoe broke a third-floor window, and the fire chief had to pay the irate apartment tenant sixty cents to fix it.

Strong drivers were needed to control the horses. Drivers were required to wear seat belts—the first on any vehicle—for the jolting ride could throw them from the seat. While answering one alarm, the driver of Pittsburgh's No. 4 engine either forgot to fasten his belt or broke it. He pitched forward and landed on the pole between the horses. Unnoticed by the firefighters riding on the fuel pan, the engine continued driverless for more than a block until somebody saw the empty driver's seat, threw a board under the wheels, and stopped the steamer. As a result of the near tragedy, brakes were developed that could be operated from the front and rear.

Racing to fires was risky, and horses occasionally could not avoid collisions or stumbling and sprawling. Drivers sometimes had no choice but to sacrifice their horses to avoid a pedestrian. Horse ambulances and horseshoeing wagons became part of some large city fire departments' growing fleet of apparatus. Loss of a horse would throw the firehouse into mourning.

Horses lasted from four to sometimes more than ten years. Philadelphia horses got annual vacations, many years before firefighters did. Fairmount Engine apparently started the practice in 1858 during the hot summer months, and it later became traditional among other Philadelphia companies.

It was a sad day in the firehouse when the department veterinarian pronounced a horse unfit for further duty. Retired horses were sometimes given less strenuous duty in city parks or were sent to farms where they lived out their days doing absolutely nothing.

Some horses were sold at public auctions. Every firehouse had its favorite story of the horse who could not resist the call to duty. A milkman was making a delivery on New York's Bowery when the galloping horses sped by with their clanging steamers, ladder trucks, and hose wagons. The old nag bolted after them and the milkman ran after a trail of broken bottles and spilled milk until he caught up with his horse, who was standing calmly while the steamers worked on the fire.

In the autumn of 1872, a highly contagious and deadly disease diagnosed by veterinarians as epizootic, a form of distemper, spread from horses in Montreal and Toronto to those in American cities. Within twenty-four hours, three hundred horses were dead in Buffalo. The epidemic spread to many cities, including New York, Philadelphia, Newark, and Jersey City. Horses died by the hundreds. Transportation stalled. Milk and other deliveries halted. Cities were paralyzed. But the worst worry was fire.

By late October, four of Boston's firehorses were dead, and twenty-two unfit for duty, out of a total of seventy-five to ninety horses in the department. Until the epidemic ended and it became safe again to bring healthy horses into the city, many of the heavy steamers had to be dragged by firefighters and citizen volunteers temporarily mustered into the department. Boston's luck held for several weeks until 7:24 P.M., Saturday, November 9, when Box 52 was pulled at Sumner and Lincoln Streets in the heart of the city's commercial district.

Boston firefighters and volunteers did the best they could without the speed and mobility the horses had provided. The Great Boston Fire raged sixteen

Boston's Engine 18 fascinates youngsters as the horses pull the steamer to a fire in 1923. During the Great Boston Fire of November 9, 1872, many engines had to be pulled by hand when the horses fell sick from an epizootic disease. The disaster was later called the Epizootic Fire.

hours, destroyed 776 buildings, left 20,000 jobless and 1,000 homeless, and caused $76 million in damage. Fourteen were killed, including eleven firefighters. On the centennial of the castastrophe, John P. Vahey, a Boston district fire chief, wrote a monograph renaming the Great Boston Fire. He called it the Epizootic Fire. It is history's only conflagration that was named after a horse disease.

16
"CHICAGO IS IN FLAMES!... SEND HELP!"

The oppressive Indian summer heat and high humidity hung like an ominous cloud over tinder-dry Chicago that Sunday evening, October 8, 1871. During the previous fourteen weeks only a smattering of rain had dampened the Queen City of the West. What relief the showers brought to Chicago's 334,270 sweltering residents was quickly blotted up by southwest winds, which blew almost constantly from off the parched prairies. A layer of smoggy haze from prairie fires, and smoke from the smoldering ruins of a disastrous fire the night before, blanketed the city and turned the sun into a red globe as it set over the pink horizon.

The previous night's fire was one of the worst in the city's history, the topper to more than two dozen blazes during the past week. Starting after 10:00 P.M. in the Lull and Holmes planing mill, 209 Canal Street, it burned four blocks of buildings, including huge coal yards that were still glowing. The fire also destroyed Pioneer Hook and Ladder No. 1. With Liberty Engine No. 7 in the shops for repairs, Chief Fire Marshal Robert A. Williams was down to only sixteen engines—twelve Amoskeags and three Silsbys—plus three hook and ladders, six hose wagons, and a hose elevator—a rickety contraption, seldom used, that lifted hoselines to fires in upper floors of downtown buildings. A second hose elevator was out of service.

The firefighters were exhausted after seventeen

Cyrus McCormick's Reaper Works and the Chicago Steam Sugar Refinery, on the Chicago River, burning during the Great Chicago Fire of 1871. The fire raged for more than thirty hours and left one-third of the city in ruins. Hundreds of stores and factories and 17,450 homes were destroyed.

Opposite: *The firestorm swept into Chicago's downtown business district and destroyed the Chamber of Commerce* (top) *and the Crosby Opera House* (bottom). *Building bricks, laid in winter with freezing mortar, did not hold well, especially under stress of the firestorm. No American fire had generated so much heat—more than 3,000 degrees Fahrenheit.*

hours of continuous duty at the mill fire. Many had suffered facial burns, and more had gone off duty with seared and swollen eyelids. At best, there were no more than 125 firefighters fit for duty in a department with a normal strength of 219.

Fire was no stranger to Chicago. During the past year the city had averaged two alarms a day, far more than New York, a city three times larger. Distressed by continuing high fire losses, insurance companies had, only a week earlier, organized the Chicago Fire Insurance Patrol under Ben Bullwinkle and equipped a wagon with salvage covers and other gear for minimizing damage from fire and water.

Part of the explanation for Chicago's bad fire record was the city's unparalleled prosperity. It had that year moved ahead of St. Louis as the nation's fourth largest city. Chicago's twenty-seven banks held $13 million in deposits. More than 1,100 factories churned out everything from furniture to the grain harvesters in Cyrus McCormick's gigantic plant that supplied farmers throughout the west.

Chicago already was the nation's grain basket. A yearly avalanche of up to 12 million bushels of wheat and corn flooded into the city's seventeen grain elevators. The Union Stock Yards had recently opened, and its annual receipts were running to around 17 million hogs and half as many cattle and sheep.

Over twelve thousand vessels docked at Chicago that year, more than New York, Philadelphia, Baltimore, Charleston, San Francisco, and Mobile combined. The transcontinental railroad had been completed two years earlier, and the city, with its ten railroads, was the gateway to the west and the Pacific northwest. Every day, 120 freight and nearly as many passenger trains entered and left the city.

This phenomenal growth made Chicago a plum ripe for disaster. Fully two-thirds of its 60,000 houses were of wood, many merely slapdashed together to shelter the 35,000 immigrants who flocked every year into the city from northern Europe, especially Ireland and Germany. Even the sidewalks were wooden, and the streets were mostly paved with wood blocks. Brick and stone buildings were mainly those of up to five stories in the downtown business district known today as the Loop. Here again, construction was not the best. Bricks were laid in winter with freezing mortar and did not hold together well, especially under stress of flames or strong winds.

The T-shaped Chicago River separated the city into three divisions. Except for heavy industry along the river, the sprawling North Division was mostly residential. The city's retailing and commercial operations were based in the South Division, along with a huge slum area of wooden tenements called Conley's Patch. Irish, German, and Scandinavian immigrants settled mostly in the West Division's one- and two-story frame cottages. They included Patrick O'Leary, a laborer, his wife, Catherine, both around thirty-five years old, and their five children.

For $500 the O'Learys had bought the rectangular lot at 137 DeKoven Street between Jefferson and Clinton. On it they built two cottages, one behind the other. The front cottage was rented to the Patrick McLaughlin family, and the O'Learys lived in the other. At the far end of the lot, about forty feet behind their cottage, was a small barn with a peaked roof that butted on an alley. From this barn Mrs. O'Leary ran a neighborhood milk route and kept five cows, a calf, and a horse to pull her milk wagon.

There are conflicting accounts of how the fire started. They range from arson by radicals who had vowed to burn all cities in order to achieve social ideals, to spontaneous combustion in a load of timothy hay delivered that afternoon to Mrs. O'Leary's barn. Mrs. O'Leary told neighbors and others that she was in the barn when the fire started, but recanted her story five days later and said she had finished milking at 4:30 and was in bed with a sore foot.

Her story was thoroughly investigated by many, and the overwhelming evidence led to the conclusion that Mrs. O'Leary, carrying a kerosene lamp, entered the barn around 8:30 P.M. If she had finished milking at 4:30, why was she in the barn? Some say she was looking in on a sick cow; others, that she always made a final check of her animals before retiring. The likeliest probability is that Mrs. O'Leary went to the barn to get some milk for the McLaughlins, who were having a party and needed it for an oyster stew or punch.

Mrs. O'Leary set the lamp on the floor, and after delivering about half a pint into her bucket, the cow, resenting the overtime work, kicked over the lantern with its right hind foot. The lantern broke, the spilled kerosene was ignited, the flames quickly spread through the hay, and the story of history's most famous cow was born.

Mrs. O'Leary's screams brought her husband and neighbors, who formed a bucket brigade and tried to free the animals. Only the calf was saved. Nobody thought to turn in an alarm, although the

Destruction was virtually total in Chicago's business district as a wall of flames swept in a northeasterly direction, until they reached the city limits at Fullerton Avenue. The effect of the fire is shown in this view looking north from City Hall.

nearest firebox was a short distance away. Ten minutes later, William Lee ran to turn in an alarm. Instead of going to the nearest box, he ran more than three blocks to Canal and Twelfth Streets. To prevent false alarms, only Bruno H. Goll, who operated a corner drugstore, had a key to Box 296. Goll unlocked the box and pulled the hook. For some unknown reason, the alarm was never received at the Courthouse fire alarm headquarters. The time was now 9:05. The O'Leary barn had been burning for around half an hour and the fire was spreading to other barns and shacks along the alley.

In the third floor of the Courthouse, slightly more than a mile to the northeast, Fire Alarm Operator William J. Brown was entertaining his sister, Sarah, and her girl friend, Martha Dailey, with his guitar. Sarah noticed a glow in the southwest. Her brother passed it off as a rekindle of the coal yards burned during the Lull and Holmes fire. He resumed playing. Mathias Schaffer, the man on fire watch in the Courthouse tower, also noticed the glare. He, too, dismissed it as a rekindle.

On Maxwell Street, six blocks south of the O'Learys, the bone-weary firefighters of Little Giant Engine No. 6 had returned from the Lull and Holmes fire only a few hours earlier. They went to bed while Foreman William H. Musham stood floor watch and Firefighter Joseph Lauf climbed to the station's tower to stand the first fire watch of the night. Lauf immediately saw the fire and notified Musham, who turned out the company. Horses were hitched, the boiler furnace was torched, and the basement water heater connection snapped apart, as the 900-gallon Amoskeag rolled out of the station followed by its horse-drawn hose reel.

At 9:21, going on an hour after the fire started, Schaffer took another look. The glow was more vivid. Focusing his spyglass, he decided there was indeed cause for alarm. He whistled down the speaking tube to Brown and called, "Strike Box 342, Canalport and Halsted!" Box 342 was more than a mile south of the O'Learys. Brown tapped out the number, firehouse gongs clanged, and three engines, two hose wagons, and two hook and ladders hurried in the wrong direction, while firefighters stationed closer to the O'Learys went back to bed.

Focusing on the glow again, Schaffer realized his blunder, but Brown refused to strike the correct box number. "It will only confuse the companies," he argued. "They'll see the fire and go to it." About this

Lager Beer

time, another O'Leary neighbor ran to Goll's drugstore. "The fire is spreading very rapidly!" he told the druggist. Goll took a look at the barefooted youth with his drab pants, red flannel shirt, and unkempt bushy head of hair and decided the youth was insane. "Help is on the way," said Goll. "I just heard an engine pass Twelfth Street." But to play it safe, he pulled Box 296 again. That alarm was not received, either.

Little Giant made good time up Jefferson Street and quickly got a stream going onto half a dozen frame houses and sheds. With luck and the help of other companies that would arrive shortly, Foreman Musham expected to bring it under control soon.

Fire Alarm Operator Brown, meanwhile, became increasingly worried about the gathering glow. He decided to call out more apparatus by sounding a second alarm. At 9:31, Brown struck Box 342 again. Within seconds, three box alarms registered in Brown's office, including the box nearest the O'Learys. Brown ignored all of them.

Foreman Chris Schimmels of Chicago Engine No. 2, a Silsby, had seen the O'Leary glow as he pulled out of his station after Box 342 hit. But orders had to be obeyed, and he yelled to the driver to continue to Canalport and Halsted until he realized Box 342 was false. Turning around, they headed toward the O'Leary blaze. Almost immediately after arriving, their hose burst and a spring broke in the pump. The Silsby was completely disabled. Twenty minutes later the firefighters managed repairs, only to discover they had used all their coal and Little Giant could spare none. The nearest supply was at the firehouse, eight blocks away.

Waubansia Engine No. 2, also a Silsby, arrived at Box 342. Foreman Mike Sullivan and his men turned to go home and gawked at the flickering orange glow lighting the sky to the north. Waubansia arrived at the O'Leary fire just as its boiler steam pressure ran out. They would have to start from scratch.

With the second alarm, Third Assistant Fire Marshal Mathias Benner followed the glare to DeKoven Street. By now flames had spread to grocery stores and saloons on Jefferson. Marshal Benner ordered Musham and his Little Giant firefighters to start a hoseline on Jefferson Street. Benner commandeered some spectators and told them to take over Little Giant's first line. But the inexperienced bystanders soon panicked, dropped the hose, and fled. The hose burned, dooming the O'Leary block.

When Chief Williams arrived, he found flames gnawing in a northeasterly direction. The tall, forty-three-year-old spade-bearded chief was not overly alarmed. This was a nasty fire, but only two blocks of small buildings were blazing and the flames were pointing toward the Saturday night burn where they would surely run out of fuel. Williams was widely recognized as an aggressive and competent fire chief whose experience went back to his years as a volunteer. He knew he was operating short of apparatus and with exhausted men, but no department in the United States had more modern equipment, and no department could boast more highly motivated firefighters. To play it safe, however, Chief Williams pulled a third, or general alarm, a few minutes before 10 o'clock. The general alarm called out the rest of the department.

The fire was eating toward the site of Saturday's fire faster than a man could walk. The light evening breeze was blowing sparks, bits of burning shingles, and other debris three to five hundred feet in the air and broadcasting them to the northeast. People were wetting down roofs. But Chief Williams' confidence increased as the extra alarm companies began to arrive and surround the fire. The O'Leary fire was under control. But not for long.

At 10 o'clock a two-foot spear of blazing debris lanced the steeple of St. Paul's Catholic Church on Clinton, one block south of Harrison. The church blossomed into flames. Brown was among the first to spot them and struck Box 787, Van Buren and Canal. He missed by three blocks.

Chief Williams was appalled when told the church was burning. He had always dreaded a fire in that block. If ever there was a breeding place for conflagration, the St. Paul's block was it. Jam-packed around the wooden church, one of Chicago's biggest, were two enormous four-story wooden factories occupied by W. B. Bateham's shingle mills, the Frank Mayer Furniture plant, the three-story wooden Roelle Furniture Finishing Company, and an enormous house. Open areas were stacked with 1,000 cords of kindling wood and 600,000 board feet of furniture lumber stacked twenty-five feet high.

If the Bateham block went, the city would be in deep trouble. Chief Williams sent three Amoskeags—Fred Gund Engine No. 14, A. C. Coventry No. 11, and Jacob Rehm No. 4—to the fire. But three steamers could not stop those fast-spreading flames; nor could thirty. As the Bateham block fire worsened,

Brown decided to strike Box 342 again. At least he was consistent—consistently wrong.

The Bateham fire quickly melded into the O'Leary blaze, which, with its newfound strength, quickly consumed dozens more homes, shacks, barns, stores, and factories. Frank Sherman of Engine No. 9 made a valiant stand at Polk and Clinton, while stoker George Leady shielded himself from the flames with a door, the heat scorching the hair of the terrified horses that stood by obediently.

Thousands of Chicagoans streamed into the area. Mobs broke into taverns and rolled kegs of whiskey and beer into the streets. When the crowd refused to make way for the Fred Gund Engine, Foreman Denis J. Swenie told his men to turn their hose on them. Blistering heat from the Bateham block forced the steamer to take up a new position, but as quickly as the engine started pumping again the flames forced a new retreat.

At 11:30, a burning brand from Bateham's was wafted across the Chicago River and landed on the roof of the Parmelee Omnibus and Stage Company at Franklin and Jackson. The new three-story brick building was quickly enveloped. Learning that the fire had slopped over into the South Division, the heart of the city's business district, Chief Williams became deeply worried. Simultaneous major fires in different parts of the city have always been every chief's nightmare, because they force him to spread his apparatus and manpower dangerously thin.

Before climbing aboard a hose wagon and hurrying across the Van Buren Street bridge with some engines, Chief Williams ordered Foreman Swenie to abandon his dangerous position and fall back to a safer one. But Swenie stubbornly held until it was too late. The firefighters abandoned the Amoskeag, and it was crushed under a falling wall. Chief Williams was now down to fourteen engines to fight two huge fires, one of them nearly a mile long.

Half an hour later another Bateham brand flipped over the river and set fire to the Chicago Gas Light & Coke Company. Fearing a gas explosion, people stampeded. But workers shut off the valves, and as the tanks were drained, every light in the city went out. With only the fire to see by, the effect, said many, "was as if this was Judgment Day for Chicago."

The steady spray of firebrands soaring over the river caused Chief Williams to recall momentarily that his request for a fireboat had been rejected by the mayor and the Common Council. The boat could have sprayed a water curtain to stop firebrands from hurtling the river. For want of a $25,000 fireboat, $200 million of the city would go up in flames.

At 12:20 A.M., another piece of burning debris pierced the roof of a three-story frame flophouse on Adams Street in Conley's Patch. The tenement swiftly became a torch that fired other slum buildings. Flames sweeping through Conley's Patch soon amalgamated with the gas works fire and together they linked with the Parmelee blaze. The South Division was doomed and so was the North Division. A thermodynamic-meteorological phenomenon was now in the making.

Columns of superheated air shot high into the cool night atmosphere. As the hot air stabbed up, cold air rushed down, forming chimneylike drafts that developed into windstorms. Whirling masses of flaming tornadoes swirled into the business district. Five-story brick buildings became furnaces. The poorly laid bricks could not long withstand the heat and the galelike firestorms. Buildings toppled like lines of dominoes, spilling their contents and feeding new fuel to the worsening cyclones.

Chicago streets were laid out in an east-west, north-south direction. Attacking from the northeast, the flames forked around intersections and swept up streets, incinerating paving blocks, sidewalks—everything. Buildings literally melted, and State Street trolley tracks twisted into molten curlicues. No American conflagration had generated so much heat—more than 3,000 degrees Fahrenheit.

James H. Hildreth, a former alderman, urged Chief Williams to blow firebreaks with gunpowder. Williams wanted none of it, but Hildreth convinced Mayor Roswell B. Mason otherwise. With Bullwinkle's Fire Insurance Patrol wagon they loaded powder at the city armory. Bullwinkle wondered if he could satisfactorily explain to his insurance company bosses why he destroyed buildings he was supposed to save. Charges were set in the four-story Union National Bank, at Washington and LaSalle. The blast merely blew out windows and made it easier for firebrands to enter. Soon the bank was burning. Hildreth next tried to blow up the Nixon Block at LaSalle and Monroe, with similar results.

In the Courthouse at Randolph and Clark, watchman Schaffer was stomping roof fires while Mayor Mason, in his office below, was sending telegraph messages to mayors of other cities: "Chicago is in flames! . . . Send help!" Within hours, more than

Opposite top: *Pumper built by Rumsey & Company around 1860. This type of rig was dubbed a piano—for its big water box—or a squirrel tail, because of its curved suction hose.* Opposite bottom: *This Rumsey was named a crane neck, because its arched frame made it easy to turn.* Below right: *Chicagoans flee the flames via the Randolph Street bridge.*

twenty-five engines from eight states were speeding to Chicago aboard railroad flatcars.

The fiery blizzard bombarded the Courthouse with blazing timbers. One pierced the tower, which quickly resembled a huge flaming derby hat. Another chunk of burning debris whizzed through a broken window and set a fire that Schaffer could not put out. Schaffer, Mayor Mason, and everybody in the building fled, but not before they set the Courthouse bell tolling. At 2:05 A.M., the hands of the tower clock melted and the five-ton bell went crashing, with a resounding clang, clear down to the basement. Mason, a mayor without an office, decided he had done all he could and went home.

In the Sherman House hotel across from the blazing Courthouse, John R. Chapin, a *Harper's Weekly* artist, watched from his window as the fire devoured "the most stately and massive buildings as though they had been the cardboard playthings of a child. . . . One after another they dissolved, like snow on a mountain." Chapin fled as flames stormed into the Sherman House. The five-story Tremont House—where Lincoln and Stephen Douglas had stayed during their famous debates—fell before the onslaught. So, too, did the Chicago Times building, where workers were preparing a special fire extra edition. A block south, the Post Office and the Customs House came crashing down and more than $2 million in currency inside turned to ashes.

With the tempest rampaging in the South and West Divisions, it was now the North Division's turn to burn. Almost as if the fiery monster had a brain, it aimed its attack at its worst enemy—the waterworks on Chicago near Michigan. A hint of its plan came early that morning when sparks landed on the paint and carpentry shop of Lill's Brewery across from the waterworks. The shops burned to cinders.

At 2:30 A.M., the flames, for lack of a fireboat's water curtain, spilled across the river into the North Division. First to go was a train of tank cars filled with kerosene on the Chicago & Northwestern Railroad tracks along North State Street. Flames next ignited Wright's Stables, half a block long, near State and Kinzie and spread from there into freight houses and homes. The North Division became a maelstrom.

Almost as if it had been reenergized by the North Division fire, the O'Leary-Bateham blaze burst into renewed frenzy. A sheet of flame bridged the river and touched off a South Division lumberyard near Polk. Churning forward, the flames made no

distinction between freight sheds; dwellings; the Chicago, Rock Island & Pacific Railroad depot; and long trains of passenger cars.

Columns of flaming tornadoes continued to swirl through the city's main retailing district along Lake Street. Looting flourished despite the thunderous crashing of walls all around. A looter was killed at Randolph and Wabash when struck by a bolt of cloth thrown from a window. Jacob Klein tried to stop two looters in his store and had his skull bashed in with a coal shovel. Wagon drivers pocketed a hundred dollars to haul whatever businessmen managed to salvage; some draymen dumped the stuff when they accepted higher bribes. Horses to pull wagons were scarce and many firehorses were stolen, unnoticed by firefighters until they went to move their rigs to better positions. They were forced to pull the apparatus themselves.

Chicagoans fled by the thousands. The exodus from burning and soon-to-be-burning areas added to the pandemonium, and fire apparatus bogged down in masses of humanity clogging the streets. A young lady clutched an empty bird cage; another, a feather duster. Two men pushed a wooden cigar store Indian up LaSalle Street. A woman was forcibly removed from her Adams Street house twice; she ran back a third time and vanished in the smoke and flames. Solomon Witkowsky was last seen at a window of his home at Van Buren and Harrison firing a revolver into the flames. One by one, most of the two dozen swinging bridges connecting the three divisions of the city fell flaming into the river.

At 3:20 A.M., a twelve-foot-long burning javelin penetrated the roof of the city's new 38-million-gallon waterworks. Built of cream-colored stone, with tall towers, the pumping station looked like a Rhineland castle. Within the hour, the waterworks crumbled into the flames as engineers shut down the pumps and fled. When Chief Williams arrived, he realized for the first time that he was licked and Chicago was dead. It would not be long before water in the nearby 175-foot tower reservoir ran out. The tower remained standing, however, as a monument to the Great Chicago Fire.

By dawn, thousands were seeking refuge along Lake Michigan's shoreline. With heat and smoke sweeping over them, husbands scooped holes in the sand, buried their wives and children up to their necks, and dashed back and forth from the water's edge with cooling buckets. In the West Division the fire was mostly out, and neighbors gathered at 137 DeKoven Street to gawk at the carcass of a cow and the charred remains of a lantern. Part of the barn remained standing, and the O'Leary cottages were among the few buildings in the neighborhood that escaped damage!

But in the North Division the windstorm of fire was increasing. Holy Name Cathedral at Chicago and State burned soon after daybreak. At 7:00 A.M., two grain elevators along the river erupted into flames and sent more fire cascading into freight yards, lumberyards, and Cyrus McCormick's reaper factory. "Several tons of pig iron . . . ran together like taffy in the sun," wrote Robert Cromie in his excellent book, *The Great Chicago Fire.*

In the downtown South Division, firefighters were waging a last desperate battle as water petered out in the mains. The six-story department store of Marshall Field and Levi Leiter fell to the flames after Titsworth Engine No. 13 pumped the mains dry while trying to save it. Crumbling, too, was the new eight-story Palmer House hotel, tallest building in the city, and the Chicago Tribune where, until the last, publisher Joseph Medill hoped to put out a fire extra. Crashing down in flames were Woods' Museum—which held Lincoln's catafalque—Crosby's Opera House, Dr. Florenz Ziegfeld's Chicago Academy of Music, and Booksellers Row on State Street between Madison and Washington.

Hildreth, still determined to blow the fire out, chose the Wabash Avenue Methodist Episcopal Church at Harrison Street. Rector Simon McChesney pleaded with him, and parishioners prayed, but the belfry was already blazing. William Haskell, a former professional gymnast, climbed hand over hand up the side of the church, dousing the flames with buckets of water that were passed to him. The church was saved; the fire would travel no farther south, and the Union Stock Yards would be saved, too. Hundreds of spectators cheered Haskell, and a collection was taken up for him, but he disappeared before the reward could be given.

Chief Williams and his men—joined now by three steamer companies from Milwaukee and one from Springfield, Illinois—tried to stop flames rolling steadily northward, but they were powerless as the blistering hot, hurricanelike gales pushed them backward, and they surrendered block upon block of frame dwellings and stately homes. Flames traveled at the rate of half a mile an hour along three ranks. In the front rank, whole neighborhoods of houses were smoking. Houses immediately behind that rank were burning fiercely. In the third rank, buildings were burning themselves out, and there was little use in attacking ruins. Beyond that was a deep belt as far as the eye could see of nothing but smoldering ashes and stark chimneys.

At noon, flames swept into Lincoln Park, where the Chicago Historical Society—repository of Lincoln's walking stick, John Brown's pike, and the original Emancipation Proclamation—stood in the path of the impenetrable wall of fire. By late afternoon the building and all its historical treasures would be gone. At 5 o'clock, the brig *Fontinella,* its tall masts and spars ablaze like a flaming Christmas tree, drifted downstream, slammed into the Chicago Avenue bridge, and set it afire, turning it into a molten skein of tangled ironwork and cutting off the escape of many trying to flee the North Division.

Around 11 o'clock that night the flames reached Fullerton Avenue, the northernmost city boundary, and a few drops of rain began to fall. And then more. Sometime after 2 o'clock, Tuesday morning, October 10, the Great Chicago Fire fell back exhausted.

Chief Williams and the smoke-grimed remnants of his badly beaten fire department trudged wearily home and left the final wetting down to firefighters who were arriving from Cincinnati, Indianapolis, Louisville, Detroit, St. Louis, Pittsburgh, Philadelphia, and even New York City. New York's engines

The fire department was not up to peak efficiency when the Great Chicago Fire started. A major fire the previous night had destroyed a hook and ladder, and the firefighters were exhausted. Chief Robert Williams was down to only sixteen engines, twelve of them Amoskeags of the type shown in this advertisement by the United States' largest maker of steamers.

would remain several weeks until Williams reorganized his department.

The Great Chicago Fire burned for more than thirty hours and destroyed one-third of the city's property. It carved a swath more than five miles long and one mile wide. Destroyed were 17,450 homes and hundreds of factories, stores, and other buildings. Only 120 bodies were recovered, but official estimates put the death toll at closer to 300. Nearly 90,000 people were homeless and tens of thousands were thrown out of work. Damage came to $200 million, only $88 million of which was insured. Fifty-seven of the 250 insurance companies doing business in Chicago went bankrupt. Some paid only three cents on the dollar.

Almost unnoticed in the awesome calamity that stunned the world was a catastrophic loss of life from Wisconsin and Michigan forest fires that burned while Chicago did. At least 1,200 people perished when fire tornadoes, similar to Chicago's, swept out of the timberlands and overwhelmed more than a dozen communities, including Peshtigo, Wisconsin, and Manistee and Holland, Michigan.

The O'Learys perhaps regretted that their cottages escaped. Public reaction was fearsome and newspapers pilloried them, factors that no doubt partially explain why Mrs. O'Leary changed her story about how the fire started. The *Chicago Times* charged that the O'Learys set the fire out of spite because they had been taken off the public dole. With three incomes, it was obvious the O'Learys did not need it. "During her testimony," said the *Times*, "the infant she held kicked its bare legs and drew nourishment from mammoth reservoirs." The O'Learys were never held to account, and they faded into obscurity.

In 1922, on the fifty-first anniversary of the Great Chicago Fire, the week in which October 8–10 falls was proclaimed by the President of the United States and the Governor General of Canada as National Fire Prevention Week under the continuing sponsorship of the National Fire Protection Association. Where the O'Leary barn stood is the block-square training academy of the Chicago Fire Department. Outside the front door stands a monument to the fire, a spiraling metallic flame.

That Chicago recovered quickly from the conflagration is credited largely to such civic boosters as publisher Medill, who wrote in an editorial, "Let the Watchword henceforth be: Chicago Shall Rise Again." Medill used the slogan a few weeks later when he ran for mayor, campaigning on the Fireproof Ticket. He won in a landslide, and the city later named a fireboat after him.

17
BIG STICKS, TALL TOWERS, AND SODA

The Great Chicago Fire coupled with Boston's conflagration jolted America into the realization that no city was immune from destruction. These holocausts produced a host of fire protection improvements.

The most immediate was the rapid development of chemical engines. In April, 1864, French scientists had demonstrated that a mixture of bicarbonate of soda, sulfuric acid, and water created a pressurized gas, carbon dioxide. The liquid was propelled by its own pressure through hoselines. Because the chemical solution was 150 percent heavier than air, it removed the oxygen necessary for the fire to burn and thus smothered it.

Among the most prominent builders of wheeled chemical engines were the Babcock Manufacturing Company of Chicago, the Charles T. Holloway Company of Baltimore, and the Champion Manufacturing Company of Louisville. At first these engines were pulled by hand, but around 1872 Chicago became the first city with horse-drawn chemical engines.

The apparatus consisted of one or two horizontal or vertically mounted 35-to-100 gallon tanks containing water, bicarbonate of soda, and small bottles of sulfuric acid. The rigs also carried at least one reel of hose. The chemical reaction occurred in several ways. In one, a plunger pierced the acid bottle. Another released the acid by pulling a lever. Still another consisted of inverting the tanks. All chemical

Top: *Twin Seagrave water towers batter a Chicago fire in 1955.* Center: *Answering an alarm in Brooklyn, a 1914 Garford tractor pulls a 1907 Seagrave tower.* Above: *An Anderson chemical wagon used in Phoenix, Ariz., around 1910.* Opposite: *In an illustration from* Harper's Weekly, *August 6, 1892, a New York water tower battles a multiple-alarm blaze.*

DELUGE
WAGON
ENGINE
1
1654-H

Opposite top: *Hoselines are tangled like spaghetti along the 400 block of South Broadway in Los Angeles, as the city's fire engines and a Gorter water tower battle a 1913 blaze in a commercial building.* Opposite bottom: *A Christie front-wheel drive powered this thirty-two-foot water tower, a 1925 American LaFrance, of the Pittsburgh Fire Department.*

tanks had a paddle, which agitated and helped to mix the solution. Tanks could be independently charged and operated to provide a continuous stream.

Chemical engines offered a wide range of uses. They were ideal for extinguishing small fires, or as a first aid unit until the steamers began working. Before chemical engines, firefighters had largely used 2½-inch-diameter hose; but on minor fires, this was like killing a fly with a sledge hammer. The one-inch-diameter hose of chemical wagons now kept water damage to a minimum. They were useful, too, in suburban or rural areas where water was scarce.

Fire departments rapidly accepted chemical engines and eventually bought a great many. Babcock boasted in 1875 that carbon dioxide was "30 times as effective as water, the 200 gallons of the first-class engine being equal to 6,000 gallons of water. Besides, it uses the only agent that will extinguish burning tar, oil, and other combustible fluids and vapors." Chemical engines were no panacea, but these copper and brass rigs became commonplace throughout America for more than half a century and put out at least 80 percent of all fires in most communities.

Fearing another epizootic epidemic among horses, some cities bought self-propelled Amoskeags. At first, rounding corners was difficult for these engines, because both power-driven rear wheels turned at the same speed. N. S. Bean, Amoskeag's superintendent, solved the problem by inventing differential gearing, a principle later adapted for automobiles. The engineer operated the throttle while he stood on the fuel pan behind the boiler, and the driver turned the steering wheel. The engines had steel tires with iron studs to increase winter traction and reduce skidding.

Learning from Chicago's costly experience when the Great Fire bridged the river, Boston, on January 1, 1873, put in service the first iron-hulled boat especially constructed for firefighting. Designed by Boston's fire chief John S. Damrell, the steam tug *William F. Flanders* had two Amoskeag pumps capable of pumping 2,000 gallons a minute. New York followed two years later with the 106-foot-long wood-hulled *William F. Havemeyer,* a boat with four Amoskeags that put out 6,000 gallons a minute.

Rapidly growing downtown districts required better water supplies, and Rochester, New York, in 1874, was the first of many cities to install high-pressure water systems to supply the increased volumes and pressures needed for downtown fires.

That year is also remembered for two other major improvements in fire protection. Henry Parmalee invented the first automatic fire sprinkler head system and installed it along ceilings in his New Haven piano factory. If a fire occurred, the heat melted a plug in each head and water sprayed onto the flames. That summer in Baltimore, the American District Telegraph Company began offering subscribers eleven types of service. By cranking a telegraphic call box, a subscriber could summon a messenger, a policeman, a doctor, a taxi, or firefighters. ADT officers were located as close to subscribers as it would take a young boy to run in about three minutes. If the call signaled a fire, a blue-uniformed messenger ran to the nearest firehouse to turn in the alarm, while another youngster ran with a fire extinguisher strapped on his back to the subscriber's business or home to do what he could until firefighters arrived. The ADT firm spread across the country and along with other companies eventually offered protection linked to sprinkler systems. When water began surging through the system, an alarm was automatically transmitted to the nearest ADT office, which called the fire department.

What firefighters needed most were longer and better ladders, and methods for attacking fires in the upper floors of the nation's buildings, which were growing increasingly higher. Ordinary seventy-five-foot extension ladders, hand-raised by nine men, were clumsy and heavy brutes to lift, and were dangerous to climb because they broke easily. America's first practical apparatus-mounted, self-supporting aerial ladder was patented by George Skinner of New York. Its three wooden sections telescoped when not in use and were mounted over the rear axle. In use, the truck had to be positioned at a right angle to the building, which limited its usefulness in narrow streets. Skinners, as these trucks were called, operated somewhat like scissors, the front and rear wheels automatically moving close together when the ladder was raised. They went up to 101 feet by means of a portable extension at the top.

Chicago got the first Skinner, an 84-footer, about a year before the Great Fire. A cage was mounted on this truck, designated as Hose Elevator No. 1, to provide a platform for operating a stream. Historians disagree as to whether the rig could claim the distinction of being America's first water tower for firefighting. In any event, the cage proved unsatisfactory and was soon removed. Skinners were flimsy contraptions, difficult to handle, and few firefighters liked them.

An exception was Phelim O'Toole, tillerman of the St. Louis Fire Department's Skinner Escape Truck. O'Toole, thiry-one years old and a native of Dublin, was a former sailor accustomed to keeping his balance while perched high up on the yardarms of tall masts of ships rolling in heavy seas. The shaky heights of the Skinner did not intimidate him.

Shortly after 1:00 A.M. on April 11, 1877, flames engulfed the block-square Southern Hotel facing on Walnut Street in St. Louis. O'Toole climbed to the highest rung and rescued twelve people. Afterward, he publicly apologized to one of the men he had saved—because in the excitement of the rescues, he said, "I swore at him in a way that I oughtn't to have done." When O'Toole died three years later, his casket was carried to the grave atop the Skinner. Among the mourners walking beside the truck was Joanna Halpin, one of the women he had rescued.

In 1873, Paolo Porta of Milan invented an aerial ladder truck and sold the United States rights to Mrs. Mary Bell Scott-Uda, who received an initial order for three from the Fire Department of New York. The Scott-Uda wooden aerials were in eight separate sections that were stacked in the bed of the wagon; the base section was attached to the wagon's frame. Preparatory to raising the aerial, each section was connected with bracing rods. Counterbalancing weights were extended to prevent the wagon from tipping over, and the ladder was raised by a system of cranks and cog wheels.

Chief Eli Bates of New York arranged a demonstration in June, 1873, for fire chiefs from seven other cities. From that meeting came the idea to form an association of chiefs that would assemble for regular exchanges of fire protection ideas. Chief John S. Damrell of Boston was host to the first meeting of the National Association of Fire Engineers on October 20–22, 1873, which became the International Association of Fire Chiefs in 1926. Damrell was chosen the first NAFE president, and Chief Patrick H. Raymond of Cambridge, Massachusetts, was elected recording secretary. Chief Raymond was the first recorded black fire chief in America.

New York firefighters soured on the idea of using Scott-Udas, however, after September 14, 1875, when one of the ladders snapped during a public demonstration, killing three firefighters who had been climbing it. A scandal involving the sale of the ladders to New York effectively ended Scott-Uda sales in the United States. A few cities bought them, but they were rarely used. Eleven years would pass before the Fire Department of New York would buy another aerial ladder.

The city, meanwhile, continued to experience tragic fires for want of effective ladders. Shortly after 10:00 P.M. on January 31, 1882, flames swept through the World Building at Park Row and Nassau Street. Ground ladders were thirty feet too short to save twelve people who were trapped on upper floors. Chief Bates learned that Foreman Chris Hoell of St. Louis's Hook and Ladder No. 6 had that year patented a new type of ladder, the Hoell Life Saving Appliance, and he invited Hoell to New York to

Daniel D. Hayes, a San Francisco Fire Department machinist, patented the first successful aerial ladder. It was raised by a horizontal worm gear turned by a long handle cranked by up to six men. The gear moved a nut forward to raise the ladder. The LaFrance Fire Engine Company built this 55-foot big stick in 1888 for the Baltimore Fire Department.

demonstrate it. Hoell's scaling ladder was around eight feet long and consisted of a centerpost with rungs extending from each side and an L-shaped hook at one end.

In the demonstration, Hoell hooked the arm of the ladder over the sill of a second floor window, climbed to the window, stood on the sill, and hooked the ladder onto the third-floor sill. Floor by floor, Hoell scaled the outside of the building. Bates was so impressed that he bought three scaling ladders for each hook and ladder. Hoell's scaling ladders became better known as pompiers, the French word for firefighter, probably because scaling ladders similar to Hoell's were earlier used in France.

New York firefighters got their first chance to use the scaling ladders shortly before noon, April 7, 1884, when smoke and flames shot up two dumbwaiter shafts and mushroomed along upper floors of the seven-story brick St. George's Flats, 223–25 East Seventeenth Street. Elevator operator Louis Costaing, age sixteen, was trapped on the top floor. While Hook and Ladder No. 3 firefighters manhandled the seventy-five-foot extension ladder into position, three others, including John Binns, grabbed the scaling ladders. Binns scrambled up the side of the building and rescued Costaing, who lived to tell the story of how he became one of the first to be saved by a pompier. The near-tragic incident prompted Alder-

man Waite to propose to the Common Council that "no building in New York ought to be more than 60 feet in height."

Daniel D. Hayes, a machinist in the San Francisco Fire Department, built the first successful aerial ladder truck, but it took him many years to convince everybody of its value. On February 23, 1868, while serving as superintendent of steamers of the San Francisco Fire Department, he patented the Hayes Hook & Ladder Truck and Fire Escape Combined. The eighty-five foot wooden aerial was raised by a single horizontal worm gear turned by a long handle, manually operated by four to six men. As the gear turned, a large nut moved forward and raised the ladder. Its turntable mounting enabled it to be swung into almost any position.

San Francisco bought the rig for $3,000, but Chief F. E. R. Whitney apparently had second thoughts about using it, so Hayes's aerial sat gathering dust in No. 1 Engine's station and was seen only in parades. During the Fourth of July parade in 1871, however, the truck was following No. 1 Engine down Market Street when an alarm was sounded for a Washington Street fire. David Scannell, who had just been named fire chief, told No. 1 Engine to bring the Hayes. The firefighters raised the big stick, and the aerial "demonstrated beyond all shadow of doubt the superior excellence of this apparatus," as recorded in the *History of the San Francisco Fire Department.*

Recognition outside San Francisco came slowly. Hayes built only about five aerials for Pacific coast cities. Eastern departments were still under the cloud of the Scott-Uda scandal. In 1882, Hayes sold his patents to the LaFrance Fire Engine Company, Elmira, New York. The LaFrance brothers, Truckson and Asa, had been selling fire engines for only nine years, but the LaFrance name had become identified with quality. Their endorsement helped to make LaFrance-built Hayes aerials nationally popular. Not until June 5, 1886, did Hook and Ladder No. 3 of New York get New York's first eighty-five-foot big stick; but soon there were eight Hayes aerials in the city and fourteen in Brooklyn.

Imitators quickly joined the race to build better aerials, which firefighters began calling trucks, as distinct from pumpers or engines—when a firefighter says "truck," he specifically means an aerial ladder. Aerial ladder improvements came fast. In Detroit, Frederick S. Seagrave was manufacturing wood ladders for use in northern Michigan orchards. Encouraged by rural volunteers, he began in 1886 to build aerial ladders along the lines of Hayes's. The Seagrave name also became famous for excellence in fire apparatus of all types.

After moving his plant to Columbus, Ohio, Seagrave patented on January 22, 1901, a spring hoist device for raising ladders faster. The initial lifting power was provided by twin coiled springs; the ladder was extended the rest of the way by cranking a worm screw. Seagrave's invention revolutionized aerial ladder construction, and similar devices were developed by other manufacturers.

In 1886, the Fire Extinguisher Manufacturing Company of Chicago, successors to the Babcock Company, began building Babcock aerials, which were raised by two vertical worm screws on each side of the ladder's turntable base. With the tillerman's seat over the ladder (not under, as in Hayes's design), better visibility was possible. The company built the first successful one-hundred-foot aerial ladders, in 1882. It also built the first all-steel aerial ladder; trucks went to St. Paul and Seattle. Another make was the Gillespie Patent Turntable Aerial Ladder Truck, a four-section wood ladder built after 1889 by the Warwick Machine Company, Warwick, New York. Fire Chief E. F. Dahill of New Bedford, Massachusetts, perfected a device for raising aerials quickly with compressed air. Many ladders were soon outfitted with Dahill Air Hoists.

In 1895, in Seneca Falls, New York, the apparatus builders Gleason & Bailey began making Dederick Aerial Ladders, which were raised by means of a cable passing around a drum, the forerunner of today's method for raising aerials. Four years later, a Kenosha, Wisconsin, volunteer, Peter Pirsch of James S. Barr Hook and Ladder Company No. 1, began building ladder trucks and other fire apparatus. The Pirsch name became synonymous with superiority. Of all the early aerial ladder manufacturers, only LaFrance, Pirsch, and Seagrave remain in business.

At midnight, December 31, 1875, New York firehouse gongs struck "1-7-7-6" followed by "1-8-7-6," and America's one-hundredth birthday celebration began in earnest. Firefighters observed the centennial with parades and other demonstrations of their new ladders, chemical engines, and steamers.

In that centennial year, two brothers—Abner and Albert Greenleaf, who owned a nickel plating works in Baltimore—and John B. Logan, a machinist they employed, hit upon a solution to a century-old firefighting problem: how to produce large volumes of water for fighting fires in upper stories of tall buildings. Streams from the ground merely arced into windows, hit ceilings, and splashed ineffectively onto the flames. Powerful streams were needed to penetrate to the root of the flames before the water turned to steam. Running hoselines up ladders created problems, not the least of which was the inability to use the ladder at the same time for lifesaving.

On November 21, 1876, the Greenleafs and Logan patented a Portable Stand-Pipe or Water Tower. The tower was in three sections, mounted on a wagon drawn by two horses. The base pipe was connected to the wagon's deck. When the two other pipes were attached, they formed a fifty-foot water pipe with a nozzle at the end. The tower was raised by two cranks and gears that engaged a trunnion, which enabled it to swivel. Guy wires steadied the tower, and the direction of the flexible nozzle's stream was controlled by a rope held by a firefighter on the ground. One or more steamers pumped into inlets at the base of the tower.

The Greenleafs loaded their first water tower—three years in the building—on a flatcar and set out for New York to demonstrate it to Chief Bates. If New York accepted it, the Greenleafs expected orders from other cities. Chief Bates was impressed, but not enough to buy it. However, he agreed to take it on loan and try it out.

The chance was not long in coming. At 6:22 P.M. on November 8, 1879, an alarm box was pulled for a fire in a five-story brick building at 82–84 Bank Street in Greenwich Village. Three alarms brought out Chief Bates, steamers, and the water tower with its 1½-inch-diameter elevated nozzle. The tower was set up in front of the building and raised. Two steamers pumped into it, and water from the nozzle bored into the flames.

A New York newspaper said the tower "had a perfect sweep of the fourth and fifth floors and threw an effective stream over and on the roofs of adjoining buildings. Everyone in the vicinity appeared perfectly astonished and admitted that it was the greatest thing they ever saw, and a valuable auxiliary to the fire service. The universal verdict was that a new and important apparatus for the extinguishment of fire had been added to the equipment of the fire department." New York bought the tower and two more. Boston ordered one, too.

Improvements quickly followed. Around 1883, Fire Chief George C. Hale of Kansas City, Missouri, designed a telescoping tower raised by hydraulic pressure. He licensed several manufacturers to build it. As Hale towers became preferred by New York, Boston, Baltimore, and seventeen other cities, the discouraged Greenleafs and Logan, who built only four, sold their patents. Chicago's Fire Extinguisher Manufacturing Company, meanwhile, featured the Hale and Babcock raising principles in their famous line of Champion towers. Around 1898, a San Francisco Fire Department mechanic, Henry H. Gorter, began building towers raised by a water pump. They were used only on the Pacific coast.

As buildings went higher, towers became longer: seventy-six feet, plus a 2½-foot-long nozzle on a Gorter built for San Francisco at the turn of the century. Slightly more than a hundred towers were built, including many by Seagrave and American LaFrance, successor to the LaFrance Engine Company. The last tower built was an American LaFrance, made in 1937 for Los Angeles. Nearly every city had at least one, but no city had more than New York's fifteen. Because they had to be spotted close to burning buildings, towers were frequently crushed under falling walls; but in general, they gave long and valuable service. Apparatus buffs are partial to them and say there was no more spectacular sight during their day than water towers in action.

With their steamers, chemical engines, aerial ladders, and water towers, firefighters were confident that they were well equipped for the problems of the twentieth century. On St. Patrick's Day, 1899, flames spread through New York's Windsor Hotel on Fifth Avenue between Forty-sixth and Forty-seventh Streets. Twenty-two steamers, six aerial ladders, and a water tower fought the fire. The tower was effective, and the aerial ladders were used to make dozens of rescues. Twenty-eight firefighters were cited for bravery. "While the men of the department have made many splendid rescues and have performed many brave deeds, there has never been anything to compare with what they did at the Windsor fire," reported Chief Hugh Bonner. "I doubt if what they accomplished there can ever be equalled."

But Chief Bonner sensed a nagging worry. His men had indeed rescued dozens at the Windsor, but forty-five others had died. Was it possible that America, despite the best fire apparatus in the world, was heading for a period in which losses of life in fires would be catastrophic?

Top: *Peter Pirsch & Sons Company of Kenosha, Wis., has been famous for high-quality apparatus from the days of hand-drawn equipment to the present. This Pirsch ladder truck was acquired by Edgerton, Wis., in 1886. The longest ladder carried was seventeen feet.* Above: *Pirsch built this chief's buggy for the Chicago Fire Department in 1905.* Opposite top: *This hand-drawn chemical cart was made by Pirsch in 1916 for Centerville, Wis.* Right: *The Kissel Motor Car Company of Hartford, Wisconsin, made sporty automobiles and KisselKar fire apparatus for at least thirty-six cities, including Chicago, Dallas, and Kansas City. This 1920 KisselKar hook and ladder was fitted with Seagrave ladders. The longest was sixty-five feet. The rig also was fitted with chemical fire extinguishers and a net.*

backward. Firefighters tore at the bodies and peeled enough off the top so they could climb over the others. Hoselines snaked up the marble staircases while firefighters crawled over the mound of bodies and dragged their lines into the auditorium.

They were joined by police and reporters, who threw away their notepaper and pencils and began pulling out the coughing, spitting, vomiting men, women, and children. Many were horribly maimed. Arms had been yanked off and clothing stripped away. Heelprints gouging heads and ugly scratches mutely testified to the desperate frenzy that had suddenly turned an afternoon of Christmas merriment into mayhem. Firefighters and police would fill ten baskets with jewelry and other valuables torn from victims, five bushel baskets with women's purses, and two barrels with shoes wrenched off during the stampede.

The rear alley was a smoking, flaming hell. Newspapers would call it "Death's Alley." It was too narrow for effective aerial ladder work. Firefighters heard the pounding behind iron-shuttered doors and windows and tried to wrench them open with axes and claw bars. Above them, the unfinished fire escape door suddenly flew open. People, many on fire, were pushed onto the platform that led nowhere but down. Body after body thudded onto the cobblestones.

Another fire escape door was pried open and people were running down it when the door directly underneath was blown open by pent-up heat and gasses. Fire spewing from the door spiraled upward and engulfed people coming down the escape. Firefighters spread black nets, but few of the trapped saw them through the smoke. More jumped and survived only because their bodies were cushioned by those who had leaped before them.

The law, dental, and pharmacy schools of Northwestern University were located in a building across the alley. The structure had recently burned and workmen were finishing repairs. Students and workers pushed three scaffolding planks and a ladder from a window and plopped them against a fire escape railing. Women and children began crawling across the planks, which bowed dangerously under the weight. Several lost their balance and plunged to the alley. Nobody kept count of how many escaped across "Death's Bridge," but 125 bodies were counted in the alley.

Inside the Iroquois oven, the firefighters controlled the fire in about half an hour. But it took hours of searching for the living in the steaming, smoky murk and hauling out the dead. Two hundred bodies, piled ten deep, were discovered where stairways from the second and third floor balconies dovetailed. A husband and wife died in each other's arms. Firefighters could not pry them apart and carried them out together.

"Lights! We need more lights!" called Musham. In addition to the department's lanterns, the Edison power company sent forty arc lights. The beams stabbed the smoke as firefighters sloshed through the water searching for some spark of life.

Moans were heard under a jam of bodies. The brawny firefighters tugged with all their might to pull off the entangled corpses to reach the living. For the most part, only the people on top were burned. Those underneath died of suffocation or were crushed. Tears washed white streaks down the smoke-grimy faces of the sweating firefighters as they lifted layer after layer of dead, hoping to find some child, some woman, anyone, alive.

A firefighter emerged from the smoke with the body of a small girl. "Give that child to someone else and get back in there!" Musham ordered. In the glow of his lantern, Musham saw tears streaming from the firefighter's smoke-reddened eyes.

"I'm sorry, chief. But I've got a girl like this at home. I want to carry this one out." Musham stepped aside as the firefighter slowly made his way down the grand marble staircase.

Another was crawling across a stack of dead when he heard a boy moan. Pulling him out, the firefighter bolted from the auditorium. "Out of my way, men! Let me out! This kid's still alive!"

Dead, dying, and injured were brought out faster than seventy ambulances, fire department hose wagons, cabs, police paddy wagons, and department store delivery vans could haul them to hospitals and temporary morgues in mortuaries, saloons, and stores. Police clubbed parents and relatives milling in front of the Iroquois to clear a way for the ambulances. Bodies were laid side by side on the icy-slick sidewalk in front of the theater. Marshall Field's department store sent blankets for the dead and injured and cleared space in the store for an aid station to treat those less seriously hurt.

John Thompson's restaurant next to the Iroquois became an emergency room and morgue. Marble tabletops served as treatment tables. Fifty doctors pumped the arms of the wheezing smoke victims while nurses massaged chests and attendants administered oxygen. Screams and groans made a terrible din. As victims died, they were laid under the tables, to be replaced by a living one on top. Outside, parents beat on the door and windows.

Word of the disaster flashed across Chicago. Husbands left work and hurried to the theater to look for their wives and children. In front of the Iroquois, a teeming sea of parents who had escaped called the names of their missing sons and daughters while sobbing children screamed for absent mothers, fathers, aunts, uncles, and grandparents.

A husband found the body of his wife under a blanket. He wrapped her in his overcoat and in his shock carried her home to Evanston, a walk of nearly twenty miles. James Blackburn had become separated from his daughter in the panic and found her dead. Bundling her in a blanket, he carried her to the railroad station and took her home to Glenview.

Foy was reunited with his son. The Dimmick party escaped. Arthur Hull hurried from his office to the Iroquois and hours later identified the bodies of his wife and three children. At a hospital, the badly burned Van Ingens called Kenosha and asked friends to hurry to Chicago to look for their five children. It took hours of going from hospitals to temporary morgues, but they found them—all dead. Mr. and Mrs. Morris Egger picked out the bodies of their three daughters and two grandchildren.

Police and hospital switchboards were jammed. "Have you found a seven-year-old girl wearing a small heart-shaped locket set with blue stones?" was a typical call. Many bodies were so dismembered that Coroner John E. Traeger made an appeal that family doctors come to look for and identify the dead and injured, who came from thirteen states and eighty-six cities. Chicago's 300 dead included 102 schoolchildren and 39 teachers. Only one of the *Blue Beard* cast was lost—Nellie Reed, the prima ballerina.

Mayor Carter H. Harrison proclaimed New Year's Eve and Day a time of mourning and asked that all church bells and factory and locomotive whistles be silenced. Chicago began the New Year by burying its dead that Saturday and Sunday: horse-drawn black hearses for adults, white ones for children. Hardly a train left Chicago without at least one coffin in the baggage car.

Completing its investigation, the coroner's jury ordered Mayor Harrison, Chief Musham, Sallers, building department officials, and owners of the Iroquois bound over for possible grand jury indictments. Little came of the charges, however. Chief Musham was accused of failing to enforce fire laws and quietly resigned the following October on the twenty-ninth anniversary of the Great Chicago Fire that he had so valiantly fought.

Cities the world over examined their theaters. Out of the Iroquois holocaust came new theater fire laws, including unlocked, outward-opening doors, sprinklers, fire protection and alarm systems, and flameproofed scenery and curtains. Testifying to the effectiveness of the laws is the fact that there has never been another theater fire disaster in the United States. Investigators found little fault with the theater building. The Iroquois probably was as fireproof as possible. Unfortunately, the 602 who perished in the place were not.

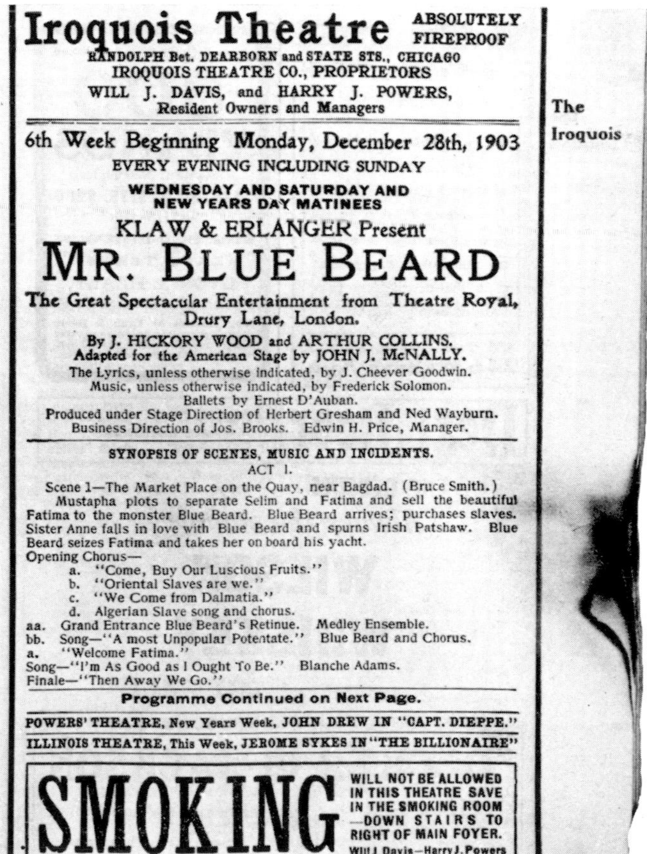

Iroquois Theatre ABSOLUTELY FIREPROOF
RANDOLPH Bet. DEARBORN and STATE STS., CHICAGO
IROQUOIS THEATRE CO., PROPRIETORS
WILL J. DAVIS, and HARRY J. POWERS,
Resident Owners and Managers

6th Week Beginning Monday, December 28th, 1903
EVERY EVENING INCLUDING SUNDAY
WEDNESDAY AND SATURDAY AND NEW YEARS DAY MATINEES
KLAW & ERLANGER Present

MR. BLUE BEARD

The Great Spectacular Entertainment from Theatre Royal, Drury Lane, London.
By J. HICKORY WOOD and ARTHUR COLLINS.
Adapted for the American Stage by JOHN J. McNALLY.
The Lyrics, unless otherwise indicated, by J. Cheever Goodwin.
Music, unless otherwise indicated, by Frederick Solomon.
Ballets by Ernest D'Auban.
Produced under Stage Direction of Herbert Gresham and Ned Wayburn.
Business Direction of Jos. Brooks. Edwin H. Price, Manager.

SYNOPSIS OF SCENES, MUSIC AND INCIDENTS.
ACT 1.
Scene 1—The Market Place on the Quay, near Bagdad. (Bruce Smith.)
Mustapha plots to separate Selim and Fatima and sell the beautiful Fatima to the monster Blue Beard. Blue Beard arrives; purchases slaves. Sister Anne falls in love with Blue Beard and spurns Irish Patshaw. Blue Beard seizes Fatima and takes her on board his yacht.
Opening Chorus—
a. "Come, Buy Our Luscious Fruits."
b. "Oriental Slaves are we."
c. "We Come from Dalmatia."
d. Algerian Slave song and chorus.
aa. Grand Entrance Blue Beard's Retinue. Medley Ensemble.
bb. Song—"A most Unpopular Potentate." Blue Beard and Chorus.
a. "Welcome Fatima."
Song—"I'm As Good as I Ought To Be." Blanche Adams.
Finale—"Then Away We Go."
Programme Continued on Next Page.

POWERS' THEATRE, New Years Week, JOHN DREW IN "CAPT. DIEPPE."
ILLINOIS THEATRE, This Week, JEROME SYKES IN "THE BILLIONAIRE"

SMOKING WILL NOT BE ALLOWED IN THIS THEATRE SAVE IN THE SMOKING ROOM—DOWN STAIRS TO RIGHT OF MAIN FOYER.
Will J. Davis—Harry J. Powers

The Iroquois

"Absolutely Fireproof," boasted this Iroquois Theatre showbill. The theater was new, and its owners said no expense had been spared in making it fireproof. But there is no way to fireproof people. More than 600 of them died in the fire and stampede.

19

SAN FRANCISCO: LEATHER-LUNGS DOUGHERTY

During San Francisco's final hours that Tuesday night, April 17, 1906, the city was bursting with wealth and revelry. In the Grand Opera House that night the New York Metropolitan Opera Company triumphed with its opening of *Carmen,* in which the role of Don Jose was sung by a young tenor named Enrico Caruso.

After-theater crowds barely noticed First Assistant Chief John Dougherty's buggy clanging past them toward the glow over the North Beach District. A tuft of snow-white hair spilled from under his helmet and his walrus moustache drooped as the formidable chief with the square face and jutting chin whipped his buggy through late-night traffic. Arriving at Bay and Mason Streets, Dougherty found the California Cannery Company's fruit warehouse fully involved, and he pulled a third alarm.

Fire Chief Dennis T. Sullivan arrived soon after and reined in his buggy alongside a throbbing Amoskeag pumper. He did not bother to ask where his assistant chief was, for you could always hear Dougherty's foghorn voice bellowing orders above the din of any fire. It was a voice rookies feared and older firefighters respected. They called him Old Leather-Lungs, though not to his face.

"I think I can hold her in about half an hour if the wind doesn't shift," Dougherty told the chief. Sullivan, one of the best leaders the department ever had, referred to his fifty-nine-year-old assistant as

The San Francisco earthquake and fire on April 18, 1906, killed 674 people, injured 3,500, destroyed 28,000 buildings, and left 514 city blocks in ruins. More than $500 million in damages resulted. This view of Market Street shows the destruction of the Call Building skyscraper.

"the Grand Old Man of the Department. He's forgotten more about firefighting than I'll ever know." Chief Sullivan left Dougherty in charge and went home. He climbed the three flights of stairs to his apartment, provided by the city over the bunkroom of No. 3 Chemical on Bush Street. Rather than disturb his wife, Margaret, he decided to sleep near the alarm bell in an adjoining room.

Before turning out the light, Sullivan scanned newspapers describing two earthquake disasters in Caucasia. The story said there had been several other severe quakes during that week, following the catastrophic eruption of the Italian volcano Vesuvius, the worst in modern times. The article went on to recall that the fault line on which San Francisco precariously perched had not slipped in nine years. Scientists had warned that the stresses normally relieved by regular tremors were creating a situation that someday would cause a disastrous quake.

At 3:45 A.M., Chief Dougherty backed his buggy into 17 Engine's house on Jessie Street. "It could have been worse," he told the firefighter on watch. Dougherty had not forgotten the dismay of the committee of twenty experts that had been sent to San Francisco six months earlier by the National Board of Fire Underwriters. The committee had been formed

San Francisco firefighters were severely hampered by the quake-shattered water system, which left them almost helpless. Here, flames destroy the Mutual Life Insurance Company building at California and Sansome Streets in the financial district. With water, the structure would have been saved.

shortly after the Great Baltimore Fire of Sunday, February 7, 1904, when 1,343 downtown buildings were destroyed with losses of $18 million. The insurance companies wanted to ferret out other bad fire risks before there were repeats of Baltimore and Chicago.

The committee had found that 90 percent of San Francisco's buildings were wooden, a far greater percentage than in any other city. They had looked with disbelief at the four- and five-story frame tenements crowding hard upon the congested downtown district. Riding cable cars up and down San Francisco's steep hills, they had wondered how the spirited firehorses ever climbed them. Time lost while answering alarms on top of these hills, compounded by the ever-present blustering winds off the Pacific, made conditions ripe for disaster. The wonder of it all was not so much San Francisco's haphazard building conditions, topography, or wind, but rather what kept the city on the face of the map.

"San Francisco had violated all underwriting traditions and precedents by not burning up," the committee reported. "That it has not done so is largely due to the vigilance of the fire department, which cannot be relied upon indefinitely to stave off the inevitable." The report was all but ignored by officials in City Hall.

Dougherty recalled how Mayor Eugene E. Schmitz had shrugged off the committee's warning. "Bunch of frightened old women," the mayor told Sullivan and Dougherty. "I'll admit this isn't the most fireproof city in the world. Lord knows we've burned her down many times. But that was back in the Gold Rush days. It can't happen again, not with all our fireproof brick buildings downtown. And I'll grant that we've got a pack of frame tenements. What those easterners don't realize is that our city is built of redwood. It doesn't catch fire or burn as fiercely as other woods. Besides, brick buildings collapse and become killers in earthquakes. And you know as well as I do what our weather is: rainy winters and damp summer nights. We never dry out enough to burn."

Rising from his desk to indicate the meeting was over, Schmitz had patted the dour-faced Dougherty on the back. "I've got the world's best fire department—five hundred eighty-five firefighters, the best bunch of Irishmen this side of Dublin." Dougherty and Sullivan knew as they left that they would never get their badly needed auxiliary saltwater service system, which was a quakeproof standby in case an earthquake fractured mains fed by the three reservoirs south of the city. Equally utopian were the fireboats the department had requested, to replace the two state harbor commission tugs that were poor substitutes for light-draft, high-powered fireboats.

Toward daybreak, lights were reluctantly flickering out and San Francisco's 450,000 residents were sleeping serenely, in the waning hours of an era they would never see again. The day dawned bright and clear, with never a hint of the unfathomable stresses pounding to a climax hundreds of miles underground and hundreds of miles along the San Andreas Fault. Firefighter James O'Neil, on watch at No. 1 Ladder, was drawing a bucket of water for the horses, when he heard a distant rumbling that hurried closer and closer.

The city out of the Arabian Nights that slumbered by day and lived by night, the upstart city that grew so fast it never lost its adolescence, the city where corruption and vice were openly flaunted, was jolted without mercy at 5:13 A.M., Wednesday, April 18, 1906, for forty-eight seconds that seemed like eternity. San Francisco shuddered and shook and creaked. Another shock hit two minutes later and was quickly followed by three more awesome temblors. Seismologists the world over gaped at recording instrument needles, which gave readings of 8.25, just shy of total destruction in the San Francisco area.

The castors on Chief Dougherty's bed trundled him across the room, just missing the open hole with its sliding brass pole. Report books spilled from the shelf over his rolltop desk. Dougherty sat bolt upright in stark disbelief at the weird creaking of nails trying to squeeze themselves out of the woodwork. Outside, chimneys and chunks of fancy gingerbread stonework adorning buildings were slamming into the street.

The tenement district south of Market Street absorbed the full punishment. Loss of life would be heaviest there. Frame houses collapsed or leaned drunkenly against each other. The ground split open and houses sunk into the crevasses, stopping only when their second-floor windows were eye-level with the street. Dozens of kerosene lamps overturned; power and trolley lines snapped and rained angry sprays of sparks into tinder-dry debris.

The walls of a four-story brick warehouse fell over, exposing a mound of furniture that still supported the roof. Another wall slammed down on No. 1 Ladder's station. Firefighter O'Neil was dead before he hit the floor. Chandeliers in Nob Hill mansions swayed crazily. Chinatown, the largest settlement of Chinese outside the Orient, panicked. The ornate and new City Hall was the most quakeproof building in town—at least that's what Mayor Schmitz had said. That its pretentiousness was all pretense was revealed as hundreds of tons of brick and ornamental stonework fell away.

Chief Dougherty shook his head for one stunned instant, then dove for his boots, pulled on his turnouts, and slid the pole to the apparatus floor, where the firefighter on watch was trying to calm the terrified horses released from their stalls when the quake triggered the chains. The front door burst open and a milkman blurted, "The restaurant on Mission across from the Mint! It's burning!" Chief Dougherty took 17 Engine and its hose wagon with him to Mission. Gobs of angry black smoke were pouring from the two-story building. Dougherty sent a firefighter to Firebox 47 at Powell and Market, to call for more help.

No. 17 Engine, a Clapp & Jones steamer, took the hydrant at the corner while firefighters stretched their hoses and waited for water. Out came only a trickle. "I can't get any pressure, chief!" said the pump operator. "The main must be broken!" No water pressure meant that San Francisco's spiderweb of mains had been snapped, as if some giant had stepped on a package of macaroni. Elsewhere, firefighters were spotting fires blossoming almost at their front doors. They tried one hydrant after another. Some worked; most did not. Dougherty knew he would have to look to the bay for most of the water he needed.

Chief Dougherty listened for galloping and the bells and whistles of the extra apparatus he had called for, but all he saw was the red buggy of Second Assistant Chief Pat Shaughnessy hurrying toward him. He knew something was terribly wrong when he saw the deep scowl on the usually carefree face of the tall, heavyset chief.

"Chief Sullivan got it bad!" said Shaughnessy. "When the quake hit I hurried over to No. 3 Chemical for orders. The firehouse was a mess. You know that ornamental cupola on top of the California Hotel next door? It fell on the station and drove the chief's apartment clear down to the apparatus floor. It missed the chief, but when he went to help Margaret he fell through the hole. The boys got him out by the time I got there, and they were leaving for the hospital. Sullivan is dying, so that puts you in command of the department."

Stunned by the loss of his friend, Dougherty barely heard the next piece of bad news. "That isn't all, John. The alarm office is wrecked, too. The circuits haven't registered a single alarm and Chief Kelly hasn't been able to transmit any." Dougherty suddenly found himself the chief of a fire department—one of the world's largest and best—that was almost completely helpless. As more than a dozen fires lifted thick clouds of black smoke into the morning sky, he could not have inherited a worse problem.

"With all those fires, we haven't got a chance of saving the tenement district. We'll have to use what water we can find and fight a delaying action. There's quite a few brick factories that'll slow the fire. We'll save some if we can. Meanwhile, let's get set up to make a stand along Market Street." Dougherty quickly sketched his battle plan. "We'll send messengers to get all the off-duty men and have them bring every available rig and length of hose. Then we'll draft from the bay and relay water up Market from the ferry terminal. The two Harbor Commission tugs can help, and the Navy's got one, too."

Market, one of the world's broadest thorough-

Ships flee the burning waterfront of San Francisco in 1906. "We'll save the city or die trying," Assistant Chief John Dougherty told Mayor Eugene Schmitz. Dougherty took command of the fire department after Chief Dennis Sullivan was fatally injured in the quake. Dougherty led the firefighters in a brave stand along Van Ness Avenue and stopped the fire.

fares, offered a natural firebreak. The street was lined, moreover, with fire-resistant brick buildings, including the Palace Hotel and the new Call Building, pride of San Francisco and nationally famous as an ultramodern fireproof structure, the posh West coast headquarters for many eastern companies.

While Shaughnessy raced off to a reported fire at Hayes and Laguna, Dougherty began mustering his companies along Market. He wondered at the irony of water becoming so scarce in a seaport surrounded on three sides by water. Dougherty felt proud of every member of the department who arrived with the city's thirty-eight steamers, as many hose wagons, ten Hayes aerial ladders, eight chemical engines, and the department's heavy artillery, the Gorter water tower.

Hose wagons were laying lines up Market when Shaughnessy returned to report the Hayes and Laguna fire out. Staring at the panorama of smoke mushrooming lazily into the sky, Shaughnessy remarked, "We're lucky the wind is only about two miles an hour. If it holds, we'll probably have the fire under control by noontime." Dougherty was not that optimistic. The fire seemed to be biding its time, patiently collecting many smaller blazes to build them into one vast conflagration. But he doubted it would grow big enough to cross Market.

Hundreds watching from Nob Hill slopes were as confident as Shaughnessy. Others wandering through downtown streets, to see the quake damage and watch the fire, never imagined that this bigger-than-usual fire—in a city famous for spectacular fires—would send them fleeing to the Presidio park.

In the shadow of the eighteen-story Call Building a small fire followed a line of least resistance and burrowed into the Grand Opera House. Flames quickly discovered the Metropolitan Opera's eight carloads of costumes and sets. Soon nothing was left of the Opera House but tradition, and the flames stormed into the brick department stores fronting on Market.

Dougherty was becoming increasingly worried while he watched the raging fires and the forlorn streams eking from the nozzles. "If only we had two good fireboats and the water system we asked for, we could do some good," he told Shaughnessy. Even as they second-guessed the fire's movement, a housewife on Hayes was satisfied that the downtown fire was no cause for worry. Returning to her apartment, she started lunch. That lunch would go down in

history as "the Ham and Eggs Fire." The kitchen flue carried the heat to the shingled roof where a chimney had snapped off during the quake. The wooden roof was soon ablaze, and the entire area north of Market—thirty blocks—was doomed and Chief Dougherty's line with it. Thirty minutes later a messenger rushed up to Dougherty. "There's a bad fire at Hayes and Gough!"

Dougherty told Shaughnessy to take two pumpers and a Hayes aerial to fight it. He paused to watch as Shaughnessy's buggy clattered up Market. He felt fortunate to have a firefighter of Shaughnessy's ability at a time like this. Shaughnessy, age forty-four, was an astute officer with raw courage. They still talked of the time he won the Merchants Association Medal for helping to save a woman's life when the Baldwin Hotel burned, November 23, 1898.

The Hayes and Gough fire was beyond control when Shaughnessy arrived. Flames cascaded down on row upon row of frame structures. Brick buildings slowed them for only a few minutes. Shaughnessy's aide, Mike Roebling, raced back to Market Street. "The fire has jumped Van Ness. The chief needs four more engines!" Dougherty's mouth fell open. "Jumped Van Ness? That's impossible!" The street and sidewalks formed an 185-foot-wide firebreak.

"If she's bad enough to jump Van Ness, Shaughnessy will need more than four engines." Dougherty ordered eight pumpers to follow Roebling. He could hardly spare the men and equipment, but he had no choice. As the horses galloped down Market Street, Dougherty noticed Schmitz hurrying toward him. "We've got to use dynamite, Dougherty. You can't let the fire go further."

"We're doing everything we can to hold it, mayor. You've got to understand we're low on water and our alarm system is out. Chicago and Baltimore learned that dynamiting causes more fires than it puts out." Dougherty pointed to the brick buildings along Market. "Concussions would break those windows and flying brands would start new fires on roofs and inside buildings for blocks around."

"I don't give a damn what happened in Chicago and Baltimore," said Schmitz. "Your way of fighting this fire isn't working. We'll try mine." Chief Dougherty bristled.

"Mayor," said Dougherty, "we'll save this city or die trying. You've made up your mind to dynamite and there's nothing I can do to stop you. Now get the hell out of my way. I've got a fire to fight!"

Dougherty's contempt was born of the disillusionment he experienced after he had been lured from the fire department into politics. He had served three terms as a state senator and later chaired San Francisco's Democratic Committee. But feeling homesick for the smell of smoke and firefighting, he quit politics and rejoined the department, although he had to start out again as a bottommost rookie. He quickly rose through the ranks, however, and was finally picked by Sullivan to be his first assistant.

Half an hour later, after hearing the first dynamite blasts, Dougherty chanced to look down Market and was stunned. Thick black smoke was puffing from the broken fourth-floor windows of the skyscraper Call Building. "The dynamite blew 'em out!" he cursed. "Our lines could never reach the fourth floor. Not with our pressure, or even if we pumped into the Gorter tower." The Call's elevator shafts provided perfect chimneys for flames, which quickly spouted from top floors and the dome.

"The Palace is a goner, too," said Dougherty, as flames poured into the rear of the hotel. "Pick up your lines and fall back." Retreat was a word unknown to Dougherty until this day, and he hated himself for giving the order. The seven-story Palace, palatial stopping-off place for nobility the world over, died regally. Especially built to withstand earthquakes, the hotel stood no chance against the fire. Its 1,500 rooms, famous art gallery, and Special Billiard and Pool Tables for Gentlewomen soon became a seething furnace that blazed until late afternoon.

"There she goes!" whispered Dougherty, as the roof caved in and the American flag vanished in the soaring flames and clouds of smoke. The sight drove away his numbing fatigue. He was bitter, and hatred boiled deep inside. No longer was this a conflagration. This was a living monster, a personal outrage to be avenged. Dougherty's rage exploded into thundering orders.

"Hit that fire harder over there, boys! Good! Now move in closer! Give it hell, men!" His fury stirred the firefighters, who knew the Grand Old Man of the Fire Department had finally met his match. But the fire bullied Dougherty and his men backward, and they dragged their hoses in retreat and set up their steamers at new positions. At nightfall, a thick smudge of smoke hung like a shroud over the city. The fire was seen sixty miles out to sea. Dougherty called his officers together for reports from all fronts.

A sweeping arm of fire was spreading into the Mission. Shaughnessy reported the Ham and Eggs

Fire completely out of control. "She'll take everything north of Market, the upper retail district, Union Square, the St. Francis Hotel, the theater district, and probably Russian Hill, too." Thirteen separate conflagrations were rampaging through San Francisco. With little water, Chief Dougherty could only fight a delaying battle. Chiefs and firefighters turned to him for some hope, some encouragement to dull the sharp pain of not having won a single round. "I don't know," he sighed, "I just don't know."

Dougherty was trying to stem the flames crackling their way slowly down California Street when a poorly planted dynamite charge scattered burning debris across Montgomery and ignited the block running through to Kearny. "We'll never save Chinatown or the Barbary Coast, either," he said, as messengers reported fires blazing for blocks behind the battle lines.

Chief Dougherty hurried over to Chinatown to see how the lines were holding and found a gigantic bonfire in Portsmouth Square. The terrified Chinese explained that the Wicked Dragon of the Earth was coming out from the center of the world as their ancestors had predicted. They claimed that the earthquake had occurred when the dragon started to move. This caused the earth to split open, and his fiery breath set off the conflagration.

Residents everywhere were trundling crates of silks, bales of spices, and boxes of tea and fine ebony into the square and igniting penitential offerings to the dragon. In Woo Tung Alley, headquarters of the Tong societies, holes were dug in the street and wheelbarrows full of money dumped into the pits. The people hoped that if they could dig far enough down, the dragon might see their offerings and change its mind about invading earth. Chinatown nevertheless burned and residents stampeded toward the Presidio.

The thirteen fires fused shortly after dawn into two juggernauts. One roared south in the Mission District. The other, far worse, gnawed toward Van Ness and beyond to the Western Addition, a sprawling residential district. Shaughnessy awaited Dougherty's plan. The chief took a deep breath. "Well, Pat, we've got only one more chance to save the city. Van Ness. We'll make our last stand there. If she crosses Van Ness, we're done for and so is the Western Addition."

Dougherty saw Shaughnessy's skepticism. "I know what you're thinking. The fire jumped Van Ness yesterday. I never thought it could happen, either. But we stopped it. And with luck we'll have a prevailing west wind at our back. I badly need you here, but I think you'd better go down to the Mission and take command."

Dougherty rode over to Van Ness, marshalled his forces, and scouted water along the final skirmish line. He was in luck. Hydrants were working for five blocks along Van Ness, and there were more along Buchanan. But how long would they last? "The big job now," he told his men, "is to lay our lines to the foot of Van Ness. We'll have the boats pump into them and our engines can boost the water the rest of the way here. We'll get General Frederick Funston to bring in his artillery and knock down the buildings along the east side of Van Ness and set backfires in the ruins."

Satisfied that he was ready for the fight of his life, Dougherty gave his men their first break in more than thirty hours. They fell asleep in the streets, on apparatus running boards, and in hose wagon beds. Wisps of smoke curled from the steamers as the engineers kept the fires low. Dougherty ached from fatigue but went to the Mission to see how Shaughnessy was doing. "We're not in too good shape," he was told. "But I guess we'll make it. How are things on Van Ness?"

"I've got water, but I could use ten times more." When Dougherty returned to Van Ness, he discovered that a freshening breeze was blowing from the east and urging flames along faster than he had estimated. Jittery firefighters watched the mountain of flame, still a mile distant, hurrying toward them. The worried silence was broken with the opening artillery salvos. The guns were reloaded and boomed again and again. One by one, mansions, apartment houses, and churches fell, and backfire torches ignited the ruins. Never in modern times had man intentionally wrought such destruction.

The sharp wind was pushing great sheets of flame and withering blasts of heat ahead of it. "Charge your lines!" bellowed Dougherty, hurrying up and down Van Ness. Dozens of hoselines spurted; then the streams turned into hard jets. The awful bellowing of the flames seemed human as they tried to drown the chief's thundering orders. "Move in close!" he roared once more. "We'll show her she's not going to get past us again!"

No general ever presented a prouder sight than Chief Dougherty racing up and down Van Ness, pausing only to bolster a line here where the fire was at its worst, or telling firefighters there to move a little

to the left. "You're doing great, boys! Stick with it!"

The battle continued without quarter through the afternoon and on into the night. News of the valiant last stand heartened people around the world. The President of France cabled a message of encouragement. "Well Done Indeed!" headlined a New York newspaper. In Los Angeles, the world's heavyweight champion, James J. Jeffries, auctioned off oranges at ten dollars apiece and more to help San Francisco.

"Hear that, laddies!" boomed Dougherty. "Jim Jeffries is selling oranges in the streets of Los Angeles for *our* benefit! What do you say about that?" The firefighters cheered. Then came a stroke of bad luck. A massive sheet of flame curled up and over Van Ness. The spire of St. Mary's Cathedral began smoking and patches of flame raced up it. The firefighters tried to hit them, but their streams lacked pressure. The fire had crossed Van Ness again.

A Hayes aerial poked its big stick up to the cathedral's roof. Firefighters scurried up it and edged along the roof to the spire. Clinging like human flies, they hacked away at burning sections. The church was saved and the monster was shoved back across Van Ness. Firefighters looking on took inspiration from this miraculous feat and flew into the attack with renewed bursts of energy. The flames retaliated, but toward midnight, victory was within grasp. A cry of jubilation rose from the spectators.

The cheering abruptly ended and the firefighters gaped in utter dismay when an enormous splinter of flame lobbed over their heads, crossed Van Ness, and touched off a string of buildings at Sutter Street. This was too much for the bone-weary firefighters. Some collapsed in the middle of Van Ness. Why continue? They were beaten.

San Francisco's darkest hour had arrived. The firefighters knew they had fought their hearts out for nearly two days and all they had to show for it was a few buildings, islands in a sea of ashes. The fight was gone from them. Chief Dougherty whipped his buggy back and forth along Van Ness, heat bubbling its red paint. "Don't give up, boys! You've held her this long. Don't quit now!"

But even Old Leather-Lungs, still vigorously fighting beside them although he was older than any of them, could do no good. San Francisco tottered on the edge of complete destruction with the conflagration inches short of total victory. Dougherty had one last ace in the hole. "Up on your feet, men!" He was vicious. "Don't be quitters! You haven't even begun to do your best. I've seen hick-town firefighters do better than you've done up to now!"

Chief Dougherty's brutal words infuriated the men as the fire never could. They had done their best and Old Leather-Lungs still was not satisfied. In rage, vowing they would make him eat his words, they took new grips on their nozzles and drove streams hard and true into the flames on both sides of Van Ness. Shrieking steamer whistles called for more and still more coal.

This was what Dougherty had hoped would happen. He had browbeaten the exhausted firefighters to a fury that made them hate him, so much that they would rather take a bellyful of smoke and heat than admit to the Grand Old Man that he could stand the punishment longer than they could.

Chief Dougherty was too absorbed with the battle to notice the tall, haggard man in the grime-covered white helmet standing beside him. "We've held her, chief," said Shaughnessy. "The Mission fire is under control." The words took a few seconds to sink in. Shaughnessy told him again. Dougherty let out a whoop that was heard for blocks. He wheeled his buggy up and down the avenue. "They've held her down in the Mission, boys. They've stopped her! This is the only hot spot left. Let's show Shaughnessy's boys we can do it here, too!"

The news provided the added elixir the firefighters needed. Although nobody knew what kept them on their feet, the streams from their hoses bored into the flames. Suddenly Dougherty felt something cool against his heat-blistered face. "Thank the Lord! A west wind!"

Under Dougherty's constant encouragement, the firefighters gradually stopped the fire. For the first time in the long struggle they were able to advance their lines. The tide of battle changed and the flames conceded defeat. The men were too numb to think much about it or even cheer. The gratitude of all San Francisco was too deep for tears. The worst was over by dawn. The losses would be catastrophic: 674 dead, 3,500 hurt, 28,000 buildings destroyed, 514 city blocks in ruins, more than $500 million in damage.

"The men performed a miracle in saving as much of the city as they did," said Dougherty.

"They sure did, chief," agreed Shaughnessy. "Every last one of them."

Dougherty looked into Shaughnessy's eyes. "We've lost our city six times. By God, we'll never lose her again." He quickly turned on his heels and proudly walked away.

Opposite top: *One of the nation's most elegant chief's buggies, from Newburyport, Mass.* Opposite center: *American LaFrance engine from Oakland, believed to be one of those ferried to San Francisco to fight the earthquake fire.* Above: *Postcard view of San Francisco burning.*

THE TRIANGLE FIRETRAP

The New York Board of Fire Underwriters called the Triangle Shirtwaist Company "a rotten risk." During the nine years the ladies' blouse makers had leased the top three floors of the ten-story Asch Building in lower Manhattan, a series of fires cost insurance companies upwards of $32,000. Repeaters like Triangle were tagged in insurance records with a red stamp, "Other Insurance Permitted," and the risk was shared by a syndicate of companies.

In 1910, fire protection in the unsprinklered Asch Building consisted of 259 water pails and a standpipe water system with hose connections on each floor. There was but one fire escape, two narrow, winding stairways, and four tiny elevators, two of them for freight only. Despite these firetrap conditions, the decade-old building at Washington Place and Greene Street, about two blocks east of the famous Washington Square arch, was in almost total compliance with existing laws.

Triangle was the nation's largest manufacturer of shirtwaists, the women's fashion rage inspired by the "Gibson girl," created by the magazine illustrator Charles Dana Gibson. The bouffant blouses were of a sheer white cotton fabric called lawn and were trimmed with lace. Open at the neck, with button-down collars, they made for a crisp, clean, and distinctly feminist look, popular in those days of agitation for suffrage and other women's rights. Triangle produced nine hundred dozen shirtwaists a week, wholesaling them for up to eighteen dollars a dozen.

The company's five hundred employees worked for as little as three dollars a week, and their pay often was the primary support of their families on New York's Lower East Side. Triangle's workers were mostly Jewish and Italian immigrant women as young as fourteen years of age, such as Rosalie Maltese, whose sister, Lucia, age twenty, and mother, Catherine, also worked at the company. The women labored about sixty or more hours a week, in the hot and stuffy cutting room on the eighth floor; in sixteen parallel rows of 240 sewing machines on the noisy ninth floor; and in the shipping room, loaded with heavy cardboard and wood boxes, on the tenth floor. Clotilda Terdanova, one of the tenth-floor workers, was looking forward to quitting in a week to get married.

Workroom doors were locked to prevent the women from sneaking out for a break. At quitting time they endured the humiliation of having their pocketbooks checked for pilfered shirtwaists; sometimes there were even body searches. Sweatshop conditions resulted in a strike, late in 1910, of Triangle members of the Waistmakers' Union, Local 25, International Ladies' Garment Workers' Union of the American Federation of Labor. Their demands included adequate fire escapes and unlocked doors. Triangle's management immediately replaced the striking workers with strikebreakers, but the dispute spread to a general walkout at all shirtwaist factories.

AFL president Samuel Gompers said, "I never declared a strike in all my life. But there comes a time when not to strike is but to rivet the chains of slavery upon our wrists. Yes, Mr. Shirtwaist Manufacturer! It may be inconventient for you if our boys and girls go out on strike. But there are things of more importance than your convenience and profit. There are the lives of the boys and girls who are working in your business."

The strike was ugly. Pickets were arrested for no other cause than glancing at police. Prostitutes were hired to provoke fights with the Triangle women, giving officers an excuse for beating the picketers with their nightsticks. By Christmas, police had arrested 723 strikers throughout the city—but no prostitutes. After thirteen weeks of impasse, most shirtwaist makers signed contracts granting a fifty-two-hour workweek and pay increases. Triangle, however, remained an open shop, and its employees were no better off than before.

The Triangle Shirtwaist fire, March 25, 1911, in New York's ten-story Asch Building. The factory's fire escape provisions were grossly inadequate. Of the 146 workers, mostly young women, who died in the blaze, many did so in leaping from windows eight to ten stories above ground.

The Triangle firetrap was no worse than most of the other 1,242 garment factories in New York. There had been forty-two shirtwaist factory fires in New York in 1910, and there would be nearly double that number the following year. By 1911, around 300,000 of the city's factory workers were crowded into factories above the seventh floors in hundreds of high-fire-hazard loft buildings, where rents were cheap and natural light saved electricity. There was, however, not an aerial ladder made that could reach above the sixth floor. Similar situations existed throughout the United States. On November 25, 1910, four months to the day before Triangle burned, a Newark, New Jersey, factory fire killed twenty-five workers, nineteen of whom leaped from upper windows.

"This city may have a fire as deadly as the one in Newark at any time," warned New York Fire Chief Edward F. Croker. "There are buildings in New York where the danger is every bit as great. A fire in the daytime would be accompanied by a terrible loss of life." Croker urged more fire escapes and installation of sprinkler systems, but manufacturers' associations said they were unsightly and too expensive. "At least teach your employees fire safety and have fire drills," Croker retorted.

A New York fire prevention expert, H. F. J. Porter, offered a fire drill educational service, but found few takers. His letter to Triangle management went ignored. Porter told the *New York Times* that one factory owner had said, "Let 'em burn. They're a lot of cattle anyway." Ida Rauh of the Woman's Trade Union League tried to bring firetrap conditions to the attention of the New York Grand Jury. Women had no business meddling in such matters, said the foreman, and gave her short shrift.

Shortly after 4:30 that balmy Saturday afternoon, March 25, 1911, the quitting bell rang, and the 130 women in the eighth-floor cutting room began lining up for purse inspection while the cutters, all male, put on their coats and left. This was an especially happy day. Saturday was payday, and many of the younger women were eagerly looking forward to shopping trips and visits with their beaux that evening. Someone lit a cigarette. One girl saw smoke swirling from the scrap bin under one of the long cutting tables piled high with cotton fabrics. Bins in the room had not been emptied for weeks and contained more than a ton of lawn scraps. Shirtwaists were the height of fashion, but they were the height of flammability, too.

There was no more popular fire engine among buffs than those built by the Ahrens-Fox Company of Cincinnati. They were distinctive for their front-mounted piston pumps and shiny silver air-chamber domes. This 1922 model pumped 750 gallons per minute. The box over the hose bed held equipment. This engine fought Baltimore fires for forty-one years until retirement.

Below: *The charred remains of a Triangle Shirtwaist workroom after the disaster. Windows were broken by panicked employees, who jumped to their deaths in an effort to escape the fast-spreading flames.*
Opposite: *Relatives identify bodies of the victims, who were taken in wooden coffins to a temporary morgue on the Twenty-sixth Street pier.*

Somebody ran for a pail of water. It did little good. More pails were dumped while other women unfolded the hose connected to the standpipe, but they did not know how to turn the water on. An automatic sprinkler system, costing only pennies per running foot, would have quickly doused the fast-spreading fire in the long bin under the table.

Before she fled, switchboard operator Dinah Lifschitz called the ninth floor to warn the 270 women in the sewing room. There was no answer. Lifschitz rang the tenth floor, got an answer, and sent one of the women to find the bookkeeper, the only one with authority to call the fire department. Flames were now swirling from the bin and igniting shirtwaist paper patterns hanging on wires. Bits of flaming lawn and paper fluttered onto the piles of cotton and into wooden wicker baskets of lace.

The frightened women and girls jammed against the inward-opening doors and more time was lost while they tugged them open. Somebody ran for the elevator. It came up, passed the eighth floor, and continued to the tenth to answer a ring there. "Stop! Stop!" the women implored. Flames were worsening and a smoky haze was filling the 150-foot-square room as the women and girls impatiently awaited the elevator. When the cage door opened, it created a draft of air that whooshed into the cutting room, flashing a sheet of fire across the entire room.

Saturday afternoon strollers along Washington Place and Greene Street heard a muffled explosion and crashing glass. Looking up, they saw smoke puffing from a window and a hurtling blob. James Cooper said it looked "like a bale of dark dress goods." As Cooper and others realized what it was, another came out the window and the two bodies splattered on the sidewalk. John H. Mooney stood for a moment of stunned horror, then ran to the corner and at 4:45 P.M. pulled Fire Alarm Box 289.

Flames racing up the Greene Street stairway swept into the gigantic ninth-floor workroom with its long rows of wooden tables and sewing machines. The 270 workers in the jam-packed room panicked and trampled each other as they bolted for the Washington Street stairway. The door to it was locked. Heat and smoke from the ninth-floor inferno boiled into the tenth-floor packing and shipping room. Workers fled up stairs to the roof, where they were rescued by ladders held by workmen and students on the roof of the next-door American Book Company and New York University. Only one tenth-floor worker was killed—Clotilda Terdanova, who panicked and dived through a window.

On the roof, the assistant cashier, Joseph Flecher, said—as quoted by Leon Stein in his 1962 book, *The Triangle Fire*—"I looked down the whole height of the building. My people were sticking out of windows. I saw my girls, my pretty ones, going down through the air. They hit the sidewalk spread out and still."

Both stairways were jammed with clawing, fighting women and girls who collided with firefighters coming up with rolls of hose. Other young women, their hair flaming, pushed onto the rear fire escape, which was wrenched from the building by the weight

Top: *The famous line of Mack Bulldogs, first built by Mack Trucks in 1915, were so named because of their snub noses. This 1915–1916 Mack pumper and hose wagon combination was one of three high pressure companies used by Baltimore firefighters.* Above: *Mack Trucks built this 1927-model pumper, which threw 500 gallons per minute, for the Thurmont, Md., Fire Department.*

of so many people. It collapsed, dumping many of the women, some of whom fell onto four-inch spikes topping a fence under the fire escape and were impaled.

The elevator operators, Gaspar Mortillalo and Joseph Zito, shuttled continuously from the lobby to the upper floors. Fortunately, other Asch Building tenants were not working this Saturday, so the two elevators could go directly to the Triangle floors. The cages held fifteen, but more than double that number pushed, shoved, and battled to get in, some jumping over the heads of those before them. When the cage doors banged shut, some of those left behind slid down the cables.

Unable to crowd into the elevator at the ninth floor, Sarah Cammerstein saw the car hesitate at the seventh and jumped on top of it. Instead of continuing to the lobby, the car started up toward flames jetting into the shaft. Screaming, Sarah pounded on the cage roof and caught the attention of the operator, who reversed the elevator and took it safely down to the lobby. Other young women plunging into the shafts crushed the roofs of the cages and wrecked the elevators.

Battalion Chief Edward J. Worth arrived within three minutes after the first alarm. Bodies were thudding onto the streets and sidewalks, despite spectators' screams of "Don't jump! Don't jump!" Dozens more workers were standing on the eighth- and ninth-floor ledges beside windows framing thick smoke and flames. Chief Worth ordered three more alarms, which called out thirty-five pieces of apparatus, including the department's two new horseless carriages—Engine 39, a pumper built by Waterous of St. Paul, and Engine 58, an automobile steamer made by Nott of Minneapolis. Engine 58, with its massive hood covering the four-cylinder piston engine, was the most famous fire engine in America; its picture had appeared in newspapers throughout the country.

Chief Worth knew that nets were ineffective for heights above the fourth floor, but what choice did he have? He ordered his men to spread them anyway. Two, three, and four people hit them at a time, and the impact tore the nets from the firefighters' bleeding hands and sent them somersaulting into their own nets. Hook and Ladder 20, the longest aerial in the department, raised its eighty-five foot big stick. Seeing it, a worker standing on the ninth-floor ledge waved her white handkerchief and called to the firefighters. But the ladder could not reach farther than the sixth floor—thirty feet short. Desperately hoping to jump onto the ladder, she stepped off the ledge, missed, and plummeted to the sidewalk.

Water in the Washington-Greene district was supplied by the new high-pressure supply system. Chief Nash ordered his steamers to pump into the high-volume nozzles mounted on water towers and apparatus, which shot streams splashing over the women's heads to cool them and the building. That did not work, either, and the young women continued to leap. Burning bodies were hitting so fast that they covered the hoselines.

In the Asch lobbies, firefighters restrained workers from leaving the building, for fear they would be killed by falling bodies. The young women stood screaming as they heard and saw body upon body come crashing down, some smashing through glass deadlights in the sidewalk and down into the building's cellar. Among the crowd outside was Frances Perkins, age twenty-nine, executive secretary of the New York Consumer's League, who was visiting friends when she heard the clanging apparatus and galloping horses. Miss Perkins said she and her friends "got there just as they started to jump. I shall never forget the frozen horror which came over us as we stood with our hands on our throats watching that horrible sight, knowing that there was no help."

United Press reporter William Gunn Shepherd had heard the explosion while walking along Washington Place. He ran to a store, found a telephone, and dictated his story as he watched the women jump. The beginning of his article became a journalism classic: "Thud—dead! Thud—dead! Thud—dead! I call them that because the sound and the thought of death came to me each time at the same instant."

The United Press cleared teletype lines to subscriber newspapers throughout the United States and fed Shepherd's story as fast as he could swallow the terror clutching his throat as he dictated, "Down came the bodies in a shower, burning, smoking, flaming bodies, with disheveled hair trailing upward.

"A young man helped a girl to the window sill on the ninth floor. Then he held her out deliberately, away from the building, and let her drop. He held out a second girl the same way and let her drop. He held out a third girl who did not resist. I noticed that. They were all as unresisting as if he were helping them into a street car instead of into eternity. He saw that a terrible death awaited them in the flames and his was only a terrible chivalry.

"He brought another girl to the window. I saw her put her arms around him and kiss him. Then he held her into space—and dropped her. Quick as a flash, he was on the window sill himself. His coat fluttered upwards—the air filled his trouser legs as he came down. I could see he wore tan shoes." Shepherd counted sixty-two leapers. Water streaming down the building turned red as it ran across the sidewalk and drained into the gutters.

Thirteen minutes after Mooney pulled the firebox, another young woman stepped off the ninth-floor ledge. As she fell, her burning dress caught on an iron hook at the sixth floor. Dangling there a few seconds, she then plunged the rest of the way. She was the last to jump. Inside the Asch, firefighters were connecting their hose to standpipes and crawling up the stairways, driving the flames back, floor by floor. It took them only eighteen minutes to control the fire.

Chief Croker led the search for the dead and injured. Eleven bodies were found jammed where escape was barred by the locked door on the ninth floor. Shortly before 7:00 P.M., a block and tackle was rigged to the edge of the roof and the canvas-wrapped bodies were lowered to the sidewalk. They came down two and three at a time while a fire department searchlight engine lit the way. Except for charred window sashes and smoke smudges, the outside of the building appeared to be little damaged. Sifting of eighth-floor ashes would produce more than two dozen wedding and engagement rings.

A crowd of more than 10,000 watched, many of them relatives moaning in Yiddish and Italian and crying as the bodies slowly came down, were laid on the sidewalks, and covered with tarpaulins until the arrival of wooden coffins. The same Eighth Precinct police officers who, a few months earlier, had clubbed and arrested the women guarded their bodies and rode in wagons hauling them to the morgue. A burglar alarm began ringing, but nobody bothered to turn it off, and its clanging continued all night.

Early Sunday morning, the firefighters removed the last of the dead. Bodies were taken to the infamous Twenty-sixth Street Pier on the East River with the lingering name, Misery Lane. The pier was the

place where more than 1,000 bodies had been taken after the steamboat *General Slocum* burned on June 15, 1904, while carrying mostly women and children on a church picnic excursion.

New York hungered for vengeance. State and local bureaucrats passed the buck, and their waffling excuses—"the responsibility for better safety regulations rests with another department"—were almost as sickening as the thuds of the bodies smacking the sidewalks. The suffragist Dr. Anna Shaw told a public meeting in Cooper Union:

As I read the terrible story of the fire, I asked, "Am I my sister's keeper?" For the Lord said to me, "Where is thy sister?" And I bowed my head and said, "I am responsible!" Yes, every man and woman in this city is responsible. . . . You men—forget not that you were responsible! As voters it was your business and you should have been about your business. If you are incompetent, then in the name of heaven, stand aside and let us try.

There was a time when woman worked in the home with her weaving, her sewing, her candlemaking. All that has been changed. Now she can no longer regulate her own conditions, her own hours of labor. She has been driven into the market with no voice in laws and powerless to defend herself. The most cowardly thing that men ever did was when they tied woman's hands and left her to be food for the flames.

Opposite: *Police untangle bodies of women who leaped from the top floors of the ten-story Asch Building when flames swept the Triangle Shirtwaist Company.* Below right: *Water-tower and high-pressure streams batter the Asch Building, although the fire is all but out. Firefighters are probably venting their rage at their inability to save more Triangle workers.*

At 1:00 P.M. on Wednesday, April 5, a massive public funeral march paraded up Fifth Avenue. Despite a heavy downpour, more than 100,000 people walked eight abreast, including members of more than sixty unions. There was only one banner, and it was carried by Waistmakers' Union, Local 25: "We Demand Fire Protection." When the marchers neared the Asch Building, the *New York American* reported, there was "one, long-drawn-out . . . heart-piercing cry, the mingling of thousands of voices, a sort of human thunder in the elemental storm—a cry that was perhaps the most impressive expression of human grief ever heard in this city." Another parade that day in Brooklyn followed the coffins of the seven unidentified Triangle women to a common grave in Evergreen Cemetery.

The Triangle owners, Isaac Harris and Max Blanck, were indicted on charges of first and second degree manslaughter. They launched a $1-million public service advertising campaign, but most newspapers returned their money. A jury found them innocent on a legal technicality. Lawsuits brought settlements averaging seventy-five dollars per victim.

But the tidal waves of demands for safety legislation forced the state to appoint a Factory Investigating Committee on June 30, 1911, and on October 21 the Sullivan-Hoey Law ordered the creation of a separate fire prevention bureau in the Fire Department of New York. Factory Committee members included State Senator Robert F. Wagner, Assemblyman Alfred E. Smith, Samuel Gompers, Frances Perkins, and H. F. J. Porter, who served as fire prevention expert. In four years, the commission's work led to thirty-six new laws in the state labor code. New York enacted America's toughest factory fire protection legislation—legislation that served as the model for the other states.

Public recognition helped Wagner's election in 1927 to the U. S. Senate where, six years later, he spearheaded the New Deal legislation of President Franklin D. Roosevelt, especially the creation of the National Labor Relations Act and social security. Smith was elected governor in 1918, served four terms, and with Roosevelt's backing, won the Democratic nomination for president in 1928.

When Roosevelt was elected he appointed Frances Perkins Secretary of Labor, a post she held for twelve years. She was the United States' first woman cabinet member. Citing the factory fire safety laws, Secretary Perkins said the 146 Triangle workers "did not die in vain and we will never forget them."

21 REQUIEM FOR THE HORSES

It was a melancholy Christmas for New York firefighters. On December 20, 1922, an alarm was received at Engine 205 from the fire alarm box in front of Brooklyn's Borough Hall. The firefighters knew what the alarm meant. When Engine 205's three black horses galloped up to the building, the firefighters saw their shiny new pumper awaiting them, its gasoline motor chugging. This was the ceremony at which the horses were exchanged for a self-propelled engine. It was the last run for the horses. The Fire Department of New York was now completely motorized.

On February 5, 1923, Chicago's firehorses, Buck and Beauty, answered their final call; and Philadelphia's white stallions pulled their chemical engine to a fire for the last time on New Year's Eve, 1927. Rochester, New York, eulogized its horses with a Fire Horse Day Parade on July 15 of the same year. In the automobile leading the parade was a bronze memorial tablet—later mounted at the City Hall annex—which read: "Our Fire Horses. Glorious in beauty and in service. Faithful friends, we cannot call them dumb, because they spoke in deed every hour of danger. Perpetual remembrance enshrines their loyalty and courage."

There were similar sad farewells throughout America, as the last horses were sent out to pasture and gasoline motors took their place at the firehouse. For the fire service, the age of the horseless carriage

The first motorized fire engine on the Pacific Coast was this 1909 Seagrave chemical rig, which Pasadena, California, bought for $4,950 when the city began to replace its horses. The engine saw service for more than twenty-one years before retirement.

24
CHEMICAL ENGINE
NO. 5.

had actually begun several decades earlier, six years after Henry Ford had built his first automobile. In 1898, a horse-drawn gasoline- or kerosene-powered pumper was made by the Waterous Engine Works Company of St. Paul, Minnesota, for volunteers who could not afford a steamer but wanted something easier to operate than hand pumps.

It is not clear who built the first motor-driven apparatus. Popular belief gives the credit to Waterous, who in 1906 made an engine with two motors—one for propulsion and another for pumping—for the Radnor Fire Company volunteers of Wayne, Pennsylvania. It is more probable, however, that the volunteers of Niagara Engine Company No. 1, New London, Connecticut, had a motorized hose and chemical apparatus built for them by American-LaFrance and in service on October 3, 1903. Even earlier, around 1897, the St. Louis Fire Department had an electric-battery-operated combination chemical and hose wagon. Around 1907, Waterous built a pumper with a single four-cylinder engine that did both jobs: it powered the apparatus to fires in Alameda, California, and it pumped about 600 gallons per minute.

With the United States entering the automobile age, the potential of motorized firefighting equipment was eagerly considered. Chief Edward F. Croker of New York could not wait for the city to get around to replacing his horse and buggy, so he bought his own Locomobile in 1901, which reporters named the "Black Ghost." Birmingham, Alabama, firefighters in 1909 raced a horse-drawn steamer against a motorized Seagrave combination hose and chemical pumper through the center of town. They could not agree which was better until five days later, when flames broke out in Birmingham-Southern College, and the motor-driven engine whizzed past the horse-drawn steamer struggling up a hill, and put out the fire.

Chiefs were amazed at their national convention in 1908 in Columbus, Ohio, when, from a starting point three miles away, a motorized Seagrave hook and ladder raced up to them and raised its seventy-five-foot aerial ladder, in the total elapsed time of seven minutes, forty-five seconds. A few minutes later, the Webb Motor Fire Apparatus Company, of Vincennes, Indiana, showed how its combination

Opposite: *During the conversion from horses to motorization, the most noticeable change was up front. In 1912, John Christie began to build front-wheel-drive tractors to replace horses. Pittsburgh used a Christie to pull this American LaFrance.* Below: *San Francisco's sixty-five-foot Water Tower No. 2 was built in 1898 by Henry Gorter and later motorized.*

engine and hose rig covered the same distance and shot water in only six minutes, eleven seconds.

Except for Detroit, there could have been no more appropriate choice for the August, 1909, annual fire chiefs convention than Grand Rapids, Michigan, near the center of the fast-growing automobile industry. More than 550 chiefs—the largest turnout in the history of the association—came to learn all about the new motor apparatus. Chief Hugo R. Delfs of Lansing demonstrated his new 650-gallon-per-minute pumper, built for $6,500 by Webb, on an Oldsmobile chassis. The rig was America's first all-gasoline engine-powered pumper.

Captain John O. Glanville, superintendent of the St. Louis Salvage Corps, told the chiefs how his autos covered three times more of the city than horses and got to fires fifty percent faster. Captain Glanville said it cost $816 a year to feed and shoe his horses, while motorized rigs covered the city better for only $481.31, including the $250 he had to spend for repairs when one of his drivers lost control of the apparatus and crashed. Fire Commissioner Waldo Rhinelander of New York reported in 1910 that the city's first motorized apparatus—a Knox high pressure hose rig—required $85 a year to operate, compared to $660 for three horses to pull it.

"What's more," another chief noted, "the Society for the Prevention of Cruelty to Animals has no spasm at seeing a motor engine facing a blizzard." Yet another chief remarked that his motorized apparatus got about eight to ten miles per gallon of gasoline—which then sold for twelve cents a gallon. "That's cheaper than oats," said another, who cautioned the chiefs to keep speeds under twenty-five miles an hour, "or you'll run the damn things into the ditch."

In 1911, the Savannah, Georgia, Fire Department became the nation's first to become completely motorized. "I did it," explained Chief Thomas Ballantyne, "by buying seven American LaFrance pumpers, one chemical engine, and four combination chemical and hose wagons on the installment plan." There were, of course, many dissenting chiefs. Motorized pumpers, they said, would never replace steamers because they could not produce pressures as high as those of steamers.

There were several established names among manufacturers of motorized apparatus: American LaFrance; Seagrave; Pirsch; and Ahrens-Fox, reorganized in 1905 by Cincinnati's Chris Ahrens and his son-in-law, Charles H. Fox, formerly assistant fire chief of the city. (Both men had worked for American LaFrance.) Ahrens-Fox pumpers were distinctive

for their front-mounted piston pumps and their shiny silver air-chamber domes. Chicago, with fifty-seven, had the nation's largest active fleet. Although no longer being built, they still enjoy a unique position in the story of the American fire engine.

More than 200 makers of motor fire apparatus entered the market to compete with the established manufacturers, and many of them remain in business today. Among the better known were the Nott Fire Engine Company, Minneapolis; Knox Motor Company, Springfield, Massachusetts; and Robinson Fire Apparatus Manufacturing Company, St. Louis, Missouri. In 1909, Robinson followed Webb by introducing a triple combination engine that offered the combined advantages of a pumper, hose, and water tank. Although highly popular today, triple combination pumpers were hotly debated when they first came out. Fire Chief E. J. Connery of New Castle, Pennsylvania, said triples were "the greatest service wagon made," but New York Fire Chief John Kenlon sharply disagreed. "Triples are a bad idea," he said. "It's like placing your eggs in one basket." Although they became commonplace elsewhere, the Fire Department of New York would have none of them until well after 1931. Other famous makers included Mack Trucks, which began in 1911 and came out with its famous Mack Bulldogs four years later.

A number of automobile manufacturers—including Ford, Chevrolet, KisselKar, Velie, and Pierce-Arrow of Buffalo—built fire engines. But since fire apparatus construction did not easily lend itself to mass-production methods, no auto maker approached the success of American LaFrance, Mack, or Seagrave. The latter company, in 1912, revolutionized fire apparatus by developing the centrifugal pump for firefighting. They sold the first—built on a Gorham chassis—to Engine 28 of the Los Angeles Fire Department. Centrifugals eventually replaced piston pumps—favored by Ahrens-Fox—and rotary gear pumps—used in the earlier American LaFrances and pumpers of other manufacturers. Eventually, nearly all engine manufacturers switched to centrifugals.

In 1914, American LaFrance made its last steamer and was booked at full capacity to produce motorized apparatus. Between 1910 and 1926 this giant of the American fire apparatus industry turned out more than 4,000 pumpers, in addition to aerial ladders, water towers, and other apparatus. No other company has produced more fire equipment. American LaFrance says it provides "everything you need to fight a fire"—including Dalmatian puppies, if that's what the fire chief wants.

With the enormous popularity of motorized

Opposite bottom: *Steam fire engines supply hoselines at this multiple-alarm fire around 1900 in downtown Los Angeles.* Below: *This 1927 Studebaker carried salvage covers to protect property from fire and water damage.* Bottom: *Los Angeles steamers appear to be puffing more smoke than the fire in this downtown-district blaze in the early 1900s.*

SALVAGE CO. 7 L.A.F.D.

apparatus, why did it take until around 1925 to replace fire horses and steamers throughout the nation? The fire service's traditional conservatism and reluctance to accept untested innovations were only part of the answer. Of greater importance was the fact that steam-powered engines were highly sophisticated and had many years of proven dependability. There could be no compromising with reliability, especially when the breakdown of a motorized apparatus could cost lives and turn a small fire into a conflagration. Fear of igniting gasoline fumes was another consideration, but certainly not as important as the enormous investment that cities had in their steamers—New York, for example, owned more than 300.

But the major obstacles to faster replacement of horses and steamers were engineering problems. Pumping engines consequently came along several years after some other types of fire apparatus. As the late Clarence E. Meek explained in the July, 1960, issue of *Fire Engineering* magazine: "Rotative speeds were slow, and to develop sufficient horsepower, engines of excessive size and weight were required. Such items as special brakes, transmissions, axles, and air starters had to be developed. Fire apparatus manufacturers had to design and build these engines and accessories themselves."

While American fire apparatus builders set about solving these severe challenges, cities continued to rely upon steamers, New York buying twenty-eight more in 1912, the last big order placed in the United States. Initially, the internal combustion engine was used chiefly to propel apparatus. Gasoline to power the pump followed, gradually replaced by diesel fuel beginning around 1964. The American fire service consequently entered the automobile era by bits and pieces.

With the gradual switchover to motorized equipment, the most immediately noticeable change in design was in the front of the apparatus. John Walter Christie, an Indianapolis-500 race car builder, dreamed of glory on the track but won it instead as a builder of tractors for pulling fire apparatus. Christie devised a front-wheel-drive vehicle that looked like a truck that had been sawed in half at the midsection, with the back end discarded. The engine was mounted well ahead of the truck's only two wheels. In February, 1912, Christie formed the Front Drive Motor Company, in Hoboken, New Jersey, and during seven years in business he produced more than 600 units. Their ninety-horsepower gasoline engines enabled cities to hitch their Christies to the apparatus and retire the horses. Christies could reach a speed of about eighteen miles per hour. By 1915, the Fire Department of New York was 50 percent motorized.

About this time another new type of fire apparatus began to appear in American cities. The concept that firefighters—lots of them—put out fires, rather than apparatus, led Detroit to form the first flying squadron in October, 1908, with a special van mounted on a Packard chassis that rushed fifteen additional men to large fires. In 1913, Chicago began to add rescue squads to its fleet. At first they primarily carried extra firefighters, but Chicago gradually equipped its squads with rescue and forcible-entry equipment. Each of Chicago's thirteen squads eventually mounted a turret nozzle, supplied by pumpers, to deliver large volumes of water at high pressure.

Shortly after a New York subway blaze sent a hundred people to hospitals—with smoke poisoning from burning insulation—New York organized its first rescue squad, which went in service on March 8, 1915. Rescue Company No. 1 was an open-type rig built in the department's shops on a Cadillac touring car chassis; it had ten firefighters assigned to it. Special Order No. 41 creating the company said its duties included "rescue work, ventilating and firefighting in places heavily charged with smoke or gas."

Rescue 1 carried pulmotors and other oxygen equipment for reviving firefighters and smoke victims; a cutting torch; a lifegun for shooting ropes to trapped victims; and two smoke helmets, which were crude air masks. The squad was the start of New York's famous rescue squad fleet manned by the elite of the department, many of whom became chiefs.

The entry of the United States into World War I and the military draft that accompanied it created manpower shortages in fire departments throughout the country. Many cities considered hiring women, and Raleigh, North Carolina, took on five in 1918. The subject arose that year at the annual chiefs' convention in Chicago. Atlanta's Fire Chief William B. Cody was outraged and took the podium to cry out against the idea, in a speech in which he "defended motherhood, sweethearts, and virtuous women generally. Until the last male member of Georgia is dead and gone, there never shall be any woman working in any institution we control. When you seek to put our mothers and sweethearts in the public work, I am against you." Although it was the consensus of the convention that firehouses were no places for females, the chiefs hooted Cody into silence.

The era following World War I was marked by an increasing number of severe fires. In Berkeley, California, a fast-spreading grass fire on September 17, 1923, ignited wood-shingle roofs, resulting in the destruction of 640 houses and leaving 4,000 people homeless. Fall River, Massachusetts—the center of United States textile manufacturing—was devastated in 1928 by a conflagration that destroyed 107 factories. On April 21, 1930, a fire in the Ohio State Penitentiary, Columbus, killed 320 convicts.

Fire losses soared. On May 7, 1931, the worst fire up to that time in Buffalo, New York, caused damages in excess of $7 million to the 106th Armory, a church, and more than fifty homes. A nineteen-alarm conflagration in Chicago, May 19, 1934, caused $6 million in damage to the Union Stock Yards and injured 166 firefighters. Later that year, on September 8, 1934, the SS *Morro Castle* burned off New Jersey with the loss of 125 lives.

One of the most memorable fires of the period occurred in the White House, on Christmas Eve, 1929, while President Herbert C. Hoover was entertaining holiday guests. Informed of the fire, Hoover told the red-coated Marine Band, which was performing for the guests, to "play something loud and cheerful." Few attending the party therefore knew of the five-alarm blaze that burned the attic and roof of the West Wing and caused heavy damage to the President's Oval Office. The fire did $135,000 damage and was the most destructive of five in the White House since the British burned the building on August 24, 1814, during the War of 1812.

Mounting fire losses demanded more powerful equipment. In 1930, American LaFrance sold to the Fire Department of New York a sixty-five-foot water tower, whose four nozzles together delivered 8,500 gallons a minute. The following year, LaFrance announced a major breakthrough: a twelve-cylinder V-block, 240-horsepower engine that increased pumping capacities from around 1,000 or 1,250 to 1,500 gallons per minute. That year, too, Pirsch sold what it said was "the world's first all-powered aerial ladder truck" to Spokane, Washington. Four years later Pirsch built the first all-powered 100-foot aluminum alloy aerial ladder for the Melrose, Massachusetts, Fire Department. Ladders went even higher. In 1941, American LaFrance made its first 125-foot aerial for the Boston Fire Department.

There were other new looks in the American fire service, too. We can only wonder at Chief Cody's reaction when Mrs. Nancy Holst was picked in 1931 to lead the Cedar Hill Fire Department in Rhode Island. She was America's first woman fire chief and later became Rhode Island's deputy state fire marshal. The women would not be denied, especially after they demonstrated their ability to fight fires and the need for fire protection in suburban areas during daytime hours, when men were at work in the city. Communities where women firefighters answered alarms during the day were to include Superior, Colorado; the Napa, Gasquet, Silverado, Modjeska, and Trabuco Canyon areas of California; and the all-woman Woodbine Ladies Fire Department of Woodbine, Texas. In 1973 the Woodbine department was led by a sixty-seven-year-old grandmother, Mrs. Verlie Gunter, and its youngest member was Chief Gunter's sixteen-year-old granddaughter. Also in the department were the chief's two daughters, a daughter-in-law, and another granddaughter.

Well before 1930, traffic congestion was delaying apparatus answering downtown alarms. Around 1936, in downtown Los Angeles, a mid-afternoon fire on Broadway—in a large, multiple-story building—raged out of control while second- and third-alarm apparatus bogged down in traffic. Firefighters lost more time hand-laying heavy hose several blocks to the fire. The incident caused Chief Engineer Ralph J. Scott to hit upon an idea to cope with the problem, by combining two pumpers into one unit.

In 1937, American LaFrance delivered the first of four of these duplex pumpers, with twin V-12 engines. Each duplex packed a wallop of between 2,000 and 3,000 gallons per minute. Teaming with the duplexes were four hose-carrying manifold wagons, an American LaFrance, two Seagraves, and a Mack. The manifolds each carried nearly 3,000 feet of hose and were spotted directly in front of fires in the downtown, industrial, and high-value Hollywood districts. The duplex engines pumped into the manifold wagons, which had connections for around nineteen hoselines. Each manifold mounted a large water cannon similar to those carried on fireboats.

World War II again depleted the ranks of American firefighters. Many served aboard United States Navy ships, including Deputy Chief Harold J. Burke of the New York Fire Department, who pioneered the development of shipboard firefighting and train-

ing methods, including the use of nozzles that shot a foglike spray. The nozzle was invented around 1936 by Battalion Chief Glenn G. Griswold of the Los Angeles County Fire Department, for use at refinery fires in the Santa Fe Springs district. A similar type of fog nozzle had been available as early as 1886, but fire chiefs had long preferred the straight-stream types. Griswold was killed while serving with the army in Italy, but his invention of a new type of fog nozzle came into almost universal use after the war.

Other firefighters enlisted in the United States Marine Corps, including Donald M. O'Brien of Engine 6, Auburn, New York, and Chicago's Joseph J. McCarthy of Hook and Ladder 11. O'Brien's lifesaving heroism on Iwo Jima won him the Bronze Star and a battlefield commission. Following the war, he became editor of *Fire Engineering* magazine and in 1965 was named general manager of the International Association of Fire Chiefs.

Captain McCarthy led an assault against a Japanese pillbox on Iwo Jima and was critically wounded by mortar fire, for which he was awarded the Congressional Medal of Honor by President Truman. When he returned to Chicago, he saw in the newspapers pictures of accident victims sprawled in snow for as long as an hour, until a police paddy wagon arrived, loaded them on foul-smelling canvas stretchers, and took them to hospitals. The Chicago Fire Department was given the job of organizing an emergency ambulance service and Captain McCarthy was put in charge. He was ideally suited for the assignment. Recalling how his life had been saved by fast and efficient first aid by Navy corpsmen, he quickly organized a fleet of twenty-five ambulances, which was later expanded.

While the firefighters were at war, thousands of civilians trained as auxiliary firefighters and worked in fire alarm offices. America was worried that Axis planes would attack United States cities, so Boston auxiliaries mounted a machine gun on a hose wagon, and Los Angeles painted its Fireboat 2 battleship gray to camouflage it from the air. Firefighters kept all-night vigils near the boat in case the Japanese fleet should steam into Los Angeles Harbor.

Out of the war came an answer to the problem of smoke inhalation, which over the years has killed hundreds of firefighters and shortened the lives of thousands more. Many years earlier—in the days when full beards were fashionable—firefighters relied on a primitive method of smoke control: dousing their whiskers with water, stuffing them in their mouths, and then breathing through their beards. A host of air masks had been in use for more than a century, but none of them were totally effective; many could not even filter out the firefighters' worst enemy, carbon monoxide gas. These contraptions ranged from Shaw Smoke Caps and Nealy Smoke Masks to the later Gibbs rebreathers and Burrell filters, to the types used in coal mines. There are vast differences between gases encountered

There were no more powerful steam fire engines built than this self-propelled model by the Manchester Locomotive Works (formerly Amoskeag) of Manchester, N.H. Boston acquired several of them in 1897. This one, assigned to Engine 38, could pump 1,350 gallons per minute. It saw service at major Boston fires for nearly thirty years.

in mining and those found in firefighting; but the fallacy of the all-purpose mask nevertheless continues to persist.

During the war, however, high-altitude flying required the development of self-contained air masks, with regulators that controlled the flow of oxygen from pressurized steel bottles. These masks were fairly easily adapted for firefighting, and in a modified form are still in use. Most recently, firefighters have been experimenting with the lighter-weight masks being developed by the National Aeronautics and Space Administration, from technology learned in the astronauts' program.

There were several reasons why effective breathing apparatus was slow to develop. Its high cost was one, but the primary reason lay in the firefighters' attitude toward it: one measure of a firefighter's manhood was the length of time he could remain in a smoky building while "taking a dose," as it was said. This foolish bravado killed many firefighters and unfortunately lingers as an inexcusable tradition in too many cities, where firefighters continue to shun masks except in the smokiest situations. Masks are even more necessary today because of the greater amounts of toxins in smoke from burning synthetics and other materials unknown in the early days of firefighting.

World War II and the several years following it saw a series of incredible fires. On February 9, 1942, workers were remodeling the *Normandie,* the world's largest luxury liner, into a troop ship at her Hudson River berth in New York, when sparks from a welder's torch ignited kapok life preservers. Before turning in an alarm, the workers fought the fire for at least fifteen minutes, with an ineptitude described in the report of the National Fire Protection Association, the following July, as having "the elements of a Hollywood slapstick comedy."

When the alarm was finally turned in, fireboats and land pumpers poured a million gallons of water into the ice-glazed ship. Early the next morning the $60-million liner capsized and rolled over dead in the water. Germany claimed the fire as a victory for its spies, but New York District Attorney Frank Hogan found no evidence of sabotage. "Carelessness has served the enemy with equal effectiveness," he said.

On Thanksgiving weekend that same year, on a Saturday night, around 1,000 people, including many servicemen, were jammed into the Cocoanut Grove night club, at 17 Piedmont Street in Boston. A fire started near an artificial palm tree in the basement Melody Lounge, but nobody called the fire department. Then a ball of flame rolling up the stairway touched off a panic. Bodies stacked up against exits and jammed the revolving door. Boston firefighters were only a short distance away dousing an automobile fire when they saw the smoke. They called for fire alarms of apparatus and manpower and used eighteen hoselines, but nearly 500 people died and 166 were injured.

In Hartford, Connecticut, two years later, around 7,000 people were attending a July 6 matinee of the Ringling Brothers and Barnum & Bailey circus when the tent burst into flames. The resulting stampede killed 168 and injured around 500. The following October 20, explosions of liquefied methane gas and the resulting fire at the East Ohio Gas Company in Cleveland killed 130, injured 225, destroyed or damaged 15 factories and 100 dwellings, and devastated twenty-nine acres, with losses in excess of $8 million. On December 7, 1946, the fifth anniversary of Pearl Harbor, Atlanta's Winecoff Hotel burned with a loss of 119 lives, only six months after the June 5 LaSalle Hotel fire in Chicago, where 61 were killed.

Certainly the most incredible fire in the United States during the war occurred on July 28, 1945, when a B-25 bomber slammed into the seventy-eighth floor of the 102-story Empire State Building. Flaming fuel spilled into offices and corridors and down an elevator shaft. Falling debris ignited a nearby loft building. The crash occurred on a Saturday afternoon when few people were in the area, else the loss of life might have been disastrous. As it was, fourteen were killed and twenty-five injured.

The crash was one of the first hints of two major problems that would confront the fire service well past the 1976 Bicentennial: firefighting in high-rise buildings far beyond the reach of the tallest aerial ladders; and airport fire protection. As the United States entered the jet age—accompanied by a series of crashes and mid-air collisions—air-crash firefighting techniques developed rapidly, and special apparatus was built to meet the challenge.

The United States was still stunned by the unbelievable story of a bomber hitting one of the world's most famous buildings when, nine days later, on August 6, mankind was stupefied by the most horrendous fire ever seen, as a boiling mushroom-shaped cloud of flames erupted over Hiroshima.

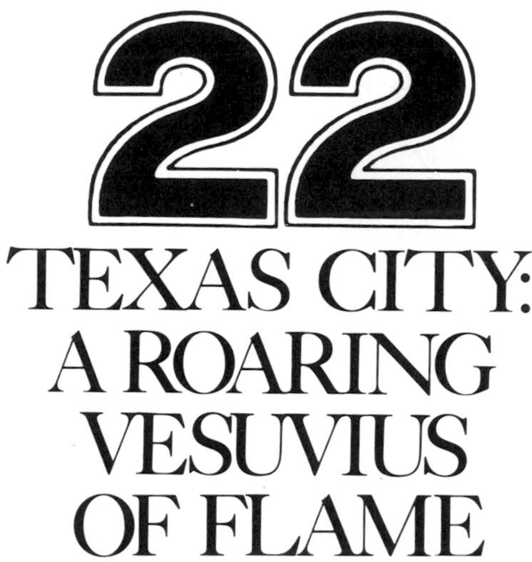

22 TEXAS CITY: A ROARING VESUVIUS OF FLAME

About 8:10 on a balmy Wednesday morning, April 16, 1947, longshoremen working in Number 4 Hold of the SS *Grandcamp* discovered smoke seeping from between bags of fertilizer grade ammonium nitrate (FGAN), a gritty substance that looks like maple sugar. The French freighter, a former Liberty Ship, had been loading for five days at its berth at Pier O Warehouse of the Texas City Terminal Railway Company. On board were 46,000 sacks—2,300 tons—of FGAN.

A crewman notified Captain Charles de Guillebon while longshoremen began lifting off sacks to find the seat of the fire. A jug of drinking water was poured without effect. Another jug gurgled into the smoke and a fire extinguisher was emptied. Still the smoke oozed. Deckhands lowered a hose. "Not too much water!" someone cautioned. "You'll damage the cargo."

Nobody thought to call the fire department, and there was no reason to suspect that the nation's worst industrial catastrophe was only an hour away. FGAN was almost impossible to burn. By itself, the ammonium nitrate was considered nonexplosive, although during World War II it had been used with TNT as a major ingredient of demolition bombs. With peace, the government's stockpile was converted into nitrogen-rich fertilizer. More than 80,000 tons of it had already been shipped without mishap through Texas City, destined by United Nations relief programs for war-depleted agricultural fields in Europe.

Texas City, ten miles north of Galveston, had prospered during the war, when its population tripled to 20,000, and afterward the economy continued strong along the waterfront's oil refineries, chemical plants, and tank farms. The city's largest employer, Monsanto Chemical Company, had nearly 500 workers as it converted from making styrene for wartime synthetic rubber to polystyrene for peacetime plastics.

By 8:30 A.M., the fire aboard the *Grandcamp* was spreading fast. Smoke, heat, and the overwhelming stink of melting ammonium nitrate drove the coughing, sweat-drenched longshoremen from the hold. Puffs of white smoke were noticed for the first time by many of the hundreds of workers in the docks, but not one of them thought to turn in an alarm; some assumed the *Grandcamp* was undergoing a routine fumigation. Nor did anyone happen to mention the smoke to Henry J. Baumgartner, who was in his office just a few yards from the ship. Baumgartner, a terminal purchasing agent, was chief of the Texas City Volunteer Fire Department.

Puzzled by the failure of water to put out the fire, Captain de Guillebon decided to smother the blaze with steam, a recognized shipboard firefighting method. It took ten minutes to replace the hatch covers, dog them down, spread tarpaulins, and plug the ventilation cowls before the *Grandcamp*'s steam injection system was turned on. The tactic was one any other officer in Captain de Guillebon's position would have chosen.

A worse mistake could not have been made. Steam might put out the burning paper sacks and wood dunnage. But as any chemist knows, ammonium nitrate, under three conditions—heat, confinement, and pressure—will become highly explosive. Sealing the hold of the *Grandcamp* not only corked the escape of heat and pressure, but rapidly accelerated the heating process. The ship was becoming a pressure cooker longer than a football field, and with no safety valve. The chemical reaction was comparable to a roller coaster ride. Slow to climb to the peak of the steepest incline, the roller coaster passes the point of no return and roars down the other side.

But Captain de Guillebon was a seaman, not a chemist, and he would be forgiven his error, especially considering that not one of the sacks carried a warning that FGAN could become explosive. It is even more understandable, therefore, that neither the captain nor anybody else thought to ask the

The waterfront in Texas City, Texas, following the explosions of April, 1947. This was the nation's worst industrial catastrophe, in which 561 people died and 3,000 were injured. The fires burned for almost a week, causing property damage in excess of $50 million.

advice of any one of the several hundred chemists working directly across from the ship, many of whom were watching the fire with increasing fascination.

Time was running out on Texas City at 8:33 when Police Chief W. K. Ladish received a call that smoke was coming from a ship in the docks. Ladish triggered the city's siren calling out the volunteers. Terminal officials sounded theirs, too, and called Galveston for tugs in case the situation required the *Grandcamp* to be taken into the gulf and scuttled.

Chief Baumgartner had headed the volunteers for twenty years and knew from past shipboard fires that steam was effective; he concurred with Captain de Guillebon's decision. Chief Baumgartner was unable to speak French, but he managed to get the captain to understand that he wanted to see the ship's manifest, to determine what else might give trouble if the fire spread. He learned that the *Grandcamp*'s cargo included 5,900 balls of sisal twine; 9,335 bags of shelled peanuts; 380 bales of cotton; farm machinery; an automobile; a large quantity of oil-well drilling rods; and sixteen cases of rifle bullets.

The wailing sirens of Texas City's four fire engines, together with the lazy plume of darkening smoke, attracted hundreds of spectators, including many school children who were on half-day sessions. Among them was the fire chief's son, Harold, who liked to go to fires. He knew the department had just bought a new fire engine, which had yet to get its baptism in fire. Harold began peddling his bicycle toward the column of smoke.

Police kept spectators off Pier O. The crowd was in a festive mood, but the gaiety changed when word spread that ammunition was aboard. Many people left and a great number of lives were saved because the 16 cases of bullets caused more alarm than the 46,000 bags of ammonium nitrate. Fred Brumley and Charles Norris took off from Texas City Airport in a small plane and joined another sightseeing aircraft circling high over the *Grandcamp*.

Going on 9 o'clock, the situation was rapidly deteriorating. As steam continued to spew into the hold, the hatch covers were straining against their dogs, tarpaulin covers were smoking, and the firefighters felt the deck's heat through their thick-soled boots. Below them an ominous trembling told that the molten FGAN was coming to a boil. The peak of the roller coaster ride was close at hand.

Suddenly, the hatch covers blew off and a fountain of golden smoke spouted from the hold. Bits of flaming paper sacks soared over the *Grandcamp,* were carried high into the air, and came fluttering down on the decks of two nearby ships, the *Wilson B. Keene* and the *High Flyer,* the latter being loaded with ammonium nitrate. Deckhands ran out hoselines while longshoremen battened hatches. The *High Flyer*'s turbine engines were down for repairs and she would have to be towed to safety if the situation worsened.

The smoke boiling from the *Grandcamp* soon turned dark copperish red, and the stink, the fumes, and the heat drove firefighters off the ship and onto the pier, where they played their streams onto the vessel. Then balls of fire rocketed like Roman candles from Number 4 Hold, along with a roar like a blast furnace. Water draining through scuppers hissed into steam as it streamed down the red-hot hull.

The volunteers were joined by fire brigades from Monsanto and the Republic Oil Refining Company. They hooked up their firefighting foam-generating equipment, but the point of no return had been reached and the only hope was to scuttle the ship. The terminal vice president, W. H. "Swede" Sandberg, hurried to his office, called Galveston again, and was assured that tugs were on the way. Sandberg hung up just as the roof fell in on him.

At 9:12 A.M. the *Grandcamp* blew up once, twice, three times, and everything and everybody around it vanished in a roaring Vesuvius of flame. Burning bales of cotton, popping ammunition, shelled peanuts, the automobile, oil-well drilling rods, and hunks of the ship shot thousands of feet into the clear blue sky and came cascading down upon the demolished, blazing waterfront and the industrial areas beyond. The blasts scooped an enormous crater out of the North Slip and created a massive tidal wave. The wave swept up the *Longhorn II,* a thirty-ton oceangoing barge, sent it skimming along the crest, and plopped it 150 feet inland. Texas City's new fire engine, a twisted wad, whanged down onto the *Longhorn.*

The blasts were felt and heard for 150 miles. In Denver, more than a thousand miles away, the seismograph needle at Regis College jiggled. The Monsanto board chairman, Edgar M. Queeny, later reported that chemists calculated that the *Grandcamp* packed a wallop equal to the detonation of 250 five-ton blockbuster bombs. Comparing the blasts to those of Hiroshima and Nagasaki, Queeny said those at Texas City probably were more severe, because the

Texas City could have made effective use of a fireboat—such as this one in New York—when a series of explosions ignited many fires along the waterfront. New York's Marine Division, largest in the nation, at one time had as many as ten fireboats to protect its gigantic port.

atom bombs exploded in the air while the *Grandcamp* blew up at ground level.

Hundreds of people were slaughtered: Captain de Guillebon and nearly all his crew; 59 longshoremen; 227 Monsanto chemists, technicians, secretaries, and construction workers; dozens of spectators; and the occupants of the two sightseeing airplanes, which witnesses said were "shot out of the air like ducks." Mr. and Mrs. Hollie O. Youngman were driving along a highway two miles from the *Grandcamp* when a razor-sharp chunk of the ship sliced through the windshield of their coupe and decapitated them. "I was blown twenty feet off my bicycle," said Chief Baumgartner's son. "I got up and started running. The second time it exploded, I was again blown about twenty feet. I ran all the way home as fast as I could. I knew my Dad was in the middle of it all." Chief Baumgartner and all 26 of his firefighters were killed and every one of the city's fire engines was obliterated.

The blasts mowed a swath of death and destruction twelve blocks wide and twenty blocks long. Twelve warehouses collapsed or were severely damaged. Strings of freight cars lay on their sides. A flatcar, flicked into the air, landed upside down. Eight bodies were under it. The *Grandcamp*'s one-ton propeller shaft was hurled like a spear more than two miles, before burrowing eight feet into the ground between two houses. The thirty-foot-long iron drilling rods, each weighing over a ton, were flung 13,000 feet, arrowing into the earth and bending like twisted hairpins.

Monsanto was instantly engulfed in mountainous clouds of thick black smoke and ugly flames, billowing thousands of feet over the sprawling forty-acre complex of storage tanks and processing, laboratory, and office buildings. Hundreds of autos blazed in the parking lot. From broken pipelines and ruptured tanks gushed thousands of gallons of benzol, ethylene, and propane gas, which ignited and blocked any escape. Workers survived the blasts only to be cremated in the withering heat, or drowned in the tidal wave of mud and water surging through the plant.

More flames were spouting among refineries and oil storage farms, where tanks were crushed by the blasts or pierced by red-hot missiles. The ten tanks of the Humble Pipeline Company farm, filled to their fifty-five-million-barrel capacity, erupted into flames, and the awesome black column of smoke stabbed miles into the sky. Dozens more fires bloomed from blazing cotton and balls of twine, as they unraveled and landed like flaming spiderwebs in widening pools of gasoline, oil, chemicals, and flammable cargo spilled from flattened warehouses.

Every clock in Texas City stopped dead at 9:12.

Part of the destroyed Wilson B. Keene *in the Texas City harbor. Sixteen hours after the first explosions at the docks, there was another mighty blast, which split the* Keene *in two. The bow section, hurtling over a warehouse, crashed down on a string of boxcars and flattened them.*

Hardly a window remained and some were shattered in Baytown, twenty-five miles to the north. Nearly a thousand students at Danforth Elementary and Central High Schools—both more than a mile from the *Grandcamp*—were sprayed with flying glass. Miraculously, no one was killed, but hundreds were cut.

Texas City's business and residental districts were severely damaged. The tornadolike blasts ripped away storefronts, peeled bricks from walls, and collapsed the roofs of two theaters and a department store. Houses were smashed to kindling or shoved off foundations, doors were ripped from hinges, furniture thrown across rooms, and wallpaper torn to strips. Pete Peterman, manager of Michael's Jewelry Store, was in the back of his shop when the front of it "came toward me like a shower of rain." A passerby later brought him a hatful of diamond rings he had picked up from the sidewalk.

In the moment of stunned silence that followed the blasts, Texas City's survivors gawked in dumb disbelief as dead seagulls rained from the sky. And then the city reacted. Rescuers hurried to the docks and in Galveston a light flashed in the telephone company headquarters. Plugging into it, the operator heard a woman's voice over the Texas City line: "For God's sake, send the Red Cross!" Within fifteen minutes, busloads of doctors and nurses were on the causeway to Texas City. Galveston's John Sealy Hospital prepared for a flood of victims. By fortunate happenstance, the Galveston chapter of the American Red Cross had that morning received 210,000 war surplus surgical dressings, which were immediately made ready.

Picking their way into the smoking, burning waterfront—despite the danger of further explosions—rescue workers came upon hundreds of victims staggering, crawling, or wandering in a daze. Many were nude and covered with an oily slime masking hideous injuries, which the medical team director, Dr. Clarence F. Quinn, described as "every conceivable wound." From this day would come countless stories of rescues and miraculous escapes, including the Monsanto office worker blown from a fifth-floor window who suffered only a broken ankle. Fred Grissom, a Monsanto draftsman, was watching the fire from his window at the time of the explosion. Blinded by flying glass, he groped his way to the street and bumbled into a construction worker whose legs were fractured. Grissom picked the man up. With the draftsman's good legs and the worker's good eyes they made their way out of the inferno.

Fire apparatus streamed into Texas City from Galveston and dozens of other communities. Even if the Texas City department had not been wiped out, the firefighting problem would still have been insurmountable. Firefighters discovered they could not get close enough to the blistering heat, thick smoke, and deadly fumes to do any good with their hoselines. Even if they could have, it would have been of no use, since the terminal pump house had been flattened, the water mains were shattered, the hydrants sheared off, and the sprinkler systems wrenched apart.

A temporary morgue was set up at McGar's Motor Service Garage and the lubrication racks were turned into embalming tables. Row upon row of white-sheeted bodies were laid in Central High School's gymnasium, where orange and black crepe paper streamers remained from Friday night's prom. The feet of identified bodies were tagged with yellow parking tickets, their names on one side and "You Have Violated a Traffic Law" on the other. By mid-afternoon, army, navy, and national guard units were hurrying into Texas City. Plasma, embalming fluid, radio command post equipment, bulldozers, gas masks, and relief supplies were rushed into the area. Much of it was airlifted, some from as far away as California and Massachusetts. Two billion units of penicillin—virtually the nation's entire supply—was flown to Texas City and Galveston. The antibiotic saved countless lives.

Toward dinnertime, eight hours after the explosions, the task of searching for survivors and victims was continuing. There had been no more explosions, and a glimmer of hope arose that the worst was over. Emergency water supply repairs enabled Foamite to be used on some of the blazing oil tanks. Elsewhere, some fires were burning themselves out, and Texas City residents were making their homes habitable for the night.

But at 6:00 P.M., all optimism vanished. The *High Flyer* was burning. The pungent stench of its blazing 2,000-ton sulfur cargo permeated the blanket of smoke over the waterfront. Unless the *High Flyer* was towed to sea and scuttled, its 961 tons of ammonium nitrate surely would explode. With nightfall, a sense of imminent doom fell over the city. A sound truck, blaring orders to evacuate, raced through the streets. Residents hastily threw together what belongings they could, and streams of automobiles, trucks, and buses drained Texas City of all life except for firefighters and rescue, relief, and medical workers.

Hours passed and still the *High Flyer* did not

blow up. Fires boiling from Monsanto, demolished warehouses, oil tanks, and refineries etched the darkness and cast a glare that could be seen for miles. Around 10 o'clock, volunteers manned four tugs and gambled that time still remained to pull the *High Flyer* to sea. The debris-littered water in the Main Slip shimmered in the flames as the tugs picked their way through smoke, heat, and acrid fumes. The blasts had snapped the *High Flyer's* hawsers and the ship had been dashed across the slip, slamming broadside into the *Keene*. Even with acetylene torches, towlines, and the best of luck, the job of freeing the *High Flyer* would take hours. But the volunteers decided to try.

Their efforts were briefly rewarded early that morning, and the *High Flyer* was pulled clear of the *Keene*. The tugs were starting out of the slip with the reluctant *High Flyer*, when Roman candle balls of fire began rocketing from her, just as they had from the *Grandcamp* before it exploded. Chopping the towlines, the volunteers rang for full speed, and the tugs churned out of the Main Slip and into the safety of Galveston Bay.

At 1:10 A.M., nearly sixteen hours to the minute after the *Grandcamp* blew up, the *High Flyer* exploded like a clap of thunder. The blazing orange glare lit up Texas City as if the sun had risen. Galveston and cities for hundreds of miles around quaked. The *High Flyer* ceased to exist. Later, only scattered parts of it could be found, among them a four-ton turbine engine, which had soared a mile before smashing through the pump house roof of Republic Oil.

Slicing like a meat cleaver, the blast split apart the *Keene*. The bow section flew end over end over the two-story Pier B Warehouse and, crashing down, mashed a string of boxcars. The blast pulverized the concrete warehouse, largest on the waterfront, and destroyed whatever had been salvageable in the docks following the *Grandcamp* explosion. Wheat spouted from an enormous debris-punctured grain elevator. Casualties, on the other hand, were miraculously light; only one person was killed.

"Daybreak revealed a sickening sense of destruction . . . pitch-black columns of smoke spiraled skyward for 3,000 feet or more and were visible for 30 miles. They burned continuously for almost a week," said the report of the National Board of Fire Underwriters. The final death toll was 561, with more than 3,000 injured. In addition to the industrial losses, more than 3,300 homes and 130 commercial structures were destroyed or damaged. Property losses exceeded $50 million.

Investigations by the National Board, the U.S. Coast Guard, and other agencies generally agreed that it was impossible to determine when and how the fire started. The Board's report noted that "every common fire safety rule was being violated. . . . This tragedy is to be labeled as 'needless,' and that it was preventable with a minimum of ordinary and properly directed effort. Prompt deluging of the burning material with heavy streams of water or immediate flooding of the hold would have avoided this terrible incident."

Following the disaster, changes were made in the ammonium nitrate manufacturing process and in regulations governing its handling and shipment. Bags were required to carry yellow warning labels. But four months after Texas City—while investigations were continuing—the SS *Ocean Liberty*, carrying a cargo of fertilizer ammonium nitrate from Baltimore, caught fire near Brest, France. Steam was again used, and the *Ocean Liberty* blew up. Twenty were killed and 500 injured.

FIREPOWER!

Los Angeles waterfront firefighters were jittery. The devastating explosions in the Texas City docks nine weeks earlier had reminded them of the hazards in Los Angeles Harbor, one of the nation's major handlers of petroleum and other flammables. After Texas City, fire department and port authorities throughout the United States were reviewing waterfront fire safety regulations.

The bulwark of Los Angeles harbor fire protection was—and still is—Fireboat 2, the queen of the department's fleet of five. One of the world's most powerful fireboats, it pumps 13,500 gallons a minute through thirteen turret nozzles, including the largest, called Big Bertha, which shoots 10,000 gallons a minute by itself.

At 2 o'clock that Sunday morning, June 22, 1947, there was no unusual activity along the forty-five-mile waterfront, which was lined with refineries; warehouses; lumberyards; chemical plants; shipyards; and oil storage tank farms, including the Shell Marine Oil Terminal about a quarter of a mile north of Berth 227, where Fireboat 2 was stationed. The 10,000-ton tankship *Markay* was being loaded at Shell with tens of thousands of barrels of butane blend. Unknown to anyone, highly flammable vapors were escaping from Number 5 Tank as nearly 3 million gallons of gasoline and other liquid dynamite sloshed in the *Markay*'s nine compartments. At 2:06 A.M., the fumes somehow ignited and the *Markay* blew up. The

Los Angeles's Fireboat 2, which can pump 13,500 gallons a minute through thirteen turret nozzles. On June 22, 1947, when the huge tanker Markay *exploded and burned, the crew heroically rammed the fireboat through a sea of flames to cut off the spreading fire.*

explosion and others that quickly followed split the tanker in half, killing twelve crewmen and terminal workers.

The whooshing roar and concussions rocked the timber pilings supporting the wooden firehouse and jolted Acting Captain Jack Gordon and the thirteen crewmen of Fireboat 2 awake, as a flaming glare lit their bunkroom. At first they were too stunned to move. Then, realizing they were facing the firefighting job of their lives, they pulled on their turnout clothing and boots, grabbed their helmets, and ran down the gangplank to the boat.

Brainard "Choppy" Gray, the pilot, nosed the fireboat from its cavernous shed and into the turning basin. Gray had been a firefighter for twenty-four years, but he had never seen anything like this. "I saw a fury which I had imagined only an atom bomb could cause," he said. "Vivid billows of flames boiled and churned from the *Markay.* The fire whipped hundreds of feet into the sky, then darkened as it ran out of oxygen, only to burst into renewed frenzy when it sucked in more air. Great gobs of black smoke rolled up into mushroom-shaped clouds."

Blazing butane floating on the water spread a blanket of flames completely across the slip and under wooden wharves, where two city-block-long warehouses were quickly engulfed. The sea of flames then floated upstream, threatening warehouses, refineries, shipyards, and the U.S. Borax and Chemical Company.

Fireboat 2 was within 500 feet of the tanker when heat popped three windows in the pilot house and put out all lights on the starboard side. Gordon picked a spot to attack. "It was futile to open up on the *Markay,*" said Gray. "We could have pumped the harbor dry and still not put out that fire." Boat 2's best approach was to open up on the burning wharves and warehouses across from the *Markay.* Tons of water gushed from Big Bertha, while the tower turret and deck guns bored into the flames. Paint blisters swelled on the fireboat's hull as Gray maneuvered closer.

When Chief Engineer John H. Alderson arrived to take command of more than twenty-four pieces of apparatus, he knew the only way to keep the fire from spreading up the slip toward more industries was to order Boat 2 through that sea of flames to attack the fire head on. His decision could mean sending the fourteen firefighters to their deaths. There was, moreover, the fear that fumes from the boat's gasoline-powered engines could ignite and blow up the boat. "It has to be done," said Chief Alderson. "There is no other way." It was a tough decision and an even tougher maneuver for Boat 2 to execute. How Captain Gordon and his men did it is still being told and retold in Los Angeles fire stations more than a generation later.

Aiming Big Bertha and the other guns into the flaming water, they plowed an open path into the 1,200-foot-long blanket of fire. Their first attempt failed. "Smoke was so thick, I couldn't see the compass," said Gray. They tried again as Gray rang for full speed ahead. Boat 2's guns pushed aside the flames and it vanished into the thick smoke. To Captain Gordon and the crew, it seemed like an eternity, but suddenly Boat 2 burst into the clear, and the furnace was behind them. Gray brought the boat about, and the firefighters swiveled the turret guns into action against the burning wharves and warehouses. The fire was stopped, and hundreds of millions of dollars worth of waterfront property was saved. Boat 2, built in 1925, had repaid its original $214,000 construction cost many times over.

Fireboat 2, still going strong after several remodelings, celebrated its fiftieth birthday during the United States Bicentennial. The fireboat is the oldest piece of apparatus in active service in the Los Angeles Fire Department and probably will last another generation. There were fireboats in America as early as 1800, when New York volunteers mounted a pump on a scow and rowed the nation's first fireboat to fires. In 1872, Boston put into service the first iron-hulled, steam-powered fireboat, the *William H. Flanders.* Since then, there have been more than 120 fireboats built for American cities. They pack the mighty punch required for large waterfront fires. Fireboat 2, for example, has the firepower equivalent of around ten fire engines. Fireboats are especially useful as floating pumping stations to supply water to land-based fire apparatus—as Fireboat 2 did on August 8, 1972, when it provided more than 13,000 gallons a minute through seventeen hoselines to apparatus battling a chemical tank farm fire at the General American Transportation Company.

Of all fireboats, none was more unique than the one built in 1908 for Chicago and named the *Joseph Medill,* for the mayor elected following the Great Chicago Fire. To solve the problem of how to hold a floating fireboat in place with the back-pressure force of its powerful streams tending to push it away from

Turret guns of the Chicago fireboat Joseph Medill *shooting water into a blazing LaSalle Street warehouse. Three firefighters and a member of the Chicago Fire Insurance Patrol were killed in this fire on Jan. 21, 1951, when a wall collapsed. Sixty-nine pieces of apparatus fought the blaze.*

the fire, the *Medill* was equipped with anchoring spuds in the bottom of its hull. The spuds were power-driven into the river bottom and anchored the *Medill* while it pumped. Other fireboat firefighters solve the back-pressure problem by adjusting the propeller speed and shooting streams in the direction opposite from those they are aiming at the fire.

Still another innovative approach to waterfront protection occurred in 1917, when the San Diego Fire Department put in service its seaplane, Aerial Truck No. 1, to protect the harbor. The purpose of the 110-horsepower, twenty-four-foot-long flying boat was to carry fire extinguishers quickly to alarms in isolated areas of the waterfront and to put out small fires before they became large. The department had originally used the airplane in 1915 for aerial inspections of fire zones. San Diego's seaplane is believed to be the first use of aircraft by the American fire service.

The idea of using airplanes as flying fireboats never caught on, but there was a vital role for aircraft in the fire service. In 1919, Major Henry A. "Hap" Arnold—who later became the first commanding general of the United States Air Force—was looking for ways to stimulate public interest in airpower. Arnold chanced to meet Regional Forester Coert du Bois of the United States Forest Service in a San Francisco restaurant. Between them they envisioned unlimited opportunities for firefighting aircraft, starting with aerial fire patrols over forests in California's Sierra Madre mountain range. Eventually, bombers and helicopters carrying firefighting chemicals and water became indispensable for fighting forest and brush fires. The aircraft also provided fast means for rescue and for airlifting and parachuting firefighters and equipment into remote areas.

An early problem of fighting fires with boats was that of communicating with them after they had left

their berths. Megaphones and flag signals were used at first. On February 4, 1911, Boston began using a red light mounted in the fire headquarters tower at 60 Bristol Street. A flashing light told fireboat skippers they were not needed at the fire and could go back. On December 23, 1913, the Fire Department of New York experimented with a two-way wireless telegraph between Manhattan fire alarm headquarters and the fireboat *James Duane,* but the idea was abandoned because of the cost of hiring round-the-clock telegraphers.

The first fire department radio system in the United States was installed in Boston in October, 1923, to connect the alarm office with the fireboats. Although radio was to become one of the firefighters' most valuable tools, the American fire service took to it slowly. The reasons were partly due to federal laws restricting licenses and to doubts of radio's reliability. In Buffalo, for example, chiefs' cars were equipped with police radios for calling in extra alarms. Following his radio message, the chief sent his driver to the nearest fire alarm box to confirm the call by tapping out a similar message on the telegraph key in the box. For many years, the Chicago Fire Department's radio system was a two-way police unit in the car of Father William J. Gorman, the department's Catholic chaplain and an avid fire buff. However, after fireboats and chiefs' cars were equipped with them, radios gradually became an integral part of all apparatus, although the trend did not accelerate until well after World War II.

Since 1875, when the Fire Department of New York got its first steam fireboat, the *William F. Havemeyer,* the city has had more than twenty-two fireboats. As many as ten were in service at one time, manned by around 500 firefighters of the Marine Division, the largest group of its kind in America. As other cities did, New York named its boats after mayors and other well-known personalities: Senator Robert F. Wagner and Governor Alfred E. Smith; famous firefighters, like Zophar Mills; an astronaut, John H. Glenn, Jr.; and a fire buff, Harry M. Archer, the legendary physician who hurried to fires and risked his life countless times while treating injured and trapped firefighters. Strangely, New York never got around to naming a fireboat after its most famous fire buff, Mayor Fiorello H. La Guardia.

New York's fireboat, *Firefighter,* is the world's largest and most powerful. With an overall length of 134 feet, it has a 32-foot beam and is diesel-electric powered. Its eight monitor nozzles give it a firepower of 20,000 gallons a minute. Until 1962, the boat had another nozzle mounted on a hinged 55-foot elevating tower, but it proved unwieldy and was removed.

The *Firefighter* was designed by a naval architect and fire buff, William Francis Gibbs, of the marine designing firm Gibbs & Cox. It was built at Staten Island's United Shipyards for a cost of $924,000 and was launched on August 28, 1938, while Mayor La Guardia stood proudly nearby. Berthed today near the St. George Ferry Terminal, Staten Island, the *Firefighter* has fought many of New York's worst waterfront and ship fires, including the one on the *Normandie.*

Opposite: *New York's* Firefighter, *the world's most powerful fireboat, packs a wallop of 20,000 gallons per minute.* Left: *New York's fireboat* John D. McKean *supplies water to land-based engine companies through these discharge outlets.* Below: *The engine of the Super Pumper can deliver 8,800 gallons per minute.*

The *Firefighter* won everlasting fame early in the morning of June 2, 1973, when the container ship *Sea Witch* sliced into the *Esso Brussels* tanker—which contained two million cubic feet of crude oil—near the Verrazano Bridge connecting Brooklyn and Staten Island. Explosions spread fire through both ships. The *Firefighter* was the first fireboat to arrive and found a tower of flames scorching the ten-story bridge and a blanket of burning water longer than thirty football fields.

Opening up on the *Sea Witch,* the *Firefighter*'s eight guns knocked down the flames. Through the smoke, the firefighters saw crewmen trapped on the fantail. Using the boat's monitors to push away the sea of burning oil, the firefighters raised a boarding ladder and rescued thirty-one crewmen, although sixteen others perished.

About the time Gibbs designed the *Firefighter,* he envisioned a land-based fireboat, a mobile pumping station to solve a problem that had plagued firefighters for years. Major fires, distant from unlimited harbor or other supplies, required large volumes of water at effective pressures. Many conventional pumpers drawing from the same water main often reduced the pressure, and ineffective streams fell short or vaporized before hitting the heart of the fire.

Gibbs's idea lay dormant for years because pumps that could do the job were too heavy to be hauled to fires without damaging streets. Hose was another problem. There was none light enough for easy handling and yet sturdy enough to withstand tremendous pumping pressures. By 1960, however, modern manufacturing methods and exotic chemical and oil refinery processes in large industrial centers were resulting in fires of an intensity never before known. During this period the British Admiralty developed powerful lightweight diesel engines for patrol boats, and U.S. Navy research resulted in lightweight hose. Gibbs's land-based fireboat now became practical and the Fire Department of New York proceeded with the idea.

Starting in 1963, Mack Trucks, with Gibbs & Cox as consultants, designed and built an $875,000 fire engine system that is the most powerful in the world. "The water horsepower is equivalent to that of 20 regular pumpers," said John LeHocky, Jr., Mack's project chief engineer. This mobile pumping station could supply water to a city the size of Galveston, with enough water in reserve to provide the needs of another city of 3,000 population. The system, which went into service in October, 1965, consists of six units: the Super Pumper; the Super Tender, with a gigantic water cannon; three Satellite hose carriers with smaller cannons; and a station wagon for the Super Pumper System's officer.

The Super Pumper is a thirty-four-ton tractor and semitrailer about the size of an aerial ladder truck and similarly maneuverable while riding on eighteen tires. The heart of the Super Pumper System is located in the trailer's forward compartment: a Napier-Deltic diesel engine rated at 2,400 horsepower at 1,800 rpm (revolutions per minute). Directly coupled to the engine is a six-stage DeLaval centrifugal pump built of stainless steel to permit use of fresh or salt water. Depending upon firefighting requirements, the Super Pumper can deliver 8,800 gallons per minute at 350 pounds per square inch at the

pump discharge—for high-volume saturation of fires—or 4,400 gpm at 700 psi, for high-pressure penetration.

Drawing water from a source 1,000 feet from a fire, the Super Pumper can supply thirty-five hoselines, from ten to twenty-two high-volume nozzles, or four master streams—a total wallop of 37 tons of water a minute when the system is fully operating. Compared to conventional fire engines, the Super Pumper's pressure is nearly five times greater and produces more than four times as much water. It can be supplied by as many as four hydrants, but preferred usage is by drafting from waterfront locations or working in tandem with a fireboat supplying water to it. The pumper carries 2,000 feet of polyester-jacketed hose with an internal diameter of 4½ inches, compared to standard 2½-inch hose. Each fifty-foot length weighs only 115 pounds, including lightweight aluminum couplings.

The Super Tender is similar in size and appearance. Mounted on the quickly detachable tractor, however, is a huge water cannon which, when the tractor is maneuvered within range of the fire, can shoot a stream 600 feet, although it operates best at 450. This Stang Intelligiant cannon is ideal for deep penetrating punches at major fires or demolition of walls of fire-weakened buildings that could collapse and kill firefighters. The Tender also carries 2,000 feet of the polyester hose.

The three Satellite tenders are standard hose carriers with a water cannon mounted amidships. Fittings for the cannons include 2,000 gpm Black Widow fog nozzles. Each Satellite carries more than 2,000 feet of hose, to give the Super Pumper System a total of around two miles of hose.

The Super Pumper and Tender are centrally stationed together and the Satellites are strategically housed in high-fire-risk areas. One or more Satellites generally arrive at fires in advance of the Super Pumper and Tender. Hose is laid from the water supply to the fire and the Satellites take up their positions with their cannons prepared for action. When the Super Pumper and Tender arrive, the firefighters need only to complete the hookup and

Opposite: *The liner* Normandie *burned and capsized in February, 1942, after a million gallons of water were pumped into her by fireboats and land engines.* Left: *The Big Bertha nozzle of the Super Tender shoots a powerful stream into a burning Brooklyn tenement.* Below: *The Super Pumper is the world's most powerful engine and can lob a stream of water 600 feet.*

begin pumping. The Super Pumper generally does not go to the fireground, as conventional pumpers usually do, but to a predetermined source of adequate water—which might be as much as ten blocks away.

Two months after the Super Pumper System went in service, a five-alarm fire erupted in a Bronx candy factory, on the cold Sunday night of December 5, 1965. As firefighters completed hooking up the Super Pumper System, the fire was worsening, despite several dozen streams shooting into the two-story building. Fire Chief John T. O'Hagan and Deputy Chief Maurice Ratner, who supervised the design and construction of the system, ordered Satellite 2 to approach within sixty-five feet of a window—as close as heat would permit. The Satellite's huge cannon was swiveled for action where the flames were most severe.

Three blocks away, the Super Pumper drew from three hydrants. The 2,400-horsepower diesel engine whined (its pitch is so high that its four operators must always wear earmuffs and communicate with each other through sound-powered telephones), and water surged through the 4½-inch hose and into the Satellite's big cannon. Gushing 3,000 gallons a minute—still not the full 8,800 gallon capacity—water deluged into the flames. "There was an awesome splashing inside," said Chief Ratner. "It sounded like Niagara Falls." In less than ten minutes the Super Pumper System battered the flames into submission. During the next year the System's cannons were used at sixty major fires with the same degree of effectiveness.

Many cities could use a Super Pumper System, but New York's one-of-a-kind probably will never be duplicated because of its high initial cost. The Chicago Fire Department's John F. Plant designed two heavy deluge wagons which were built in the department's shops. First to go into service, in 1968, was the stubby Big Mo, with two huge nozzles supplied by standard pumpers through thirty-two water intakes. Shortly after it went into service, it lobbed a stream to the seventeenth floor of a burning high-rise building. Three years later, Plant designed a larger unit, with two gigantic, hydraulically operated nozzles that can be elevated to around twenty-one feet. The rig has two smaller nozzles on the front and a Waterous pump rated at around 3,000 gallons per minute. Built to throw a stream about 1,200 feet, the massive apparatus was named after its designer: Big John.

Opposite top: *It takes firepower to put out major fires, but it also takes manpower to move in and complete the job, as these New York firefighters are doing.* Opposite below: *Heavy streams battle a New York tenement blaze.* Above: *Chicago's Big Mo mounts a powerful attack upon a burning industrial building. Fire Commissioner Robert J. Quinn said the Big Mo was built "to help us quickly put out fires that used to take many hours to control." Soon after Big Mo went into service in 1968, it shot a 1,700-gallon-per-minute stream—about seven tons of water—230 feet into the air, to fight a fire on the seventeenth floor of a high-rise apartment building under construction.*

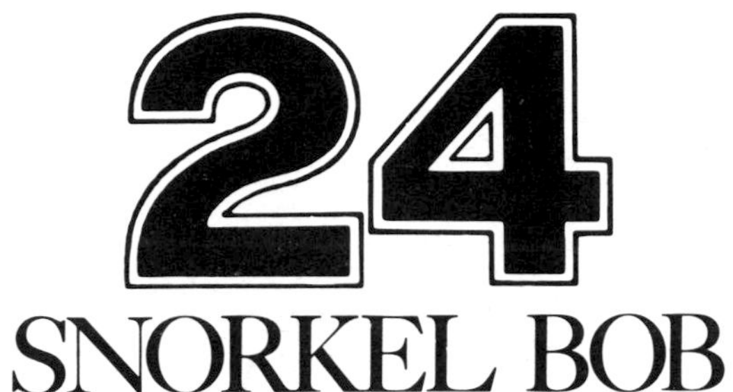

SNORKEL BOB

Monday afternoon, December 1, 1958, was crisp and cold in Chicago, the kind of day firefighters call "fire weather." Strangely, there had been few alarms. In his City Hall office, Fire Commissioner Robert J. Quinn remarked about the unusual quiet to his secretary, while he studied plans for the department's Snorkels, a new type of apparatus that had already proved to be one of the department's most effective pieces of equipment.

The wiry and athletic chief had been commissioner for a year and had been looking for something to replace the department's three antiquated water towers, which manufacturers were no longer making. With deep fascination, Quinn had watched tree trimmers and electric-sign repairmen using trucks with two hydraulically operated elevating arms that lifted them in baskets high in the air. The workers quickly moved themselves up and down, in and out, swung from side to side, and rotated 360 degrees.

Quinn was intrigued by the possibilities for firefighting and described his ideas to Edward J. Prendergast, the department's chief automotive engineer. "Suppose we mounted a nozzle in the basket and attached several lengths of hoseline to it. We could pump into it just as we do our water towers. These platforms will provide the maneuverability and versatility we lack in water towers that remain stationary. We'd be able to sweep the entire fire floors and at better angles, too. What's more, these same characteristics of platforms would make them ideal for rescuing people from upper floors."

The Pitman Manufacturing Company, Grandview, Missouri, builder of aerial platforms, agreed to cooperate in an experiment to test one for firefighting. Pitman was the American licensee for the platform invented in 1951 by Ted Thornton Trump of Oliver, British Columbia. Trump named his invention the Giraffe and built it primarily for orchards, where workers called it a cherry picker. About three years later, firefighters of New Westminster, British Columbia, lifted a hoseline in a Giraffe and used it to fight a store fire. But practical development of elevating platforms for firefighting went no further until they sparked Quinn's innovative curiosity.

In September, 1958, Pitman delivered a fifty-foot elevating platform mounted on a General Motors Corporation chassis, and the platform was outfitted in the Chicago Fire Department shops. Tests showed that engines pumping into base-mounted water inlets could—through lengths of 3½-inch diameter hose of the type used by fireboats—produce a stream of 1,200 gallons per minute, through a 2-inch diameter nozzle, at a maximum pressure of 100 pounds psi.

The platform got its first real test at 1:00 A.M. the following October 18, when it was called to a four-alarm lumberyard fire on Chicago's south side. Firefighter John Windle, operating the nozzle from the basket, helped to bring the blaze under control in a fraction of the time normally expected for a fire of equal magnitude. "I can't believe how quickly and accurately it worked," said First Deputy Fire Marshal James A. Bailey. "It really plastered this fire in a hurry." Chief Fire Marshal Raymond J. Daley added, "In thirty-three years of firefighting, I never saw anything as effective and maneuverable."

When reporters asked what this weird contraption was called, Windle said, "It's Commissioner Quinn's Snorkel." Newsmen remarked that this was an unlikely name for a fire apparatus.

"Snorkels operate underwater," said one.

Windle replied, "That's exactly where I've been for the past hour—up there in the basket and under water from other streams." From then on, the elevating platform was known as Quinn's Snorkel, and the commissioner soon became known as Snorkel Bob, for his pioneering development of one of the most versatile pieces of fire equipment ever devised.

A 65-foot Seagrave water tower on duty in Chicago. It had been fighting fires for more than thirty years when, in 1958, the city's fire commissioner, Robert J. Quinn, hit upon the idea of adapting elevating platforms for fire department use. With their superior firefighting and rescue capabilities, the platforms eventually replaced the water towers.

WATER TOWER

Opposite: *The Mount Loretta Church blazing on the night of December 19, 1973. The building was engulfed in flames before New York firefighters, hampered by distant water supplies, could go into action.* Below: *New York firefighters battle a Bronx fire on August 22, 1974.*

Few firefighters outside Chicago knew the Snorkel existed that cold December 1 afternoon, six weeks after the lumberyard fire. There was nothing secretive about it, although Commissioner Quinn wanted to learn more from practical experience before he extolled the Snorkel's virtues to chiefs in other cities. Consequently, it had yet to receive national attention. All that was about to end within hours.

The final lesson of the day had begun at Our Lady of the Angels Roman Catholic School on Chicago's northwest side, and classes were to be dismissed in half an hour. The unsprinklered two-story brick building was nearly half a century old and although it met existing fire and building regulations, it was in fact a crowded firetrap, as the National Fire Protection Association said in its January, 1959, analysis, "The Chicago School Fire." In the six rooms on the second floor were 329 children in the fourth through eighth grades.

In Room 209, an arithmetic lesson had just started for the eighth graders. A student raised his hand. "I smell smoke!" he told the nun. Opening the door, she saw the corridor filling with smoke, and she slammed the door shut. "Boys!" she said. "Pile your books at the cracks around the doors to keep out the smoke. And you girls go to the windows." The sister looked across to the south wing of the U-shaped school. Nobody there was aware of the fire.

"Boys and girls! Listen closely! Start shouting, 'Fire! Fire! The school's on fire!'" As the eighth graders began yelling and stomping their feet, they heard a swoosh in the corridor as heated gases ignited. Flames broke through the transoms of the room's two doors and flashed across the highly combustible acoustic tiles on the ceiling. The teacher and twenty-seven of her pupils died.

Smoke also was filling the seventh-grade room across the hall as the teacher there ordered students to line up in fire-drill formation. When she opened the door to the corridor, she found it filled with flames. The children panicked and ran to the windows and began smashing them. In Room 210, the fourth graders were beginning their geography lesson when they were startled by smoke seeping under the door. Little more is known of what happened in this room during the next few minutes, except that twenty-nine children and the teacher perished.

In Room 212, where twenty-seven students in

the fifth grade and their teacher were about to die, the nun implored, "Stay seated, children! Stay seated!" She told them to follow her in a prayer. And with heads bowed and hands folded they stayed at their desks. That is the position in which firefighters would find many of their bodies.

The fire had now been burning around thirty minutes, having started from some unknown cause in the rear basement stairwell. Flames fed upon the wooden stairs, piles of exam books, a roll of tar paper, and stacks of old newspapers and clothing collected during a charity drive. The heat shattered a window near the basement stairwell and the cold inrushing draft of air sent smoke and flames gushing up the chimneylike open stairway. Mushrooming along the 107-foot second-floor corridor, flames swept up into the open area between the ceiling and the roof.

Fifth-grade teacher Pearl Tristano smelled smoke at about 2:35 P.M. and notified a nun, who ran to tell the mother superior, but could not find her. Miss Tristano led her pupils to safety and tripped the school's interior fire alarm, which set bells to clanging but did not send in an alarm to the fire department, although it alerted first-floor teachers, who led all their children to safety.

A passing motorist saw the smoke and ran into a grocery store across from the school, but was told there was no public telephone he could use. He ran to find one. Janitor Jim Raymond saw the smoke and flames, hurried to the rectory, and told the housekeeper to call the fire department, then ran back to help. Smashing windows with his hands, Raymond helped to lower a fire escape before he collapsed from loss of blood.

At 2:42, in the City Hall Main Fire Alarm Office, Bill Bingham answered a call from a woman whose voice was mostly unintelligible. He managed to make out that she was reporting a fire. But where? Bingham gradually pieced together only the address, 3808 West Iowa Street. The location was the rectory. The burning school was around the corner and half a block away on Avers. Operator Bingham looked up the location and dispatched the nearest companies—Engine 85, Truck 35, Squad 6, and Battalion 18. Fire Insurance Patrol 6, a salvage company operated by insurance underwriters, immediately followed them.

Commissioner Quinn glanced up and counted the clickings on the telegraph register outside his office. Engine 85's district was not an area where the department expected severe fires. No need to worry about that alarm. Immediately after the first call, the alarm office switchboard lit up with fifteen more. "Sounds like we've got something going!" said Chief Fire Alarm Operator Joseph Hedderman. He looked up the nearest fire alarm box location, opened the master key, and began tapping out the number.

Quinn heard the pinging of his alarm bell as a thin line of paper tape with red-ink dots spelling out "5–1–8–2" streamed from the register. "A still and a box alarm fire at 3808 West Iowa," Hedderman broadcast over the department radio.

Even as Hedderman was transmitting this alarm, the officer of the first arriving company, delayed by the wrong address, was radioing, "Engine 85 to Main! Give us a box. We've got children jumping from the second-floor windows of a school. Send all available ambulances!" Three more engines, another truck, and a rescue squad were by now pulling out of their stations. Quinn grabbed his overcoat and hat and hurried out the door.

Engine 85 fortunately had its full complement of five firefighters—as recommended by NFPA standards—and they could be split into two teams, else many more lives would have been lost. One team took a hoseline into the burning stairwell area while the other team raised the pumper's two ladders and began rescuing children. Truck 35 arrived seconds later and used its ladders to bring down still more screaming children, many of them suffering from burns. Squad 6 firefighters pulled in, helped with more ladders, and spread life nets. The NFPA analysis estimated that these four fully manned companies, with the aid of Fire Insurance Patrol 6's men, saved around 160 children, many of whom jumped from windows into the arms of firefighters.

Battalion Chief Miles Devine pulled up within three minutes and radioed for a second alarm which called out nine more companies, including the Snorkel. As firefighters were advancing their lines up the stairs to the second floor, a massive portion of the roof directly over the burning stairway collapsed, sending a deadly blast of superheated air and gases into the classrooms and snuffing out the lives of anyone still alive in them. The powerful puff of heat and smoke knocked firefighters down the stairs and two of them were hospitalized.

Chief Devine skipped the third and fourth alarms and at 2:57 radioed for a fifth alarm, which brought out a total of twenty-two engines, seven

Elevating platforms lift firefighters up and over fires, where they can effectively direct streams of water into burning buildings without fear that the walls might collapse on them. One of the advantages of the apparatus is that it lessens the dangers firefighters must endure.

trucks, five squads, and other apparatus. Quinn arrived minutes later and tried to make it to the second floor. "In my thirty years as a firefighter," he said, "I have never seen such thick, dense smoke pouring from a building under such pressure."

The Snorkel's elevating platform was raised to the second floor and a firefighter in the basket opened up with the nozzle. The stream did an amazing job of pushing the fire out of the second floor and roof and enabled Quinn and his firefighters to make entry more quickly into the classrooms, where, said Quinn, they "found the children, some still seated at their desks. None of us had ever witnessed a sight so terrible."

Newspapers across the United States ran banner headlines on the fire, along with huge photos showing the Snorkel in action. With 92 children and 3 teachers dead, it was America's third-worst school disaster, calling to mind an earlier one in a Collinwood, Ohio, school in 1908, where flames and smoke barreling up open stairways—just as they had in Chicago—cost the lives of 175. The nation's worst school disaster occurred on March 18, 1937, when leaking gas in a New London, Texas, high school exploded, killing 294, including 16 teachers.

Chicagoans were stunned into deep guilt a few weeks after the tragedy at Our Lady of Angels when it was found that a sprinkler system could have put out the fire when it started with no loss of life. The system would have cost about eight dollars per child. "I think you could pass the hat in that parish and get eight dollars from every father rather easily," said Dale K. Auck, fire protection division director of Chicago's Federation of Mutual Fire Insurance Companies. Fortunately, the disaster led to many improvements in school fire safety: better-designed buildings, enclosed stairways, fire-resistant materials, and automatic alarm and sprinkler systems.

Newspaper and magazine photos of the Snorkel fighting the fire caught the interest of fire chiefs elsewhere, and they began examining the capabilities of elevating platforms for their cities. Quinn, meanwhile, was quickly finding new uses for Snorkels. They were particularly effective when spotted near big brick buildings with wood-truss roofs, one of the worst hazards for firefighters. Angling their streams down into the flames, the Snorkels controlled fires in this type of building faster and at greatly reduced risks to firefighters who had, before the platforms, suffered many casualties under collapsing walls.

Still another use for Snorkels was discovered on May 18, 1959, when a Chicago Transit Authority elevated train slammed into the rear of another train. Dozens were trapped in the cars fifty feet above the street. Two Snorkels brought down as many as four victims at a time to waiting ambulances, and lifted

doctors and extrication tools on the return trip. Sixty injured were removed, many on stretchers lying crosswise on the Snorkel baskets. Again the Snorkels made national headlines.

Acceptance of Snorkels and similar apparatus came only after prolonged debate over the comparable merits of platforms and aerial ladders. The controversy was reminiscent of other controversies in the history of the American fire service: brawn power versus horse power to pull apparatus, hand pumpers versus steam pumpers, to mention only two. Many fire chiefs steadfastly clung to their traditional reluctance to interrupt the status quo, but gradually nearly all of them accepted elevating platforms as at least an ideal complement to aerial ladders. Platforms and allied apparatus are manufactured by Pitman and the Snorkel Fire Equipment Company, St. Joseph, Missouri, as well as by American LaFrance, with its eighty to ninety-foot Aero-Chiefs; Ward LaFrance; Mack Truck Aerialscopes; Sutphen Fire Equipment Company in Amlin, Ohio; and the Calaver Corporation of Santa Fe Springs, California, with its Firebird.

Elevating platforms spawned many offshoots. On December 19, 1964, the Fire Department of New York put into service the first of its fleet of tower ladders. The first was a four-section, seventy-five-footer, with a telescoping boom. These Mack Aerialscopes were chosen over the articulated-boom type of platforms because of maneuverability problems in New York's narrow streets, especially in the financial district where Tower Ladder 1 was stationed. Snorkel also developed combination aerial ladders and water towers on the telescoping principle. These Squrts and Telesqurts, as they were named, ranged from thirty-five to seventy-five feet in length and often were mounted on pumpers.

Snorkel-type apparatus, together with modern aerial ladder-mounted nozzles, gradually replaced water towers. The last to go was a Hale-patented tower made in 1897 for the Memphis, Tennessee, Fire Department by the Chicago Fire Extinguisher Company. Rebuilt several times, the tower had connections for twenty-two hoselines. It was retired on May 3, 1974, marking the end of another colorful era in the history of American firefighting.

Above: *One of Chicago's Snorkels delivers a knockout punch to a fire.* Opposite top: *This seventy-five-foot Snorkel on a Mack Truck chassis was built for the Canyon, Texas, Fire Department in 1971.* Opposite bottom: *Chicago Snorkels are used to bring down the trapped and injured victims of an elevated train crash.*

CANYON FIRE DEPARTMENT
Snorkel

CHICAGO FIRE DEPARTMENT
SNORKEL
No 5

25 BEL AIR'S DEVIL WINDS

Teletype machines in Los Angeles fire stations clattered a High Hazard warning at 8:03 on the hot, muggy, and windy morning of November 6, 1961. Strong winds from the Mojave Desert, unusually high temperatures, low relative humidity, years of drought, and dense thickets of tinder-dry chaparral brush combined to send the Fire Danger Index soaring to 98, out of a possible high of 100.

The question was not whether there would be fires in the mountainous brush areas that day, but just where, when, and how bad they would be. The teletype warning put the Los Angeles Fire Department on an immediate brush-fire alert. Alarm dispatchers began deploying companies to firehouses that were closest to the brush areas. An alarm from inside these brush belts—which covered nearly one-third of the city—would automatically call out twice the normal number of apparatus and firefighters.

Except for the extremely high Fire Danger Index, alerts were not uncommon in Los Angeles at that time of the year. Blustery hot winds are seasonal in southern California from September through March. Forming in high-pressure areas over Nevada and Utah, these winds travel hundreds of miles downhill across the Mojave Desert and are rapidly heated while squeezing through mountain passes into southern California's low-pressure coastal areas.

Southern Californians call them Santa Ana or Santanna winds, for reasons not altogether clear.

The exclusive Bel Air and Brentwood sections of Los Angeles after the conflagration of November, 1961. Starting in a patch of brush, the fire eventually spread to a nineteen-mile area. It destroyed 484 costly homes and 21 other buildings and produced losses of $25 million.

One legend says the winds were named after the Mexican General Antonio Santa Anna, whose cavalry whipped up dust storms similar to those caused by the winds. Another holds that the name derives from *Santantas,* an Indian word meaning "devil winds." Whatever the case, the winds roaring out of Newhall Pass and gusting to over fifty miles an hour that Monday sent temperatures climbing into the eighties, while the relative humidity dipped to 4 percent at recording stations along Mulholland Drive, above the famous residential areas of Bel Air Estates and Brentwood, on the south slopes of the Santa Monica Mountains. In this area of elegant homes and estates lived movie and television stars, entertainment industry executives, lawyers, doctors, and other prosperous business and professional people.

Bel Air and Brentwood may have been two of the world's most exclusive residential areas, but to firefighters they were powder kegs begging for a spark to set them off. By 1961, thousands of homes were nestling in the thick chaparral, which stood up to twenty-five feet tall. Except for the desolate backcountry of Australia, there was no more flammable ground cover in the world. With less than three inches of rainfall that year, the oil- and resin-impregnated brush had reached the point of explosiveness. Homeowners had resisted fire department urgings to clear the brush from around their houses, and it had grown so deep in some areas that only parts of the rooftops were visible from the air. Many houses were built out over brush-covered canyons; supported by stilts, they were architectural invitations to disaster because their wood flooring and roofs made them easy prey for flames that might sweep up the canyon slopes.

The access to the area was a nightmare of narrow, winding streets, a bewildering maze climbing sharply north from Sunset Boulevard toward Mulholland, which runs along the crest of the mountain. The rugged topography of Bel Air and Brentwood is marked by a series of deep, brush-clogged canyons and high ridges that run mostly in a north-south

direction from Mulholland to Sunset. Many streets are private and without names, reflecting the residents' desire for privacy and their wish to keep out strangers. These efforts for seclusion also kept out firefighters.

Even the most powerful fire engines come to a slow crawl as they circle up the steep streets into Bel Air and Brentwood. Two parallel ridges may be only a stone's throw apart, but because they are separated by deep canyons, their miles of streets have no interconnecting avenues. For fire apparatus to get from one street to another one parallel to it can take more than ten minutes. Of equally deep concern that November day was whether the residents of Bel Air and Brentwood could be evacuated if Santa Ana winds ever drove a fast-spreading fire through the canyons and over the ridges.

Worst of all, more than half the homes had wood-shingle roofs. Across the United States, 648 cities had laws forbidding or limiting wooden roofing, but Los Angeles was not one of them. The city had not profited from the lessons taught by a number of earlier conflagrations throughout the country. Since 1900, fifty-four conflagrations involving wood-shingle roofs had incinerated 20,428 buildings. By comparison, only 2,815 structures were lost in the forty-six disasters involving fire-resistant roofing. In its 1959 study of Los Angeles, the National Fire Protection Association of Boston bluntly predicted a conflagration if homes, especially in brush areas, continued to be built with wood-shingle roofs.

The Los Angeles Fire Department was aware of the problem. For years, its chiefs had been urging the passage of new laws, but their disaster warnings were mere whistles in the wind. Lumbering is one of California's major industries, and lobbyists and other construction interests had fought to protect the status quo. Architects, moreover, said wood-shingle roofs were better looking, and homeowners preferred them.

Most of all, Bel Air and Brentwood were lulled into a false sense of security because there had not been a major brush fire in the area for at least half a

Opposite: *One of the more than a dozen air tankers that dropped chemical fire retardants, in attempts to stop the brush fire sweeping through the Bel Air and Brentwood sections of Los Angeles.* Above: *Firefighters were able to save 78 percent of the homes inside the disaster area.*

century. Besides, the Los Angeles Fire Department was rated by professional fire agencies outside the city as among the best in the United States. If there was a fire, the department had the latest equipment, superior leadership, and enough men to put it out.

Seven minutes after the brush-fire alert on the morning of November 6, Rex Thompson and two other grading contractors were preparing to begin bulldozing a new subdivision in the brush, on the Sherman Oaks side of the Santa Monica Mountains north of Bel Air. Smelling smoke, they spotted a fire in grass clippings and trash about a hundred feet beyond the end of Stone Canyon Avenue. Leaping the street barricade, they ran into the brush and tried to stomp it out. "It was no use," said Thompson. "As soon as we hit it, flames came leaping from under our feet."

They ran to a nearby home at 3651 Stone Canyon, where Mrs. Walter Bockwoldt immediately called the fire department, while the contractors tried to stretch a garden hose into the brush. At 8:15 A.M., dispatchers in the Van Nuys Signal Office sent out a beefed-up double assignment of three engines, three water-carrying tanks, and an aerial ladder truck. Assistant Chief Henry C. Sawyer—one of the department's brush firefighting specialists—heard the alarm in his headquarters on Mulholland and left immediately. Shortly after Engine 88 pulled out of its Sepulveda Boulevard station, Acting Captain Bill Porter saw the smoke and radioed for two more engines.

The wind-driven flames were making a run up the slopes toward Mulholland when Chief Sawyer arrived. There is only one way to fight a fire in brush or a forest: Hit it hard and hit it fast with lots of apparatus, firefighters, bulldozers (to slice firebreaks), and aircraft (for reconnaissance and the dropping of chemical fire-retardants and water). At 8:26, Sawyer radioed for fifteen more engines and six chiefs, and activated the Major Emergency Plan, which immediately mobilized the entire department. Additional companies were barely pulling out of their stations when the southwesterly winds blew bits of flaming brush across Mulholland and sprinkled new fires on the Bel Air side.

Sawyer also called for air tankers to drop chemical borate, a thick solution that at the time was the best available fire retardant. Dropped along the perimeters of a brush fire, it insulated the brush against further burning. The nearest tankers were two AJ-1 Savages at Van Nuys Airport. One was down for repairs, but could get airborne within the hour. Don Campbell, a local pilot, took off in the other and headed for the column of smoke boiling up from the Santa Monica Mountains.

It was essential that Sawyer get above the fire to direct operations; the area was too vast and the canyons and gullies too difficult to see from the ground. Learning that the department's helicopter also was undergoing repairs, he managed to contact the KMPC radio news helicopter, which had been circling the area. The chopper landed, picked him up, and lifted him above the fire. What he saw was alarming. Driven by the winds, dozens of spot fires on the south side of Mulholland were spilling down into Stone Canyon, feeding upon the tall brush that had been thickening there for fifty years.

While firefighters made a stand along Mulholland, dozens more engines were directed into Bel Air from Sunset Boulevard and up Roscomare Road. From their command post at Donella Circle, Division Chiefs Robert E. Radke and Thad T. Whippo hoped they could pinch off the flames along an east-west fire road above Bel Air. While firefighters hooked up to hydrants and made ready to attack the flames tumbling down toward them, Radke and Whippo called for an air tanker drop east of Roscomare. But their optimism was short-lived. The violent winds continued to drive gigantic fingers of flame deep into Stone Canyon.

Meanwhile, in the air, the fierce winds were bouncing Sawyer in the tiny helicopter. He tried to break through the babble of radio messages to warn that the fire was racing dangeously close to a ridge where—unseen by firefighters on the ground—it could spill over into a new area. But the radio was so jammed that he could not be heard. Radke's and Whippo's call for a second borate drop could not get through either. The flames stormed into Stone Canyon, and the Donella line was lost.

Shortly after 9 o'clock, tidal waves of flames spilled into the upper reaches of Bel Air. The fire was gathering speed and chewing through the crackling brush at the rate of more than thirteen acres a minute. Half an hour later, Battalion Chief Oliver H. Howard radioed, "I've got a house burning on Stradella." The house at 2115 Stradella Road was new, unoccupied, and cantilevered over the flaming brush in the canyon below. It was the first house destroyed. Two minutes later, Chief Howard reported, "I've got a lot of houses burning on Stradella!"

Hundreds of chunks of flaming brush were

scooped up by the galelike winds and sprinkled onto wooden rooftops, igniting them. Radiated heat caused other houses to blossom with flames. Then the winds peeled off thousands of burning shingles, sucking them high into the air and scattering them far in advance of the jagged perimeter of flames zigzagging through Bel Air. Bits of charred shingles landed inside Sawyer's helicopter. This was a fire unlike any he had seen. "There was no fire line," he said. "Major fires were scattered all over Bel Air."

After knocking down fires in one building, companies quickly leapfrogged each other down Roscomare and Stradella, their work made all the more difficult because there were no interconnecting streets for two miles. Firefighters desperately protected buildings they knew they could save and were forced to abandon dozens of others already blazing. Soon, entire blocks of rooftops were bursting into flames. "One minute one house was burning, the next minute there were fifty or sixty blazing," said Chief Engineer William L. Miller, who was supervising overall direction of the fire at a command post on Mulholland. The firefighting force would grow to 2,500 at the peak of the fire, with more than 200 pieces of apparatus.

By 10 o'clock, fifty-four Los Angeles fire companies were on the lines, and mutual aid calls were bringing in more from thirty-seven communities around the city. The chief engineer of the Los Angeles County Fire Department, Keith E. Klinger, led a force of twenty-two pieces of apparatus into the area. The United States Forest Service and the California Division of Forestry answered with several dozen more, some being called in from as far as 350 miles away. Many communities surrounding Los Angeles sent apparatus into the city to answer fire alarms for as many as a dozen other large fires. Incoming companies that had never been in Bel Air struggled to locate their assigned positions in the mishmash of streets. Some got lost. Would they be able to get out of this maze if they became trapped in the thick gray smoke that cut visibility to a few feet?

The Los Angeles Police Department sent 331 officers into Bel Air to broadcast bullhorn warnings to evacuate. The hundreds of residents fleeing down the streets from upper Bel Air became caught in the jam of fire apparatus trying to go up. School buses hurried into the area to evacuate children. The miracle of the disaster was that not a single life was lost. And the majority of the injuries were to 200 firefighters, who mostly suffered eye irritations.

As fast as fire engines took up their positions, the wind-driven smoke and flames bullied them back to new spots. Pumpers throbbed for hours as the several hundred engines sent as much as 50,000 gallons of water a minute surging through hoselines snaking along streets. Panicky residents made matters worse by turning on lawn sprinklers and water taps and spraying their roofs with garden hoses. This additional demand upon water supplies—some of it made in unthreatened areas—plus broken service lines in destroyed homes, drained available water and sapped pressures. Hydrants went dry and firefighters were unable to draft from most of the hundreds of swimming pools because they could not get their rigs close to them.

Bulldozers meanwhile continued to widen firebreaks and clear thick brush from around threatened homes, working in tandem with the fleet of more than a dozen air tankers, including some of World War II vintage. At Van Nuys Airport, a team of forty-five city, county, and Air Force firefighters were mixing and loading the 125 tons of borate that would be dropped.

The flames, raging totally unchecked, slashed a jagged southwesterly course through Bel Air, then, driven by the Devil Winds, moved to the east toward thickly built-up Beverly Glen Canyon. While bulldozer blades widened firebreaks, twenty-two city and county engine companies quickly formed battle lines to protect homes along Beverly Glen Boulevard. With the aid of borate bombers, the fire's easterly jab was stopped, but not before a new peril occurred.

Far behind the firefighters, at Benedict Canyon Boulevard near Wanda Park Drive, a man threw a burning flare into thick brush, which flared up instantly. Air tanker pilots spotted the fire almost immediately and plastered it with borate, while three engines hurried in to completely surround it. The flare-thrower was quickly arrested. When questioned, he said he liked to see brush fires and had become so excited by the Bel Air holocaust that he decided to start a new one.

With the eastward spread blocked and the open expanse of the Bel Air Country Club promising to stop the southerly threat to the UCLA campus, the situation began to improve on those flanks. It was a totally different story on the southwesterly perimeter, which by noon continued to rage out of control with no hope for containment. Wind-goaded flames stormed into Hog Canyon towards Sepulveda Boulevard. Luckily, the eight-lane San Diego Freeway was

being built through Sepulveda Canyon. Grading equipment had cut a quarter-of-a-mile break, which would surely prevent the fire from crossing into Brentwood.

But luck was not with the firefighters. Shortly after noon the winds blew a storm of burning brush and shingles across the freeway and peppered the thick chaparral on the Brentwood side of Sepulveda Canyon. Instantly, the mountainside twinkled like a Christmas tree, as dozens of spot fires crackled in the brush. Now a disaster of unbelievable proportions loomed. If the fire was not stopped at Brentwood, it could go rampaging for miles clear across the Santa Monica Mountains, through Pacific Palisades, and on to the Pacific Ocean. Though he had hundreds of companies at his command, Chief Engineer Miller could hardly spare any for this new outbreak. But he had no choice, and he began pulling engines away from Bel Air and sending them west on Sunset Boulevard to Brentwood.

There was more bad news within the hour. At 12:56, the lookout in the Topanga Fire Tower reported, "Fire at forty-seven degrees! On Mulholland east of Topanga Canyon Boulevard." The fire was in Santa Ynez, seven miles west of Bel Air and traveling toward it. Now there were three major brush fires burning inside Los Angeles. Chief Miller and the others feared the worst from this new one, and they were not wrong. The Santa Ynez area was covered with brush as thick as that in Bel Air and Brentwood. If the Santa Ynez fire linked with the Bel Air-Brentwood fire, a large area of the city would be in grave danger.

Shortly after the Brentwood outbreak, the Devil Winds swept flames south toward the $10-million campus of St. Mary's College. Apparatus was quickly deployed to protect the buildings, but firefighters found that hydrants were dry from the tremendous drain on the system. A dozen 5,000-gallon water-tank trucks from the freeway construction project were rushed to St. Mary's to supply the fire engines, enabling them to save all but the fine arts building and the nuns' quarters.

As flames swept over the campus they spilled into Brentwood residential areas, where dozens of fires erupted on wooden roofs. Brentwood was a repeat of Bel Air, and the homes of the famous and wealthy crumbled into ashes. *Life* magazine called the disaster "A Tragedy Trimmed in Mink."

Fire department radios continued to chatter into

the early afternoon hours, as flames leapfrogged from street to street, leaving in their wake ashes and tall, blackened chimneys. Around 2:30 the westward-rolling flames spilled into Kenter Canyon, but half an hour later the firefighters' luck turned. The winds began to wane, and the fury of the fire slowly diminished. The last two houses to burn were on Kenter Avenue.

The gradually dissipating fire moved sluggishly west toward Mandeville Canyon, where weary Division Chief Radke built a line of sixty fire engines in the event it flared afresh. At the northernmost end of the line was a fire engine that had been pulled out of storage but probably belonged in a museum. "If it pumps, we'll use it," said Captain Les Evans. With adequate water supplies, and in an area where only thin brush covered the slopes, the exhausted firefighters could now begin to look for control.

The Bel Air-Brentwood fire died fitfully in a seesaw battle lasting into the night. By 8:00 P.M., the western and southerly spread of the flames was stopped, but final control would not come until early Wednesday, November 8. The Santa Ynez fire was controlled the next day, by a force of one hundred fire engines, after it destroyed nine structures and 9,720 acres. It burned to within less than a mile of the Brentwood fire.

The $25-million losses in the Bel Air-Brentwood disaster made it one of America's worst conflagrations. There are two ways of assessing it. The first is a negative one: 484 costly homes and 21 other buildings were destroyed inside the nineteen-mile perimeter of the fire, which blackened 6,090 acres. The other view is more positive: The combined efforts of city, county, state, and federal firefighters saved nearly 78 percent of all homes inside the disaster area. Rex Wilson of the NFPA testified before Mayor Samuel W. Yorty's fire inquiry board: "You have here in Los Angeles one of the finest fire departments in the country. It is capably administered, highly efficient, and beautifully trained. I [have seen] it in operation. You should take great pride in it."

Bel Air-Brentwood residents thought so, too. Some painted a huge "Thank You" in the street as fire chiefs surveyed the disaster area from helicopters. Out of the conflagration came many improvements, including accelerated expansion of water supplies; more fire stations, equipment, and men in the brush areas; a law requiring chaparral to be cleared at least one hundred feet from around structures; and another law forbidding wood shingles unless treated with fire-resistant chemicals.

Opposite: *Firefighters fought a seesaw battle with the flames, which raged into the night. At the peak of the fire, there were 2,500 firefighters on the line with more than two hundred pieces of apparatus.* Below: *"One minute one house was burning, the next minute there were fifty or sixty blazing," said William L. Miller, the Los Angeles fire chief who directed operations.*

As in any disaster, the question is inevitably asked: Can there be another Bel Air-Brentwood? Even the best-impregnated shingles lose their effectiveness in time from rain, wind, and sun. By 1976, the memory of Bel Air had dimmed and the Los Angeles Fire Department, for economy reasons, cut back on equipment and manpower in the area, despite homeowners' protests. The hearty chaparral has grown back, the Devil Winds still blow, and so the answer to the question is yes, Bel Air-Brentwood can happen again.

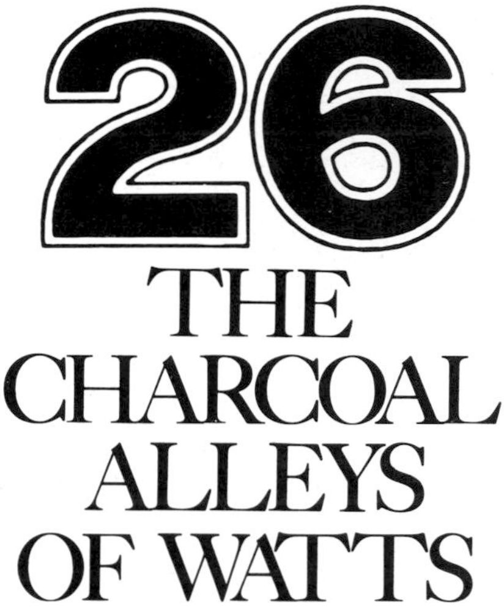

26
THE CHARCOAL ALLEYS OF WATTS

Friday, the thirteenth day of August, 1965, dawned hot and muggy in Los Angeles as temperatures climbed into the nineties. The atmosphere was tensely quiet following two nights of sporadic clashes between police and young blacks in Watts, the south central area of the city. Rocks, bricks, and bottles had been thrown, newsmen beaten, shots fired, and cars overturned and torched. Two stores were looted and burned before the roving mobs were dispersed by club-swinging police.

The residential and commercial district of Los Angeles, whose population was 95 percent black, had been simmering since Wednesday evening, when Marquette Frye was stopped for drunken driving near his home close to the Watts district. A routine arrest escalated into a brief scuffle that brought a large crowd of police and black residents. Frye, his stepbrother, Ronald, and their mother, Rena, were arrested. The incident sparked rumor upon rumor, and the area was seething with anger.

By comparison with eastern slums, south central Los Angeles looked like a paradise of well-kept single-family homes, with lawns, flower gardens, trees, and clean streets. The Urban League, a national organization dedicated to the economic advancement of blacks, rated Los Angeles first among sixty-eight cities in its minority advantages. But a ghetto does not have to look like a ghetto to be one. The population density was nearly twice that of the rest of the city.

More than 260 buildings were firebombed and burned during the Los Angeles riots of August, 1965. One firefighter was killed when a wall collapsed, and more than 180 were injured while battling fires in the thirty-two-square-mile riot zone.

Invisible boundaries confined blacks to the area. Unemployment was highest there, as was crime, and the area had more fires than any other part of Los Angeles.

Older residents were mostly resolved to their plight, but the young were not. They ridiculed President Lyndon B. Johnson's Great Society and shared a growing discontent with its promises, many of which had not been fulfilled. Sargent Shriver, director of the Office of Ecomomic Opportunity in Washington, had recently announced 120 federal anti-poverty projects, with $35 million in seed money, for areas across the country, including Watts.

But all this was too little and too late for young blacks, who had had their fill of rhetoric and unfulfilled promises. They had shown their disgust early this Friday morning when comedian Dick Gregory, a Congress of Racial Equality activist, had addressed a mob with a police bullhorn, begging them to go home. In reply, a rioter had shot him in the thigh. The ghetto lifestyle—and there was little hope of changing it—was joblessness, frequent trouble with the police, and hanging out on street corners listening to the radio. The most popular station was KGFJ, whose well-known disc jockey, Magnificent Montague, exhorted listeners with his distinctive slogan, "Burn, baby, burn!" by which he meant, "Keep cool, brother, keep cool."

By Friday morning, Deputy Fire Chief Raymond M. Hill was growing increasingly worried, although most of the fires so far had been trivial. What most concerned him were the potential dangers to firefighters and apparatus from the angry crowds, and the possibility that rioters would set major fires. On Wednesday and Thursday, there had been reports that two firefighters had been struck with objects hurled by the crowd—one with a rock, the other with a full can of beer. Apparatus going to and from alarms was dented by barrages of stones, bricks, bottles, chunks of asphalt, and crowbars. A rock smashing through the windshield of Rescue Squad 57 broke the steering wheel.

Hill, acting fire chief in the absence of vacationing Chief Engineer Don T. Hibbard, had called the Police Control Center and was assured that fire apparatus would be escorted to alarms, providing officers could be pulled from other riot duty. Before hurrying to the area to take command, Hill called the chief of Battalion 13, Paul H. Augustine, and told him to proceed with his companies to the perimeters of alarms without using sirens or red lights, to minimize calling attention to themselves. They were to wait for

Opposite and below: *More than two hundred fires were burning at the peak of the rioting. Dispatchers showed a backlog of as many as twenty fires waiting for apparatus or police escorts. Task force groups of at least two engines and one ladder truck attacked with large hoselines, powerful wagon batteries, and nozzles that shot streams down into the fire's heart.*

police, but if escorts did not arrive quickly, they were to try to put out the fires, but leave immediately if attacked.

From the department's extensive brush firefighting experience, Hill had developed an idea for forming companies into task-force groups operating out of one station. They answered alarms as a unit and worked together as a team under a task-force commander. The concept was not new. It had been traditionally used by European brigades, but only rarely by American departments, which preferred the system of sending individual companies from the nearest stations. Task forces were ideally suited for riot firefighting. Consisting of at least two engines and an aerial ladder truck, and commanded by a chief officer, they provided greater security in numbers than separate five-man companies coming from many directions.

Most of all, task forces offered quick, hard-hitting power. If there were many fires burning over a wide area, the tactics would be to knock down the flames quickly with large hoselines, powerful turret guns, and aerial ladder nozzles that could shoot streams down into the heart of the fire. For maximum safety, each task force would form a semicircle around the fire, hopefully drawing from only one hydrant and using as little hose as possible for greater mobility. There was to be no normal dousing of the last embers. "Move in fast, knock the fire down in a hurry, pick up your lines, and make yourselves available for another fire," Hill instructed.

Friday morning was almost suspiciously quiet, and by 1:00 P.M. some firefighters were becoming cautiously optimistic when only two fires had been reported, in automobiles. All that ended at 1:09 as alarm bells sounded for a fire in a looted dry cleaning store at 107th Street and Avalon Boulevard. Task force firefighters approached cautiously while looking for police escorts. There were none. Bricks and rocks began bouncing off the hoods and sides of the apparatus. The firefighters returned to their station, but not for long.

Half an hour later, fires were breaking out all along the 103rd Street business district of Watts. There were more blazes than one task force could handle, and reinforcements were called. As task forces laid their hose lines and began attacking fires, there was the repeated sound of smashing plate glass,

jangling burglar alarms, and the crowd chanting "Burn, baby, burn!"—giving Magnificent Montague's slogan a quite different meaning.

Smoke shrouded the heavily congested street, and apparatus moved slowly to avoid hitting looters hurrying away with chairs, tables, cases of liquor, and clothing, some in pairs and threesomes to carry television and stereo consoles, sofas, and mattresses. The police were hopelessly outnumbered. "The situation is completely out of control," said Police Chief William Parker.

As soon as a task force put out one fire, another would take hold—to their right, their left, behind them, and for block upon block along 103rd. There were more fires than five task forces could handle. An enormous column of ugly smoke boiled high into the afternoon sky, as, one by one, looted stores on both sides of 103rd went up in flames. The street was so destroyed by fire that a newscaster named it Charcoal Alley.

At the same time, still more puffs of smoke were billowing for eleven blocks along Avalon, and Molotov cocktails were igniting looted stores north of Slauson, over a mile north of Watts. If it was the mob's pleasure to permit the firefighters to attack the fires, it did so. But for the most part, it ruled that firefighting could not begin until buildings were thoroughly looted. Police were inundated with hundreds of reports of rioting, looting, and shootings. Firefighters could only begin to attack a blaze when it was well under way or if the police were present.

At 5:00 P.M., Acting Governor Glenn M. Anderson activated the National Guard, but it would take hours before the vanguard of an eventual force of 13,500 arrived. Lootings and cocktail-bombings continued into the early evening.

With more fires in the area north of Watts, Chief Hill set up a second command post at Fire Station 22, Vernon Avenue and Main Street. Firefighters saw rioters slug an attendant at a service station across the street from the firehouse and begin filling bottles and cans with gasoline. There was no longer any question in anybody's mind. It was going to be a long, hot, difficult night.

By 9 o'clock, fires were blazing along Central Avenue, the area's main business thoroughfare. The entire fire department was mobilized, and more companies were ordered into the area. A steady stream of new fires was erupting throughout the thirty-two-square-mile riot zone. Looting, rioting, and burning had spilled across the city line into areas east of Los Angeles, and the Los Angeles County Fire Department was called into action.

At 10:45, task forces rushed to a major fire raging in a looted drugstore, liquor store, and the huge Shop-Rite Market at 120th Street and Central. Mobs of jeering crowds were restrained only by shotgun-carrying deputy sheriffs, who guarded the hydrants. The three buildings were well involved and more task forces were called. The deputies were soon called to a worse disturbance, but even with their protection removed, the firefighters were too committed to pick up and leave. Rioters raced up and down Central, trying to sever hose lines and skimming their cars close to firefighters, forcing them to dodge to escape being hit. Rocks and bottles hurtled from out of the darkness, pelting the firefighters and their apparatus.

After the fire had been controlled, and just as the men were picking up their hose, the front wall of one of the buildings collapsed, burying two firefighters. One of them, Warren E. Tilson, was killed instantly. The other, Robert Laxague, was pulled from the debris by firefighter Frank J. Harrison, Jr., for which Harrison was awarded the department's medal of valor, becoming Los Angeles's first black firefighter to win this highest honor.

A short while later, at a blazing market near the Los Angeles Sports Arena, two firefighters were injured when a gunman fired his pistol at them.

By midnight, still more fires were burning and others were being started. At the busy intersection of Broadway and Manchester Boulevard, seven stores were burning, including the headquarters of the Twenty-first Congressional District Coordinating Council on Economic Development and Opportunity. At 1:00 A.M., Saturday, some forty-five task forces of one hundred engines and twenty-six ladder trucks were shuttling from fire to fire, constantly under attack. Los Angeles firefighters were experiencing something unknown in America since the New York Draft Riots during the Civil War, when volunteers were harassed and stoned for two days while fighting blazes set by mobs.

Chief Hill estimated that more than two hundred fires were burning, most of them large. Command post dispatchers showed a backlog of as many as twenty fires waiting for available apparatus or police escorts. Shotgun-carrying officers rode apparatus, and task forces followed National Guard jeeps mounted with machine guns. Dispatching priorities were given to fires where life hazards were great and to fires in large structures. Lowest priorities went to burning automobiles. Alarms from fireboxes were ignored because most of them were false and were often pulled to lure firefighters into ambushes. By 7 A.M., the fire department had logged more than 1,000 alarms, including one which sent Squad 22 to deliver a baby.

Dawn promised another day with ninety-seven-degree temperatures. Alarms dwindled during the morning hours, and firefighters began hoping the worst was over. But that was far from the truth. By mid-morning the rioters attacked with renewed fury. A gigantic supermarket at Washington Boulevard and Central was looted and firebombed. Mobs of rioters swarmed into two- and three-story brick and frame buildings lining Central and Broadway for sixteen blocks. The frenzied looting was followed by the inevitable Molotov cocktails, and building after building went up in flames. Larger buildings were now involved, and the fires blazed more fully and furiously.

Elsewhere in Los Angeles, streets were mainly deserted as people stayed indoors, watching the fires, filmed by newsmen in helicopters, on television. Irving Luckerman sat at home watching the television broadcast of the burning of his hardware and paint store, which he had operated for thirty-five years. On Broadway near Forty-eighth, looters broke into the Friendly Furniture Store and plundered lamps, night tables, and sofas before splattering Molotov cocktails. The store bloomed into one of the most spectacular blazes of the day. The mobs cheered, but other black residents living nearby wept, as they sprinkled their wooden rooftops with garden hoses to try to keep them from igniting.

At Forty-third and Central, looters picked the Shoppers Market clean, blew open the safe, and escaped with its cash before setting the store ablaze. Central Avenue, from Santa Barbara Avenue to Forty-ninth, was a maelstrom of teeming mobs scurrying among blazing buildings that sent towering columns of smoke billowing thousands of feet into the sky. Central became Charcoal Alley No. 2. Paralleling it to the west was Broadway, where twenty-three buildings were burning furiously and six more were catching fire—Charcoal Alley No. 3.

From a helicopter over the area, James P. Bennett of the *Los Angeles Herald-Examiner* reported: "The whole scene looked like a crazy patchwork of hatred and devastation. Looters were . . . carrying their booty to cars past beleaguered firemen fighting fires in other shops. . . . At least three firemen were observed from the air to go down under a barrage of rocks and bricks. . . . Firemen were forced to abandon their efforts to put out the flames. . . . In one case, several firemen tried to run to safety, leaving their equipment behind. Looters moved in and removed hoses from the trucks and did a snake dance with them." Lou Mack, a photographer riding with Bennett, said, "It looks like all the fires of hell down there."

Although a twelve-hour curfew beginning at 8:00 P.M. was declared, firefighters expected the worst with nightfall, as south central Los Angeles was silhouetted by the glare. Around 10:30, a task force was fired upon from rooftops, as they attempted to put out flames in a two-story building near Forty-eighth and Broadway. The chief of the Eighth Battalion, Kenneth R. Long, ordered his men out. They returned, after police and National Guardsmen had swept the area, to discover that flames had spread to a neighboring house. The gunfire started again. Chief Long's task force was pinned down behind a concrete wall, in a no-man's-land of crossfire between snipers on one side and Guardsmen and police on the other.

"The people whose house was burning just stood there and looked at us," said Long. "By the time the police gave us the OK to come back again, the apartment house was gone. Flames were coming from a structure behind the apartment. The attic was beginning to go on the family's house. We did the best we could, but the gunfire was increasing." A tear gas grenade thunked off a wall and landed near the firefighters, felling six of them. Chief Long's task force abandoned the area to the flames.

A massive pall of smoke blanketed south central Los Angeles at dawn, Sunday, as bone-weary and begrimed firefighters girded for a third day of rioting. There were many fires, but the worst was now over. Even as the rioting and fires flickered out during the next two days, scores of attempts were made to explain the unexplainable, but nobody could. By Tuesday, Los Angeles was burying its dead. At Firefighter Tilson's funeral service, Fire Department Chaplain Robert Gaar said, "I would to God that we as a people, white or black, could look each other in the eyes and say, 'You are my brother.'"

Investigators meanwhile were tallying damages. Of the 261 buildings destroyed, most were supermarkets and liquor, furniture, and clothing stores. Damage exceeded $45 million, and thirty-four people were killed, including Tilson and a deputy sheriff.

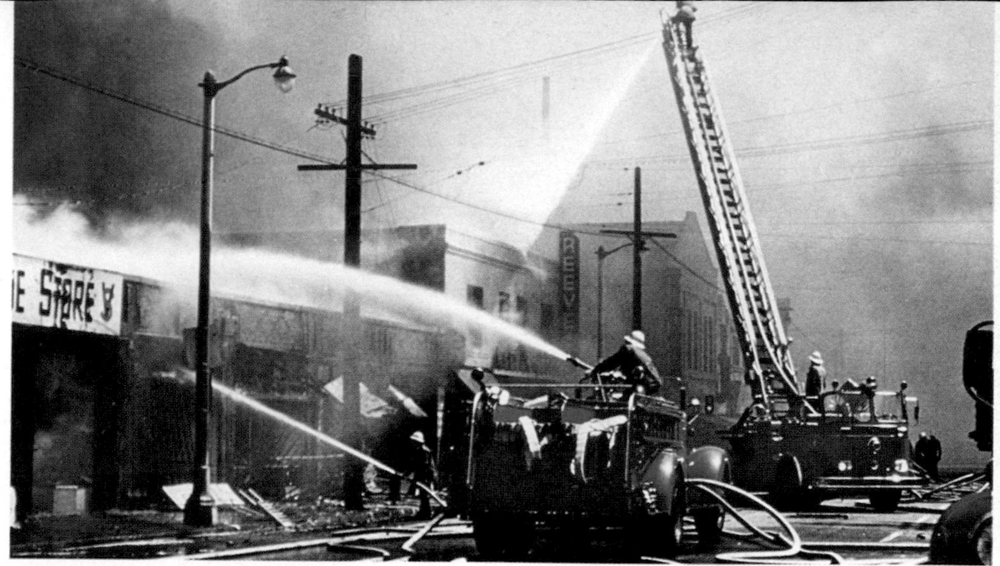

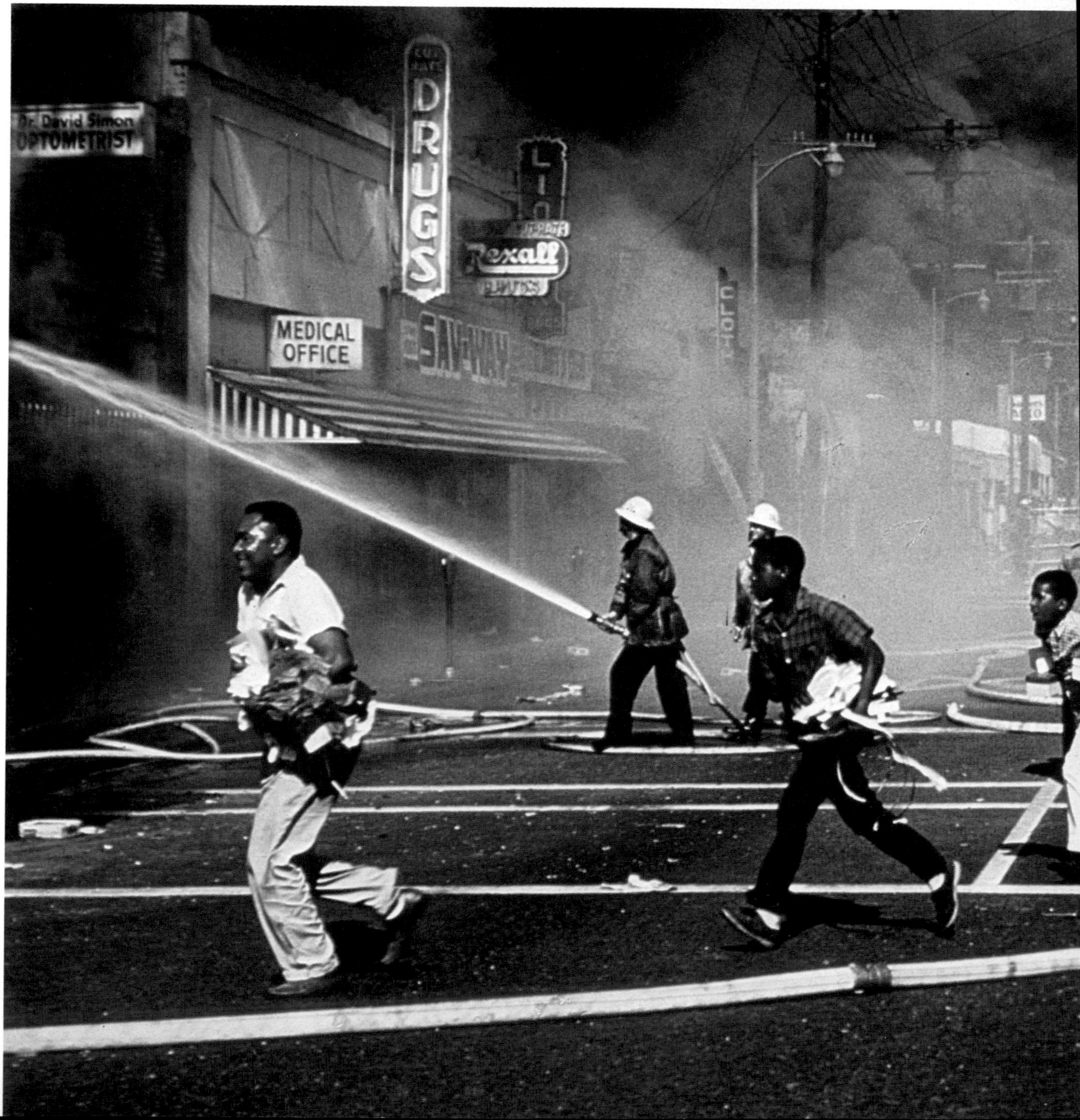
Dr. David Simon
OPTOMETRIST
DRUGS
Rexall
MEDICAL
OFFICE

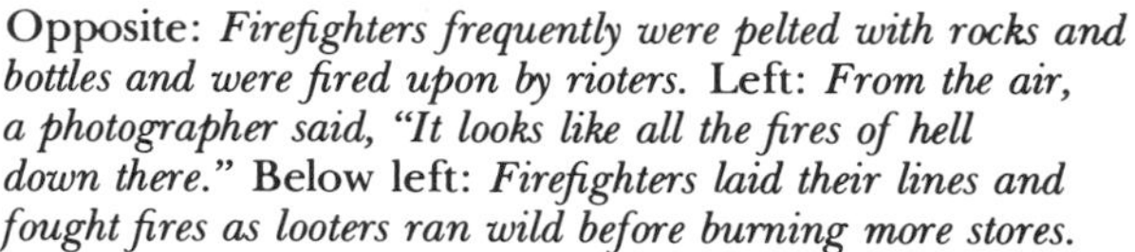

Opposite: *Firefighters frequently were pelted with rocks and bottles and were fired upon by rioters.* Left: *From the air, a photographer said, "It looks like all the fires of hell down there."* Below left: *Firefighters laid their lines and fought fires as looters ran wild before burning more stores.*

More than 4,000 people were arrested and over 2,000 guns were confiscated. More than 180 firefighters were hurt fighting the fires, 32 of them injured by rioters. The success of the task forces prompted Hill to make them standard for all types of Los Angeles firefighting after he became chief engineer the following year.

Watts was a foretaste of what awaited American firefighters during the turbulent 1960s. In 1967, firefighters battled riot-caused fires in seventy cities, the worst of them in Detroit that hot summer when forty-one persons were killed, 1,300 buildings destroyed, and damages exceeded $80 million. On April 4, 1968, Dr. Martin Luther King, Jr., was assassinated in Memphis. Fierce flaming riots quickly erupted in Chicago, Washington, Detroit, and Boston.

Through it all, the American firefighter was mostly bewildered. Why, he asked, had he suddenly become the target of rock-throwers and snipers? Why was he being lured to fires touched off in empty buildings that were booby-trapped with missing stairway planks, or holes cut in floors and covered over with tar paper? And why were floors purposely weakened to cause them to collapse under his weight when he crawled through smoke?

Nobody figured out why ghetto residents no longer looked upon firefighters as courageous saviors who always stood ready to risk their lives and perhaps die while protecting them. There were many explanations, the most frequent one that the firefighter was a symbol of authority, especially in the white-dominated American fire service with its traditional conservatism.

Whatever the cause, departments began protecting firefighters, by enclosing cabs and other riding areas of apparatus with plastic bubbles and other shields. Recruitment programs to encourage blacks and other minorities to become firefighters were started. The AFL-CIO International Association of Fire Fighters began a massive public education program based upon the theme, "Fire Fighters Fight Fires, Not People."

A VERY SPECIAL BREED

The ingredients for disaster began to take form at 12:45 A.M., Sunday, August 17, 1975, when the tanker *Afran Neptune*—berthed at the Gulf Oil Refinery on the Schuylkill River in Philadelphia—began pumping a blend of Venezuelan crude oil and naphtha into Tank 231 deep inside the refinery. During the next five hours, tens of thousands of barrels of flammable materials gushed into the huge tank.

The forty-eight-year-old refinery, one of the oldest and largest in the United States, was notorious for severe fires, but there was no hint at dawn that the worst one of all was about to explode. Philadelphia firefighters had lost count of the number of times they had been called to the 723-acre complex to help Gulf's brigade put out fires there. They could recall twelve big ones during the past decade, the most recent a six-alarmer the previous May 16.

Shortly before 6:00 A.M. that August morning, a hazardous situation was in the making. The crude oil and naphtha had been sloshing into Tank 231 at the rate of 12,000 barrels an hour for five hours. But the Gulf employee in charge had failed to monitor the filling of the tank, and—unknown to anyone—the 73,000-barrel tank was now dangerously overfilled—a thirty-eight-foot-tall bomb. Its internal floating roof was rising rapidly, and hydrocarbon vapors were escaping through vents. These vapors, freed from confinement, became insidious in the extreme as they rode the light breeze looking for a place to ignite.

Shortly after this photograph was taken, a massive flareup at the Gulf Oil Refinery swallowed Engine 133 and everything around it. Eight Philadelphia firefighters were killed, five of them when they dashed into the flames to try to rescue the others.

Opposite top: *A 1974 Ward LaFrance pumper used in downtown Philadelphia. It can throw one thousand gallons per minute and has a fifty-four-foot articulated water tower.* Opposite bottom left and right: *Thick clouds of black smoke boil from the blazing tanks of crude oil and naphtha at the Gulf Oil Refinery in Philadelphia, following a series of explosions.*

Invading Boiler House No. 4 and its tall brick smokestack a few yards away, the vapors found what they were searching for near No. 41 boiler.

The vapors ignited at 5:57 A.M. and streaked back to the tank, where they touched off still more vapors. The tank's floating roof plopped down, forcing the liquid dynamite to overflow and spill down the side. The intensifying flames spread a widening pool of fire inside and outside the dike surrounding the tank. Burning crude and naphtha gushing into the dike area caused pipelines to collapse and fueled the fire with benzine, aviation gasoline, and jet fuel. Heat split open the roof of a nearby tank containing fuel oil, and more vapors burst into flames.

Gulf firefighters were instantly called, but the *Afran Neptune* continued to feed 1,000 more barrels into Tank 231 before the pumps were shut down. Six minutes after the tank blossomed into flames, loudspeakers in Philadelphia Fire Department stations blared, "Attention! Box 5988. Penrose Avenue and Lanier Street. Gulf Refinery." Racing down the Schuylkill Expressway, Engine 60, the closest of ten companies sent, saw the thick black smoke and called for the second alarm at 6:09.

Battalion Chief Arthur Foley also saw the towering black loom-up. He quickly ordered the third and fourth alarms. The fifth alarm had gone in by the time Joseph R. Rizzo, the Philadelphia Fire Commissioner, arrived, and he sent in the sixth at 6:52, calling out a total of more than 200 firefighters, twenty-seven engines, five ladder companies, two fireboats, and other specialized equipment, including chemical foam apparatus and fire department rescue ambulances.

Philadelphia and Gulf firefighters quickly surrounded Tank 231 and began covering it and the immediate vicinity with a blanket of flame-smothering foam. Engine 133's huge deluge foam gun opened up on the fire near Y Avenue and Fourth Street. To the north, the cannon of Engine 160 began lobbing more foam, while to the south a woman firefighter from the Gulf department was zeroing in on the flames with the turret gun of the refinery's foam truck. Other firefighters soon snuffed the fire in the fuel oil tank and showered streams of cooling water to prevent radiated heat from igniting other tanks, especially the 80,000-barrel naphtha tanks above Y Avenue.

Orangish yellow balls of flame were still boiling from the roaring fire around Tank 231, and a thick column of ugly black smoke stabbed high into the sky, but Commissioner Rizzo was satisfied that the fire had been surrounded by the foam blanket. He declared the fire under control at 8:44 A.M. With so much apparatus at Gulf, the rest of the city was short on fire protection, so Rizzo kept the firefighters of the C platoon on duty at the refinery—they were to have gone off at 8:00 A.M.—and returned about ten engines and the five ladder companies to their stations, where they would be manned by other firefighters coming on duty at 8 o'clock.

Rizzo himself stayed at Gulf. Even when contained within the dike surrounding the tank and blanketed with foam, a refinery fire remains treacherous. Until the flames are completely snuffed, there is always a chance that the foam blanket will be penetrated or will dissipate and release vapors hungry for reignition. This is exactly what would happen at Gulf later that day.

Gulf workers began the slow process of draining the tank, but the best they could hope for was the draining of 1,000 barrels by later in the afternoon. Around 10:00 the same morning, Rizzo noticed a rising floodtide of water and foam outside the dike and along Y Avenue. It was of such tremendous volume that sewer pumps were unable to carry it off. Nobody told the commissioner that the valve inside the dike around Tank 231 was still open and that it was allowing thousands of gallons more of foam and water to enter the antiquated sewers. By noon, the flooding along Y was worsening, and the thick blanket of foam extended for a city block, all the way to Fifth Street. Rizzo sent Engine 16 to begin suctioning from the sewer box at Fifth and Y; it was to discharge the foamy water into another diked area and later into sewer pumps near the two-story brick Administration Building. Still the flooding worsened.

Though contained, the tank fire was still as bad as when Rizzo had first arrived. Was it being fed by some unknown source? Rizzo ordered the shutdown of all pipelines running through the area. That did not help. He also ordered the valves closed on all nearby storage tanks. Gulf workers closed those outside the dike area, around the two 80,000-barrel naphtha tanks above Y Avenue, but somehow they neglected to close valves on the outside of both tanks. (In the open position, the valves would permit the release of flammable naphtha.)

Around 3:00 P.M., Gulf officials were becoming increasingly worried about electric power lines on Y

Crack in the tall brick smokestack of the boiler house at the refinery. Flammable vapors escaping from an overfilled tank of oil and naphtha were carried by a breeze to the boiler house, where they ignited. The initial explosions split the smokestack.

Avenue. If the lines should snap from the heat, they could fall into the street and shower it with sparks, which might ignite any flammables in the foam blanket. To ward off this danger, they shut down the electrical substation; and this caused the sewer pumps—which had been carrying off the excess foam—to stop operating. Rizzo ordered the pumps switched on again, but before they were, the foam blanket deepened even further. Engine 133 was inundated by the goo. Rizzo sent a 1,000-gallon pumper to aid Engine 16 with suctioning.

Into this knee-deep mess of foam and water was flowing—unknown to anyone—a steady and intense stream of hydrocarbons. Investigators never determined its source. These deadly and highly flammable materials were concealed by the heavy mattress of foam. Flames and black smoke spouting from inside and around Tank 231 were as fierce as ever, but the danger now was in the blanket spreading along Y Avenue and growing deadlier by the minute.

Shortly after 4:30, Commissioner Rizzo and Gulf Manager Jack Burk were standing on a catwalk near Engine 133, which was throbbing hot after hours of continuously pumping a fountain of foam into Tank 231's dike area. Standing in the deep foam surrounding the engine were Firefighters Ralph Campana, John Andrews, and Robert J. Fisher. Lieutenant James J. Pouliot and Firefighter Carroll K. Brenek were plodding through the foam river toward the engine.

Many of the firefighters were exhausted from the exertion of trudging through the thick foam all afternoon while lugging and rolling drums of chemical concentrate to feed Engine 133's insatiable deluge gun. On the grass near the Administration Building, a group of men were resting and drinking coffee. Among them were George Schrufer, Hugh J. McIntyre, and a young black rookie, David Schoolfield, a firefighter for only four months. This was Schoolfield's first big fire. McIntyre was a veteran who had seen his fill of severe fires. After twenty years in the service, he could have retired the previous month, but there was something irresistible about firefighting, and he stayed. That night he was planning to leave for a two-week vacation with his wife.

At 4:40 P.M., the deadly vapors ignited and flames suddenly flared up near Engine 133. Campana, Andrews, and Fisher were engulfed as the huge flashover raced down Y Avenue with the speed of a wind-driven prairie fire. Pouliot, Brenek, Schrufer, McIntyre, Schoolfield, and others plunged into the inferno to rescue the three burning firefighters.

"I had worked with some of these men," Schrufer said later. "I knew them and I could see their faces and they were on fire. Four or five of them were burning. Their heads and their arms and their coats. Everything was flaming. They were slipping and falling underneath the foam. I don't know whether they were trying to put out the flames or tripping over hoselines under the foam. All I know is that I was not able to get to them. It was a holocaust." Schrufer and Schoolfield, suffering critical burns on their faces, arms, hands, and thighs, were themselves pulled from the flames by other firefighters.

Company officers took roll call after roll call. Who was missing? In the pandemonium, nobody knew, but as the minutes passed firefighters were certain that six of their own were somewhere in that sea of flames and thick clouds of coal-black smoke.

During those minutes of horror, Commissioner Rizzo snapped orders for the seventh, eighth, and ninth alarms and called for five more rescue ambulances. By now Engine 133 also was enveloped in flames. In no more than a minute, Y Avenue had become a river of fire from Fourth to Fifth Streets, where the two suctioning engines became torches. The flames, feeding upon still more vapors and other flammables, turned up Fifth, and in three minutes there was fire stretching a block north to Pennypacker Avenue. Still another stream of flame shot north on Fourth Street, overwhelming the foam-throwing engine there and consuming everything around it. Snaking along nearby G Avenue, under the Penrose Bridge, the fire traveled another 500 feet.

The conflagration worsened as a main pipe from one of the naphtha tanks ruptured. The open valve that someone had neglected to turn off began feeding the flames with 80,000 barrels of naphtha. More pipelines in the area broke from the heat, and thousands of barrels of flammables erupted to join the mountain of flames, which swept into the doomed Administration Building and scorched the underside of the 125-foot Penrose Bridge over the Schuylkill.

Then, at 5:37, as Commissioner Rizzo was calling for the tenth alarm, the fear of every chief—simultaneous large fires—became a reality. Battalion Chief Edward Hampson was reporting another large fire, in a three-story paper warehouse fifteen miles away. Hampson knew as well as Rizzo how critical the situation was at Gulf, but at 6:00 P.M., he was nevertheless forced to call a second alarm for the warehouse fire.

One minute later, Rizzo ordered the eleventh alarm, calling out a total of forty-nine engines, eight ladder companies, nine rescue ambulances, three fireboats to supply water to pumpers, and hundreds of firefighters. Although nobody asked them to do it, many Philadelphia firefighters reported for duty from their homes and weekend resorts along the nearby New Jersey shore. Deputy Commissioner Harry T. Kite was on vacation, but hurried back.

Later that night Rizzo left the fire for a task that is the worst any chief can face. In twenty-eight years as a firefighter, he had never lost a man under his command. "What do you tell their widows?" he asked reporters. "I know how I feel in my heart. But the words. What words do you use? You wonder what God is doing sometimes."

Rizzo returned to Gulf and stayed until 1:00 A.M., when he left Deputy Commissioner Kite in charge and went home. The fire raged throughout the night, but at 5:38 A.M., nearly twenty-four hours after it started, Kite declared it under control. Rizzo returned at 6:00 A.M., and later that morning three Gulf employees, including two members of the refinery fire brigade, managed to close the valve on the huge burning naphtha tank, in an act of extreme courage. The fire at Tank 231 was not extinguished until eight days later, ending one of the worst refinery disasters in American history, with a cost of $10 million in property damage.

On Monday, as the fire was checked along Y Avenue, firefighters began searching for bodies. Six of their fellow firefighters were dead, and two more died in the hospital in the following two weeks. The deaths of these eight—five of whom perished while trying to rescue others—marked one of the worst losses of firefighters' lives in the history of the department. It brought to 320 the number of Philadelphia firefighters killed in the line of duty since 1791. Funeral services for five of the dead were attended by nearly the entire Philadelphia fire department, plus over 5,000 firefighters from as far as Quebec.

On August 20, the *Philadelphia Evening Bulletin* ran an editorial that said: "The firemen, husbands, and fathers were heroes before they began fighting a fire that was once regarded as under control. They became heroes when they took the job. They reaffirmed that dedication every day they reported for work and every time the fire bell sounded. They were of a very special breed."

Volunteer Firefighter Benjamin Franklin, who founded the city's first fire company in 1736, would certainly have agreed.

EPILOGUE

Considering the progress of fire protection in the United States—from three-gallon bucket brigades to an 8,800-gallon-a-minute pumper—it is tempting to speculate on what future historians will be writing about fifty or even a hundred years from now. First, however, we must look at where we stand today. Despite what are acknowledged to be the world's best-trained firefighters, using the world's best apparatus, America's fire record as we enter our third century is appalling.

The United States has proportionately more and worse fires than any other nation. Fires kill around 12,000 people a year, mostly children and the elderly. America's death rate from fire is 200 times higher than Canada's, 400 times higher than England's, and 650 times higher than Japan's. Annual property losses exceed four billion dollars, according to the National Fire Protection Association.

How can this be, if the American firefighter is as good as he is and if there is no better apparatus than that produced by American industry? The answers are many. Most of all, it takes more than good fire protection to solve the problem of fire. Our record is poor because of public apathy, carelessness, and ignorance. We believe that fire is something that burns somebody else's home or child; that insurance covers any losses; that sprinkler systems are too costly. But exactly the opposite is true.

Before examining the direction of firefighting in the future, we must first look at the primary problem today. The worst fire hazard in the United States is the home. Private homes burn with a frequency—one about every thirty-eight seconds—and an intensity unknown in bygone days. The explanation is partly in the flammable construction materials we use, but even more in the wide variety of combustibles inside our homes, including plastics and other synthetics—everything from carpeting to drapes to furniture and clothing. Moreover, when houses and their contents burn, they give off a number of lethal gases in addition to deadly carbon monoxide.

If you are going to die in a fire, the chances are that death will occur in your bedroom between the hours of midnight and 6:00 A.M. Probably you will die not from the flames, but from the poisonous smoke, which acts as a deadly sleeping pill that usually kills before firefighters have even left their stations. Fire experts agree that about half of those who die in fires—six thousand people a year—would survive by the simple installation of a heat- or smoke-detecting device, which costs about forty dollars. Quickly detecting heat and smoke buildup, this device sets off an alarm that will most likely awaken you well before you are put to sleep forever by the smoke. Couple one or more of these inexpensive detectors with a prearranged family fire escape plan, and the chances are excellent that you will survive the fire.

This suggests that the future of fire protection lies in greater emphasis upon fire *prevention* and public education, especially about false alarms, which are a serious problem in every city. In 1975, for example, New York had 204,241 false alarms, more than half the total alarms for the year. When a fire company is called out to a false alarm, the serious spread of real fire and the loss of life can be the result. Ironically, false alarms occur most often in areas where there are many fires. Too large a share of fire department budgets now goes to firefighting. But fire prevention is hard to sell. It is not glamorous; legislators and the public are far more impressed by pictures of firefighters bravely battling flames. The fact of the matter is that a fire represents a breakdown in fire protection.

One possible solution would be to follow the traditions of some other countries, by invoking the Napoleonic Code, which says, in effect, that fires are caused by careless people. When a fire breaks out, the burden of proof is upon the homeowner or businessman to show that he is not at fault. The system works well in other countries, as their fire record attests. But the code would be difficult if not impossible to sell to an American public oriented toward fire insurance. Short of a national commitment to fire prevention—somewhat along the lines of that against polio or for landing on the moon—fire deaths, injuries, and catastrophic losses will undoubtedly continue.

Surely, there will be vast improvements in apparatus. There is not a piece of firefighting equipment made today that cannot be improved. For example, firefighters are experimenting with nozzles containing built-in transmitters that electronically send instructions to the pumper, which quickly and automatically provides desired water flows and pressures. And there will be improvements in chemical additives that increase the efficiency of water both as an extinguishing agent and as a carrier for new agents.

Today there are aerial ladders with sliding baskets that can reach as high as twenty-four floors to rescue people trapped in high-rise buildings. Without question, the problem of this type of fire will continue to worsen until—though hopefully before—a catastrophic loss of life teaches the lesson that sprinklers are essential. And yet, high-rise buildings continue to be built without adequate fire protection. A case in point is the World Trade Center in New York City, unsprinklered buildings that have experienced more than their share of fires in the few years since they were built. In 1975, the 110-story structures had 27,000 occupants, plus 50,000 more coming and going during business hours—making them a city of 77,000 people. When a major fire occurs, will firefighters be able to save people on the upper floors? If the elevators fail, as they usually do in a high-rise fire, how are the people to escape? How effective will firefighters be—or can they be—by the time they climb 100 or more flights of stairs while lugging their heavy equipment?

The application of computer technology to the fire service has been slow. But while some of the early uses have been disappointing—notably in Los Angeles, where a computerized alarm dispatching system was a fiasco—problems most assuredly will be solved. Already in operation, on a small scale, are computerized systems which, while apparatus is on its way to a fire, transmit diagrams of floor plans and other details about the burning building, to alert officers to special hazards, the location of fire escapes, and problems that might be encountered.

The entire field of electronics offers abundant opportunities for firefighting applications. Sensors that penetrate smoke and pinpoint trapped victims or hotspots where firefighting efforts should be concentrated are being used. Satellites are measuring fire hazard conditions in forests and beaming the data to ground stations, where the information is used to analyze the probability of fire and its exact location. New rescue equipment also is being developed.

There is another new look in today's firehouses, and it can be expected to increase as more women enter the ranks. So, too, will blacks, hispanics, and other minority groups that heretofore have found it difficult to become firefighters. This subject will require the shattering of traditions that are as old as the fire service and a profound restructuring of attitudes as well as training programs.

And what about the firefighter? It has been noted that firefighting is America's most dangerous occupation. Recent Federal Bureau of Investigation figures and other government statistics put the death rate in the line of duty at 55 per 100,000 police officers. The rate for firefighters is 86 per 100,000.

How can the firefighter's work be made safer? First, he must be provided with better apparel, durable, lightweight, and fire-resistant from head to toe. There are programs designed to do just that. He must be equipped with a more efficient mask. Here again, the prospect is encouraging. The National Aeronautics and Space Administration is applying technology from the Apollo program to provide better breathing apparatus for firefighters. The problem then becomes one of making firefighters wear it, but this will undoubtedly solve itself, because smoke today is laden with far more toxins from a wider variety of combustibles than during the early days of firefighting. The major inhibiting factor to better-equipped firefighters is the cost. In these days of municipal belt-tightening, the outlook is not bright.

Traditions die slowly and hard in the fire service. Historically, there has been much parochialism among chiefs, who feel that their traditional methods are the best and only ways to fight fires. Fortunately, too, this attitude shows indications of changing as younger chiefs and other officers, many with higher education in fire sciences, introduce refreshing ideas.

It will be fascinating, fifty or one hundred years from now, to see how tomorrow's firefighters measure up to America's fire problems. But they cannot do it alone. Fire protection and fire prevention are everyone's responsibilities. As Philadelphia firefighter Raymond S. Hemmert said after eight of his colleagues were killed while fighting an oil refinery fire: "We have an obligation to fight fires, to protect lives and property . . . but so do those we protect. Minimize the risks we are called upon to take. Give us a fighting chance."

With a greater public awareness of fire hazards and a deeper understanding of the firefighter's work, which this book has tried to convey, the men who make it their business to put out our fires will have that fighting chance.

BIBLIOGRAPHY

Abriel, Warren W., ed. *The History of the Paid Albany Fire Department: A Story of Fires and Firemen from 1865–1967.* Albany, N.Y.: Argus-Greenwood, Inc., 1967.

Air Attack on Forest Fires. Washington, D.C.: U.S. Department of Agriculture Information Bulletin 229, Nov., 1960.

American Fire Marks. Philadelphia, Pa.: Insurance Company of North America, 1933.

American LaFrance. *First Water: The History of American LaFrance, Builder of Fire Engines, 1832–1972.* Elmira, N.Y.: The American LaFrance Co., 1972.

"An Aerial Fire-Truck." *Scientific American,* July 28, 1917; p. 63.

Andrews, Ralph W. *Historic Fires of the West, 1865–1915: A Pictorial History.* Seattle, Wash.: Superior Publishing Co., 1966.

Asbury, Herbert. *Ye Olde Fire Laddies.* New York: A. A. Knopf, 1930.

Auck, Dale K. *Death in the Corridors of a Chicago School.* Presentation before the 31st Annual Fire Department Instructors Conference, Memphis, Tenn.: 1959.

Babcock, Chester I., and Wilson, Rexford. "The Chicago School Fire." *National Fire Protection Association Quarterly,* Jan., 1959.

Barben, Arnold H. *Cowing & Co.'s Great Fire Engine and Pump Works, 1840–1875.* Seneca Falls, N.Y.: Historical Society, 1973.

Battles and Leaders of the Civil War. Vol. 1, p. 179; Vol. 2, pp. 40–42. New York: The Century Co., 1887.

Best, Richard. "Refinery Fire Takes Eight Lives." *Fire Command!* Jan., 1976; p. 21.

Brayley, Arthur Wellington. *A Complete History of the Boston Fire Department from 1630 to 1888.* Boston, Mass.: John P. Dale & Co., 1889.

Bridenbaugh, Carl. *Cities in Revolt: Urban Life in America, 1743–1776.* New York: Oxford University Press, 1970 (softbound)

———. *Cities in the Wilderness: The First Century of Urban Life in America, 1625–1742.* New York: Oxford University Press, 1964.

Bugbee, Percy. *Men Against Fire: The Story of The National Fire Protection Association, 1896–1971.* Boston, Mass.: NFPA, 1971.

Burns, Robert. "Eight Firemen Lose Lives in Philadelphia Refinery Fire." *Fire Engineering,* Dec., 1975; p. 20.

Bushnell, George D. "Chicago's Rowdy Firefighters." *Chicago History,* The Magazine of the Chicago Historical Society, Vol. 2, No. 4; Fall-Winter, 1973; p. 232.

Callahan, Neal, and Bruno, Hal. "Chicago Proves Value of Aerial Platforms for Firefighting." *Fire Engineering,* Aug., 1959; p. 658.

Campbell, Steve B. *Prompt to Action: Atlanta Fire Department, 1860–1960.* Atlanta, Ga.: Firemen's Recreation Club, ca. 1962.

Cassedy, J. Albert. *The Firemen's Record.* Baltimore, Md.: Firemen's Relief Association, 1925.

Casserly, Lawrence H. *The Fire Service and Its Emblems.* New York: International Association of Fire Chiefs Educational Bulletin No. 5; Apr., 1941.

Catton, Bruce. *The Coming Fury.* Garden City, N.Y.: Doubleday & Co., Inc., 1961.

Channing, William F. *American Fire Alarm Telegraph.* Washington, D.C.: Smithsonian Institution Annual Report, 1854.

———. *Municipal Electric Telegraph: Especially in Its Application to Fire Alarms.* New Haven, Conn.: B. L. Hamlen (Yale College), 1852.

Chicago Fire Department, Annual Report, 1969.

———. "Report of Progress, 1957–1962." Chicago, Ill.: CFD, 1962.

Clapp & Jones. *Steam Fire Engines Built by The Clapp & Jones Mfg. Co.* Hudson, N.Y.: Bryan & Webb, 1871.

Clevely, Hugh. *Famous Fires: Notable Conflagrations on Land, Sea and in the Air—None of Which Should Ever Have Happened.* New York: The John Day Co., 1958.

Cohen, Jerry, and Murphy, William S. *Burn, Baby, Burn!: The Los Angeles Race Riot, August, 1965.* New York: E. P. Dutton & Co., Inc., 1966.

Commemorating the Centennial of the Philadelphia Fire Department, 1871–1971. Philadelphia, Pa.: Philadelphia Citizen's Fire Prevention Committee, 1971.

Conkling, Tremaine. "When Fire Horses Pulled 'Em in Buffalo." *Buffalo, N.Y., Courier-Express,* Feb. 16, 1975; p. 12.

Conot, Robert. *Rivers of Blood, Years of Darkness.* New York: Bantam Books, Inc., 1967.

Cook County, Ill., Coroner's Jury. "Findings and Recommendations of the Coroner's Jury Concerning Our Lady of the Angels School Fire." Chicago, Ill.: 1959.

Costello, Augustine E. *Our Firemen: A History of The New York Fire Department.* New York: Augustine E. Costello, 1887.

Cromie, Robert. *The Great Chicago Fire.* New York: McGraw-Hill, 1958.

Cudahy, Brian J. "The Fireboats of New York." *Sea Classics,* Nov., 1974; p. 18.

D. A. Woodhouse Manufacturing Company. "Illustrated Catalog of Fire Department Supplies, 1888–89." Reprinted by Jacques Noel Jacobsen, Jr. Staten Island, N.Y.: 1972.

DaCosta, Phil. *100 Years of America's Firefighting Apparatus.* New York: Bonanza Books, 1964.

Daly, George Anne, and Robrecht, John J. *An Illustrated Handbook of Fire Apparatus With Emphasis on 19th Century American Pieces.* Philadelphia, Pa.: Insurance Company of North America, 1972.

Daniel, James. "How Good Are Our Volunteer Firemen?" *Family Weekly,* Mar. 24, 1968; condensed in *The Reader's Digest,* June, 1968; p. 118.

Dawson, Charles T. *Our Firemen: The History of the Pittsburgh Fire Department, From the Village Period Until the Present Time.* Pittsburgh, Pa.: no publisher indicated, 1889.

Dektar, Cliff. "'Worst' Los Angeles Fire Consumes $24 Million in Property." (Bel Air Disaster) *Fire Engineering,* Feb., 1962; p. 130.

Dibble, Ralph. "Buffalo's Volunteers." *Buffalo, N.Y., Evening News,* May 29, 1971; p. B-6.

Ditzel, Paul C. "Cast Off and Pray! Los Angeles Fireboat 2 Raced Into Action as Explosions Rocked the Waterfront." *Man's Magazine,* Vol. 8, No. 5; May, 1960; p. 16.

———. "Chicago's Ambulance Service Run by Fire Depart-

ment." *Fire Engineering,* Sept., 1950; p. 740.
———. "The Day Texas City Blew Up." *The American Legion Magazine,* Vol. 88, No. 1; Jan., 1970; p. 18.
———. "The Elevating Platform." *Fire Engineering,* Aug., 1966; p. 110.
———. *Emergency Ambulance.* Chicago, Ill.: Reilly & Lee Books, Henry Regnery Co., 1972.
———. *Fire Alarm! The Story of a Fire Department.* New York: Van Nostrand Reinhold Co., 1969.
———. *Firefighting, A New Look in the Old Firehouse.* New York: Van Nostrand Reinhold Co., 1969.
———. "The Great Chicago Fire." *The American Legion Magazine,* Vol. 83, No. 5; Nov., 1967; p. 18.
———. "The Great Chicago Fire." Chicago Fire Department, Bureau of Fire Instruction, Training Academy, 1969.
———. "Los Angeles Firemen Tackle Multiple Incendiary Fires." (Watts Riots) *Fire Engineering,* Jan., 1966; p. 47.
———. "The Man Who Saved San Francisco." *Saga Magazine,* Vol. 12, No. 2; May, 1956; p. 36.
———. "The Rowdy Early Days of the Volunteer Fire Departments." *The American Legion Magazine,* Vol. 90, No. 4; Apr., 1971; p. 12.
———. "Safeguarding Schools From Fire." *Fire Engineering,* Sept., 1961; p. 772.
———. "World's Mightiest Fire Engine." *Popular Science,* Vol. 191, No. 4; Oct., 1967; p. 96.
Dunshee, Kenneth Holcomb. *As You Pass By.* New York: Hastings House, 1952.
———. "Enjine!—Enjine! A Story of Fire Protection." New York: The Home Insurance Company, 1939.
———. *Underwriters Salvage Corps, Cincinnati, Ohio, 1886.* Cincinnati, Ohio: Underwriters Salvage Corps, 1957.
Earle, Howard. "Disaster Attends a Matinee." (Iroquois Theatre Disaster) *Family Weekly,* Dec. 28, 1958; p. 10.
"Early History of ADT Organization." *The ADT Transmitter,* Nov.–Dec., 1968; p. 4.
Edwards, Edward. *History of the Volunteer Fire Department of St. Louis.* St. Louis, Mo.: Veteran Volunteer Firemen's Historical Society, 1906.
Endres, Matt, ed. *History of the Volunteer Fire Department of Buffalo.* Buffalo, N.Y.: William Graser, 1906.
Everett, Marshall, pseud. *The Great Chicago Theater Disaster: The Complete Story Told by Survivors.* Chicago, Ill., and Philadelphia, Pa.: Publishers Union of America, 1904.
Federal Writers' Project. *Reading's Volunteer Fire Department: Its History and Traditions.* Reading, Pa.: The Firemen's Union of Reading, Inc., 1938.
"Fire Department of Cincinnati." *Harper's Weekly,* Oct. 30, 1858.
Fire Department of New York. "FDNY Centennial Issue, 1865–1965." *W.N.Y.F. Magazine,* 1965.
———. "Super Pumper Utilization." New York: Bureau of Training, FDNY, 1967.
Fire Prevention and Engineering Bureau of Texas, National Board of Fire Underwriters. *Texas City, Texas, Disaster, April 16, 17, 1947.* Dallas and New York: FPEBT and NBFU, 1947.
"The Flying Squadron System." *Fire and Water Engineering,* Vol. 74; Nov. 13, 1918; p. 355.
Forrest, Clarence H. *Official History of the Fire Department of the City of Baltimore.* Baltimore, Md.: Williams & Wilkins Co., Press, 1898.
Foster, Robert. "From Red Shirts to Green Backs: The Volunteer Era of the Los Angeles Fire Department." *The Firemen's Grapevine.* Los Angeles, Calif.: Firemen's Relief Association, Inc., Vol. 36, No. 9; Mar., 1961; p. 9.
Foy, Bryan, with Ditzel, Paul C. "The Day Chicago Cried." (Iroquois Theatre Disaster) *Stag Magazine,* Sept., 1955; p. 18.
Franklin, Benjamin. *Autobiography.* Various editions.
Gillingham, Harrold E.: "The First Fire-Engines used in America." The New-York Historical Society Quarterly Bulletin, Vol. 20, No. 3; July, 1936.
Gindele, Joseph, Battalion Chief, Philadelphia Fire Department. *Early Philadelphia Fires.* Philadelphia, Pa.: Private monograph, ca. 1975.
Glory, C. O. *100 Years of Glory, 1871–1971.* The District of Columbia Fire Department. District of Columbia Fire Fighters Association, Local 36, 1971.
Goodspeed, E. J. *The Great Fires in Chicago and the West.* Chicago, Ill.: A Chicago Clergyman, 1871.
Gray, Brainard, with Ditzel, Paul C. "Even the Water Burned." *Male Magazine,* Vol. 4, No. 6; June, 1954; p. 11.
Greenwood, Harold W., Captain, Los Angeles Fire Dept. "The Los Angeles Brush Area Conflagration, Nov. 6–7, 1961." Official Report of the Los Angeles, Calif., Fire Department, 1962.
———, and Mahoney, Eugene F., Battalion Chief, Los Angeles Fire Dept. The South-Central Los Angeles Riot Fires, Aug. 11–17, 1965. Official Report, Los Angeles, Calif., Fire Dept., 1965.
"Gulf Refinery Fire Takes the Lives of Eight Philadelphia Firefighters." *Philadelphia Fire Department News, Memorial Edition,* Vol. 24, No. 4, 1975; p. 2.
Harris, Linden T. "Volunteer Firemen and Their Engines." *United States Review,* July 23, 1932; p. 12.
"Hartford's Famous Jumbo." *Harper's Weekly,* Vol. 51; Dec. 28, 1907; p. 1927.
Hass, Bill, and Jory, Gil. *Water Towers of America.* Baltimore, Md.: Fourth Printing, privately published, July 1, 1972.
Hathaway, Charles S. *Our Firemen: A Record of the Faithful and Heroic Men Who Guard the Property and Lives in the City of Detroit.* Detroit, Mich.: Firemen's Fund Association, 1894.
Heinl, Robert Debs, Jr. "Washington—Where Only the Unusual Is Routine." *Fire Engineering,* Aug., 1967; p. 42.
Hemmert, Raymond M. "Give Us A Fighting Chance." *The Flame,* magazine of the Philadelphia City Fire Fighters Association, Local No. 22, International Association of Fire Fighters, AFL-CIO; Vol. 33, No. 2; Sept., 1975; p. 4.
The Hibernia Fire Engine Company No. 1. Philadelphia, Pa.: published by the city's Hibernians, 1859.
Hill, Charles T. *Fighting Fire.* New York: The Century Company, 1897.
"History of Smokejumping." Missoula, Mont.: Division of Fire Control, Reg. 1, U.S. Forest Service, 1966.
History of the Fire Department. Norfolk, Va.: Norfolk Firemen's Relief Association, 1915.
History of the St. Louis Fire Department. St. Louis, Mo.: Firemen's Fund, 1914.
Holzman, Robert S. *The Romance of Firefighting.* New York: Harper & Bros., 1956.
Homan, Arthur Lee; Marvin, Keith; with Helck, Peter, and Peckham, John M. "Not Without Honor . . . Being an account of the life and times of John Walter Christie." *The Upper Hudson Valley Automobilist,* Vol. 11, No. 1;

Feb., 1961; p. 5.

Houston Fire Department, 1838–1971. Houston, Tex.: Fire Department, 1971.

Howe Fire Apparatus Co.: A History, 1872–1972. Anderson, Inc., Howe Fire Apparatus Co., 1972.

Hubert, Philip G., Jr. "Fire-Fighting To-Day—And To-Morrow." *Scribner's Magazine,* Vol. 32, No. 49; 1902; p. 448.

Jackson, L. A. "Historical Development of the Fire Hydrant." *Journal, American Water Works Association,* Vol. 36; Sept., 1944; p. 928.

Jenness, Herbert Theodore. *Bucket Brigade to Flying Squadron.* Boston, Mass.: George H. Ellis Co., 1909.

Jory, Morris Gil. "The First Water Towers." *The Visiting Fireman,* ca. 1973.

Joyce, Arthur. "Fire Fighters of Yesteryear." *The Forum,* Apr., 1945.

Kearney, Paul W. *Disaster on Your Doorstep.* New York: Harper & Bros., 1953.

Kemp, Franklin W. *Firefighting By-the-Seashore: A History of the Atlantic City Fire Department, Dec. 3, 1874–March 1, 1972.* Atlantic City, N.J.: Seashore Fire Buffs, 1972.

Kenlon, John. *Fires and Fire-Fighters.* New York: George H. Doran Co., 1913.

Kennedy, John Castillo. *The Great Earthquake and Fire: San Francisco, 1906.* New York: William Morrow and Co., 1963.

Kernan, J. Frank. *Reminiscences of the Old Fire Laddies and Volunteer Fire Departments of New York and Brooklyn: Together With a Complete History of the Paid Departments of Both Cities.* New York: M. Crane, 1885.

Kiefer, Kathleen J. "Flying Sparks and Hooves: Prologue." Cincinnati, Ohio: Historical Society, ca. 1966.

King, William T. *History of the American Steam Fire-Engine.* Boston, Mass.: no publisher indicated, 1898. Reprinted by Owen Davies, publisher, Chicago, 1960.

Klass, George. *Fire Apparatus: A Pictorial History of the Los Angeles Fire Department.* Los Angeles, Calif.: John M. Ruccione, 1974.

Kloss, Edwin J. "History of Respiratory Protection in the Fire Service." *Fire Engineering,* July, 1963; p. 534.

Kogan, Herman, and Cromie, Robert. *The Great Chicago Fire.* New York: G. P. Putnam's Sons, 1971.

Laughlin, Jerry W. *Bama Burning: Fourteen Famous Fires in Alabama.* Birmingham, Ala.: privately published by author, 1974.

———. *Birmingham Fire Department: A Century of Service, 1872–1972.* Birmingham, Ala.: Centennial Book Committee, BFD, 1972.

Lehoczky, John Jr., Chief Engineer—Advanced Engineering, Mack Trucks, Inc. "New York's Super Pumper System." *Fire Engineering,* Oct., 1965; p. 116.

———. "Super Fire-Fighter." *Mechanical Engineering,* Nov., 1965; p. 30.

———. The Mack Super Pumper System. Allentown, Pa.: Mack Trucks, Inc., 1965.

Lerch, Jack. "The Towers of New York." *Engine!—Engine!,* The Society for the Preservation and Appreciation of Antique Motor Fire Apparatus in America; Summer, 1973; p. 12.

Lewis, Lloyd, and Smith, Henry Justin. *Chicago—The History of Its Reputation.* New York: Blue Ribbon Books, Inc., 1929.

Limpus, Lowell M. *History of The New York Fire Department.* New York: E. P. Dutton and Co., Inc., 1940.

Lippincott, Horace Mather. *Early Philadelphia: Its People, Life and Progress.* Philadelphia, Pa.: Lippincott Co., 1917.

Little, Kenneth, and Rosenhan, Kirk. *Chicago Fire Department Engines: 60 Years of Motorized Pumpers, 1912–1972.* Chicago, Ill.: privately published, 1972.

———. *Chicago Fire Department Hook & Ladder Tractors, 1914–1971.* Chicago, Ill.: privately published, 1971.

MacKaye, Milton. "Death on the Water Front." (Texas City, Texas, Disaster) *Saturday Evening Post,* Oct. 26, 1957; p. 19.

Magee, Dale. "LA's Super Companies." *Engine!—Engine!,* The Society for the Preservation and Appreciation of Antique Motor Fire Apparatus in America; Winter, 1973–74, p. 10.

Maguire, John E., compilator. *Historical Souvenir: Savannah Fire Department.* Savannah, Ga.: Firemen's Relief Fund Association, 1906.

Mallowe, Mike. "The Firestorm, The Untold Story Behind the Gulf Refinery Disaster." *Philadelphia Magazine,* Nov., 1975; p. 116.

Manchester Historic Association. "The Famous Amoskeag Steamers." Special Bulletin No. 1. Manchester, N.H.: Historic Association, ca. 1974.

Manchester Locomotive Works. "Amoskeag Steam Fire Engines and Hose Carriages." Manchester, N.H.: Locomotive Works, 1877.

Masters, Robert V. *Going to Blazes.* New York: Sterling Publishing Co., Inc., 1950.

Masterson, Joseph S., Ret. Fire Commissioner, Buffalo, N.Y., with Ditzel, Paul C. "Hoodoo Box Number 29." *For Men Only,* Vol. 2, No. 10; Oct., 1955; p. 28.

Mather, Increase. "Burnings Bewayled, A Sermon occasioned by the lamentable fire which was in Boston, Oct. 2, 1711, in which the sins that provoked the Lord to kindle fires are inquired into." Boston, Mass.: Oct. 7, 1711.

McQuade, James E., ed. *A Synoptical History of the Chicago Fire Department.* Chicago, Ill.: Benevolent Association of the Paid Fire Department of Chicago, 1908.

Meek, Clarence E.: "Badges, Buttons and Braid." *Fire Engineering,* Aug., 1958; p. 692.

———. "A Century of Motorized Fire Apparatus." *Fire Engineering,* Aug., 1966; p. 98.

———. "Copper & Brass, The Chemical Engine Era." *Fire Engineering,* Aug., 1959; p. 681.

———. "The Development of the Aerial Ladder from Manual to Hydraulic Operation." *Fire Engineering,* Aug., 1966; p. 118.

———. "The Development of the Chief Officer's Rig." *Fire Engineering,* Oct., 1964; p. 858.

———. "Evolution of the Fire Department Rescue Squad." *Fire Engineering,* Sept., 1962; p. 792.

———. "From Hand Cranks to Self-Starters." *Fire Engineering,* Part 1, Aug., 1960; p. 722; Part 2, Sept., 1960; p. 876.

———. "The History of Fire Department Manpower Units." *Fire Engineering,* Part 1, Sept., 1961; p. 758; Part 2, Oct., 1961; p. 919.

———. "The Legend of the Aerial Ladder." *Fire Engineering,* Part 1, Apr., 1958; p. 284; Part 2, May, 1958; p. 376.

———. "Log of the Nation's Fireboat Fleet." *Fire Engineering,* Part 1, Aug., 1957; p. 758; Part 2, Sept., 1957; p. 938.

———. "The Rise and Decline of the Water Tower." *Fire Engineering,* Oct., 1956; p. 924.

———. "Saga of the Steamer." *Fire Engineering,* June, 1957; p. 536.

Miller, David E. "A History of the Houston Fire Department, 1838–1971." *The Visiting Fireman,* ca. 1972.

Miller, Fred J. "Fire Apparatus and Fire Department Supplies, New York, 1884." Catalog reprinted by Jacques Noel Jacobsen, Jr. Staten Island, N.Y.: ca. 1972.

Morris, John V. *Fires and Firefighters.* New York: Little, Brown & Co., 1953.

Morse, John G. *Apparatus for Extinguishing Fires.* New York: D. Appleton & Co., 1895.

Murray, William A. *The Unheralded Heroes.* Baltimore, Md.: published by author, 1969.

Musham, H. A. "Beginning of the Chicago Fire of 1871." *Chicago Historical Society Bulletin,* Vol. 2, No. 4; Oct., 1939.

———. "The Great Chicago Fire, Oct. 8-10, 1871. Papers in Illinois History and Transactions for the Year, 1940." Springfield, Ill.: The Illinois State Historical Society, 1941.

Nailen, R. L., and Haight, James S. *Beertown Blazes: A Century of Milwaukee Firefighting.* Milwaukee, Wis.: privately published by authors, 1971.

National Board of Fire Underwriters. *Fire Department Salvage Operations.* New York, Chicago, Ill., San Francisco, Calif.: NBFU, 1954.

———. *The Texas City Disaster: Facts and Lessons.* New York: NBFU, 1957.

National Commission on Fire Prevention and Control. *America Burning.* Washington, D.C.: U.S. Government Printing Office, 1973.

National Fire Protection Association. "Famous Ship Fires." *Firemen,* June, 1967; p. 27.

———. "Heritage of the Fire Service." *Firemen,* Oct., 1969; p. 27.

Neil, Henry. *Chicago's Awful Theater Horror: By the Survivors and Rescuers.* Chicago, Ill.: Memorial Publishing Co., 1904.

Neilly, Andrew H. *The Violent Volunteers: A History of The Volunteer Fire Department of Philadelphia, 1736–1871.* Doctoral dissertation presented to the faculty of the Graduate School of the University of Pennsylvania for degree of Doctor of Philosophy, 1959.

Nevins, Allan, and Commager, Henry Steele. *A Pocket History of the United States.* Fifth Edition. New York: Pocket Books, 1974.

New England General Historical and Genealogical Register. "The Great Boston Fire of 1760." NEGHGR, July, 1880.

"The New York Fire Patrol." *Fire and Water Engineering,* Vol. 75; May 7, 1919; p. 1029.

Nicholson, Philip Walter. *History of the Volunteer and Paid Fire Department of the District of Columbia, 1800–1936.* Washington, D.C.: City Firefighters Association, 1936.

O'Brien, Donald M. *A Century of Progress Through Service: The Centennial History of the International Association of Fire Chiefs, 1873–1973.* Washington, D.C.: IAFC, 1972.

———. "Aerial Ladder vs. Elevating Platform." *Fire Engineering,* Mar., 1964; p. 197.

O'Brien, Robert. "San Francisco, April 18, 1906." *Collier's Magazine,* Mar. 30, 1956; p. 32.

O'Hagan, John T., Chief, Fire Department of New York. "The Super Pumper System." Paper presented to the International Association of Fire Chiefs Annual Conference. Boston, Mass.: 1966.

Oklahoma City Fire Department, 1889–1972. Oklahoma City, Okla.: Fire Department, 1972.

"Our Firemen: Historical Sketch of the New York Fire Department." New York: Souvenir of the Second Annual Reception of the Hugh Bonner Council, Order of American Firemen, 1892.

Our Firemen: The Official History of the Brooklyn Fire Department. Brooklyn, N.Y.: no publisher indicated, 1892.

Peckham, John M., ed. *Fighting Fire With Fire.* Newfoundland, N.J.: Walter R. Haessner and Associates, Inc., 1972.

Pendleton, Harry C., pub. *History of the San Francisco Fire Department . . . Their Unique and Gallant Record.* San Francisco, Calif.: Exempt Firemen of San Francisco, 1900.

"Philadelphia, City of and Gulf Oil Co." A Report of the Investigation to Determine the Cause of the Fire Which Occurred on Sun., Aug. 17, 1975, at the Gulf Oil Refinery. Philadelphia, Pa.: Dec. 31, 1975.

Pribble, Paul. "Growth of the Self-Contained Mask." *Fire Engineering,* Aug., 1966; p. 122.

The Progress Years. Los Angeles, Calif.: L.A. Fire Department, 1965.

Quinn, Robert J., Fire Commissioner, City of Chicago. "Tragedy in Chicago." (Our Lady of the Angels school disaster) *Fire Engineering,* Jan., 1959; p. 30.

Richardson, George J. *Symbol of Action: A History of the International Association of Fire Fighters, AFL–CIO–CLC.* Washington, D.C.: IAFF, 1974.

Robrecht, John J. "Fire Apparatus From 1736 to 1871." Paper presented to the 13th Annual Institute of Pennsylvania Life and Culture, June, 1969.

Rouse, Hunter, and Ince, Simon. *History of Hydraulics.* New York: Dover Publications, 1957.

Sams, Robert, and Sytsma, John F., eds. *Ahrens-Fox: A Pictorial Tribute to a Great Name in Fire Apparatus.* Medina, Ohio: published by the editors, 1971.

Seaburg, Carl. *Boston Observed.* Boston, Mass.: Beacon Press, 1971.

Sewell, Alfred L. *The Great Chicago Fire.* Chicago, Ill.: A. L. Sewell, 1871.

Sheahan, James W., and Upton, George F. *History of The Great Conflagration.* Chicago, Ill.: Union Publishing Co., 1871.

Sheldon, George W. *The Story of the Volunteer Fire Department of The City of New York.* New York: Harper & Bros., 1882.

Smith, Elmer L., ed. *Firefighting at the Turn of the Century.* Lebanon, Pa.: Applied Arts Publishers, 1971.

Smith, Jerome Irving. "Fire Engines in New York." *Bulletin, Museum of the City of New York.* Vol. 2, No. 4; Feb., 1939; p. 38.

———. "Painted Fire Engine Panels." *Antiques Magazine,* Nov., 1937; p. 245.

Stecher, Harry M. *75 Years of Service: Philadelphia Fire Department, 1871–1946.* Philadelphia, Pa.: Box 1776 Association, 1946.

Stein, Leon. *The Triangle Fire.* Philadelphia, Pa., and New York: J. B. Lippincott Co., 1962.

Snyder, William F., and Murray, William A. *The Rigs of the Unheralded Heroes: 100 Years of Baltimore's Fire Engines, 1872–1971.* Baltimore, Md.: published by authors, 1972.

Sutherland, Henry, and Hertel, Howard. "The Story of a Disaster, Bel–Air–Brentwood." *Los Angeles, Calif., Times,* Four-part series, Mar. 11-14, 1962.

Sytsma, John F. *Ahrens-Fox Album.* Medina, Ohio: published by author, 1973.

Teller, Clriabel (*sic*). *An Historical Sketch of Horace Silsby.* Seneca Falls, N.Y.: Historical Society, 1906.

Thomas, Gordon, and Morgan, Max. *The San Francisco Earthquake.* Pleasantville, N.Y.: Reader's Digest Condensed Books, Vol. 4; 1971.

Tufts, Edward R. *A History of the Salem Fire Department.* Salem, Mass.: Holyoke Mutual Insurance Co., 1975.

———. *Douse the Glim.* Marblehead, Mass.: unpublished manuscript, ca. 1975.

———. *Hundreds of Hunnemans.* Marblehead, Mass.: unpublished manuscript, ca. 1975.

Unkrich, Donald C., compilator. *History of the Kenmore Volunteer Fire Department, 1903 to 1968.* Kenmore, N.Y.: Albert N. Abgott, Partners' Press, Inc., 1968.

Vahey, John P., District Chief, Boston, Mass., Fire Department. "The Cocoanut Grove Fire of 1944." Boston, Mass.: Boston Fire Department, 1970.

———. *The Epizootic Fire.* Story of The Great Boston Fire, Nov. 9, 1872. Boston, Mass.: privately published monograph, 1972.

Valjean, Nelson. "Fire Engine Lady." San Francisco, Calif.: Firemen's Fund Insurance Group, 1954.

"The Volunteer Fire Department of Old New York, 1790–1866." Scotia, N.Y.: *American Review,* 1962.

Walker, Harold S. "Chemical Engines." *Raleigh, N.C., Volunteer Firefighter,* Aug., 1958; p. 18.

———. "Two Early Aerial Ladder Trucks." *Firemen,* Feb., 1963; p. 14.

Walker, Hubert, and American LaFrance, technical consultant. "Aerial Ladders or Elevating Platforms—Recognize Their Strong Points and Limitations." *Fire Engineering,* Aug., 1964; p. 612.

———. "American LaFrance History Parallels Growth of the Fire Service." *Fire Engineering,* Oct., 1959; p. 946.

———. "Story of the Fire Pump." *Fire Engineering,* Part 1, Aug., 1966; p. 116; Part 2, Sept., 1966; p. 32; Part 3, Oct., 1966; p. 46.

Walsh, Thomas P. J., Battalion Chief, Marine Division, Fire Department of New York. "The Sea Witch . . . and a cauldron of fire and death!" *W.N.Y.F. Magazine,* Fourth Issue, 1973; p. 4.

"Waterous Enters 75th Year Of Aiding Firefighting Fraternity." *Fire Engineering,* Apr., 1961; p. 292.

Wells, Robert W. *Fire at Peshtigo.* New York: Prentice-Hall, 1968.

Wendt, Lloyd, and Kogan, Herman. *Chicago—A Pictorial History.* New York: E. P. Dutton, 1958.

Werner, William. *History of The Boston Fire Department and Boston Fire Alarm System: Jan. 1, 1859, through Dec. 31, 1973.* Boston, Mass.: The Boston Sparks Association, Inc., 1974.

Wheaton, Elizabeth Lee, compilator. *Texas City Remembers.* San Antonio, Tex.: The Naylor Co., 1948.

White, John H., Jr. "The Steam Fire Engine: A Reappraisal of a Cincinnati 'First.'" *Bulletin of the Cincinnati Historical Society,* Vol. 28, No. 4; Winter, 1970; p. 317.

Woolley, Roi B. "Ammonium Nitrate Explosion Held Cause of Texas Disaster." *Fire Engineering,* May, 1947; p. 294.

INDEX

ACKNOWLEDGMENTS

One of the oldest traditions in the American fire service is the strong bond of camaraderie that exists among firefighters. Learning of my intent to tell their complete story for the first time, various individuals and groups enthusiastically united to cooperate and to offer encouragement and inspiration: fire chiefs, firefighters, fire service organizations, and that dedicated legion of fire buffs who have done so much to preserve the colorful history of the American fire service. Of the many who helped me, I must particularly make special note and grateful acknowledgment of:

James H. Blomley, Everett, Massachusetts, who made his library of firefighting books available to supplement my own collection.

The Boston Sparks Association, especially Dick Bangs, District Chief Vin Bolger of the Boston Fire Department, Gustaf A. Johnson, Bill Noonan, James P. Teed, Edward Tufts, Dennis E. Williams, and the many other Sparks who facilitated research in Massachusetts.

The Fire Department of Chicago, Robert J. Quinn, commissioner; Bill Quinn, assistant to the commissioner; Division Marshal George Schuller; and Capt. Marty Harlow.

The Fire Department of New York, John T. O'Hagan, commissioner and chief; Lt. Ceaser (Sandy) Sansevero, executive assistant to the commissioner; Lt. Paul Stolz, librarian, The Assistant Chief Clarence E. Meek Library; Capt. Jerry Staats; Lt. Tom Houston of the FDNY Museum; and Firefighter Matthew Ryan.

Fire Engineering magazine, James F. Casey, editor; Richard Pratt Sylvia, associate editor; and Dorothy P. Ferguson, managing editor.

George F. Getz, Jr., president of the Hall of Flame, National Historical Fire Foundation, Scottsdale, Arizona.

Barry M. Goldwater, Jr., United States congressman, Twenty-seventh District, State of California; and Kenneth L. Black, administrative assistant, for their personal assistance in facilitating my research in Washington, D.C.

Stephen G. Heaver and Stephen G. Heaver, Jr., president and curator, respectively, of the Fire Museum of

Maryland, Lutherville, Maryland.

The Home Insurance Company, New York, Richard Doyle and Bud Siegfried.

The Insurance Company of North America, Lynne A. Leopold, Vivian Brawner, and Ann Schubert Goldsmith of the INA library and archives.

The International Association of Fire Chiefs, Washington, D.C., Donald D. Flinn, general manager, and the many member–chiefs for their suggestions and encouragement.

The International Association of Fire Fighters, AFL–CIO–CLC, Washington, D.C., William H. McClennan, president; and the many officers and members who assisted, especially Donald W. Wallace, president, and Capt. Jim Perry, vice-president, Local 112, Los Angeles City Fire Fighters, and Raymond M. Hemmert, president, Local 22, The City Fire Fighters Association, Philadelphia.

The International Fire Buff Associates, Inc., Baltimore, Maryland, and its many members who provided assistance and encouragement.

The Library of Congress's many staff members who aided, most notably, Lester Jayson, director, congressional research service, and Mrs. Adoreen McCormick, legislative liaison officer.

The Los Angeles County Fire Department, Richard Houts, chief engineer.

The Los Angeles Fire Department, Kenneth R. Long, chief engineer. I must particularly cite the cooperation of Deputy Chiefs John C. Gerard and Anthony E. Giordano; Battalion Chiefs William R. Blair, Les Evans, and Leo Najarian; Capt. Tim DeLuca, departmental adjutant; Capt. Warner Lawrence, Ret.; and Firefighter Hamilton M. Wakeman. I would be deeply remiss if I failed to acknowledge the constant encouragement of my "home company," the officers and firefighters of Fire Station 87, especially Task Force Commander Herman H. Roth and Captain Mickey Plante.

The National Archives, Washington, D.C., notably Joseph Doan Thomas.

The National Fire Protection Association, Boston, Robert C. Barr, F. James Kauffman, Paul R. Lyons, John Ottoson, and Richard D. Peacock.

Donald M. O'Brien, former general manager, International Association of Fire Chiefs, who kindly read the manuscript and made suggestions for improving chapters where his historical expertise is unquestioned.

Philadelphia Fire Department, Joseph R. Rizzo, commissioner. A writer could ask for no finer cooperation and hospitality than that provided by Commissioner Rizzo, his chief officers, and the firefighters of that department.

Albert H. Redles of Philadelphia, that most famous of all fire buffs, who has gone to more than 57,500 fires throughout the world. During the research and writing of this book, this loyal friend has been a constant source of help and encouragement with his deep interest in the fire service and fire prevention. There is no better friend of firefighters than Al Redles.

The Society for the Preservation and Appreciation of Antique Fire Apparatus in America, Syracuse, New York. Their many members were generous with their knowledge and made their vast store of information available for my use.

Harold S. Walker, consulting fire protection engineer, Marblehead, Massachusetts. A professional historian, he graciously gave freely of his time to read many chapters with the expertise he has developed over half a century of association with the fire service. His suggestions were many, and I appreciate his unbounded enthusiasm more deeply than he can ever know.

Among the others to whom I also owe deep gratitude are: Andrew A. Ayers, Engineering Equipment Company, Chicago; Chief William M. Belinson, Eggertsville, New York, Hose Company, and Eggertsville Volunteer Firefighters James C. Schwender and Joseph E. Walterich; George Bertsch, Fire Chief, West Point Military Academy, Ret.; Hal Bruno, contributing editor, *Newsweek;* Chief Augustus V. Connery, Jr., McLean Volunteer Fire Department, McLean, Virginia; Joseph C. Findlay, Fire Chief, St. Louis, Ret.; Mrs. Gladys Hansen, history department, San Francisco Public Library; Ken Little, Chicago Fire Department historian; R. Dale Magee, associate professor, fire sciences, Pasadena, California, City College; Dan Martin, motorized apparatus historian, Naperville, Illinois; Chief C. H. McMillan, Fire Task Force Innovations, Inc., Hobart, Indiana; Mrs. Cecil R. Norman, archivist, Goodyear Tire & Rubber Co., Akron, Ohio; Paul Nadan, editor, Crown Publishers, Inc., New York, and his wife Lola, for their encouragement and hospitality; Dick Orrick, Jr., National Aeronautics and Space Administration, Washington, D.C.; William J. Patterson, deputy assistant chief, Long Beach, California, Fire Department; Andrew Quigley, publisher, *Winthrop Sun,* Winthrop, Massachusetts; Ray Redick, fire chief, Skokie, Illinois, Ret.; Warren Redick, battalion chief, Chicago Fire Department; Dolly Redick and Steve Redick; Eileen Remington, Alexandria, Virginia, *Gazette;* Alden L. Rogers, Grumman Aerospace Corp., El Segundo, California; Kirk Rosenhan, University of Mississippi, University; Shirley Patterson, executive director, Seneca Falls, New York, Historical Society; Norman F. Van Gorp, vice-president, Snorkel Fire Equipment Company, St. Joseph, Missouri; and Curtis W. Volkamer, chief fire marshal, Chicago Fire Department, Ret.

And I owe everlasting gratitude to my colleagues: Shirley Collier, who kindles creative flames in authors, for her loyalty, suggestions, and friendship—every author should be as fortunate as I am to be represented by this gracious lady; Mimi Koren, my editor, whose many skills I profoundly admire and whose constructive advice and encouragement will forever be appreciated; Marion Geisinger, who has the intuitiveness and tenacity of Sherlock Holmes in searching out photographs and other illustrations; and art director Allan Mogel. And finally, I must especially express my appreciation to Fred Sammis, publisher, Rutledge Books, for his understanding and encouragement.

Paul C. Ditzel
Northridge, California

Picture Credits

Except where specific photographers are indicated, photographs have been supplied by the institutions and individuals mentioned. Page numbers are given in boldface type. The following abbreviations are used:

BB: Brown Brothers
CFD: Chicago Fire Department
CHS: Chicago Historical Society
FDNY: Fire Department of New York
FMM: Fire Museum of Maryland
HOME: Fire Fighting Museum of the Home Insurance Company
INA: Insurance Company of North America
LAFD: Los Angeles Fire Department
LC: Library of Congress
Local 22: Local 22, the City Firefighters Association, Philadelphia
MCNY: Museum of the City of New York
NHFF: National Historical Fire Foundation
NYHS: New-York Historical Society
NYPL: New York Public Library

Half-title page INA **Title page** NYPL **Contents page** INA **8–9** NYPL **11** INA **12–13** NHFF, photo by Jeffrey Kurtzeman **14–15** NYPL **15** Massachusetts Historical Society **16–17** Worcester Historical Society **18** NYPL **19** Israel Sack, Inc., N.Y.C. **20** Collection of Jack Robrecht **21** MCNY **22** Top: Essex Institute. Bottom: NYPL **23** INA **24–25** Library Company of Philadelphia **26** All three: INA **27** Guildhall Library, London **28** Top: Historical Society of York, Pa. Bottom: INA **29** NHFF, photo by Jeffrey Kurtzeman **30** Top and bottom: HOME **31** NYPL **32, 33** Top: INA. **33** Bottom left: Israel Sack, Inc., N.Y.C. Bottom right: INA **34–35** All three: INA **36–37** Historical Society of York, Pa. **38–39, 41** INA **42–43** NYPL **44** INA **45** National Gallery of Art, Washington, D.C. **46–47** Top: INA **46** Bottom: MCNY **47** Right top and bottom: INA **49** Top and bottom left: INA. Bottom right: Philadelphia Contributionship **50–51, 55** INA **56** Top: INA. Bottom: HOME **57** Top: FMM, photo by Steve Heaver, Jr. Bottom: FMM, photo by John Garetti **58** Museum of Fine Arts, Boston, M. and M. Karolik Collection **59, 60** INA **61** FMM, photo by John Garetti **62–63, 64–65, 67** Top and bottom: INA **68** NHFF, photo by Jeffrey Kurtzeman **69** FMM, photo by John Garetti **70–71** NYPL **72–73** NHFF, photo by Jeffrey Kurtzeman **74** HOME **75** NYPL **76** FMM, photo by Steve Heaver, Jr. **77** Top: FMM, photo by John Garetti. Bottom: INA **78–79** Missouri Historical Society **79** Right: Wells Fargo Bank History Room **80–81** MCNY **82** HOME, photo by John Garetti **83** NYHS **84, 85** NYHS **86, 87** MCNY **88** NYHS **90–91** National Gallery of Art, Washington, D.C. **92, 93** Top and bottom: INA **94** FMM, photo by John Garetti **95** Top: INA. Bottom: FMM, photo by John Garetti **99** MCNY **100–101** LC **102–103, 104** NYPL **105** Top: Collection of Harold S. Walker. Bottom: INA **106** INA **107** FMM, photo by John Garetti **109** NYPL **110** INA **111** MCNY **112** NYPL **114–115** INA **116** Top: LC. Bottom: HOME **117** NYPL **118, 119** LC **120** Top and bottom: NYPL **122–123** BB **124** NYPL **125** Top: Collection of Boston Sparks Association. Bottom: FDNY **126** Top: Collection of Harold S. Walker. Bottom: Museum of Art, Rhode Island School of Design **129** INA **130** Top: Author's collection. Bottom: BB **131** BB **132–133** Fire Bell Club of New York **134** INA **135** FDNY **136** Author's collection **137** NHFF, Collection of George F. Getz, Jr. **138–139** Boston Fire Dept. **140** CHS **143** Top and bottom: NYPL **144–145** CHS **148** Top and bottom: NHFF, photos by Jeffrey Kurtzeman **149** LC **151** FDNY **152** Top: Collection of Warren Redick, Battalion Chief, CFD. Center: Collection of Jack Lerch. Bottom: NHFF, Collection of George F. Getz, Jr. **153** NYPL **154** Top: Author's collection. Bottom: Collection of Steve Heaver, Jr. **156–157** FMM, photo by John Garetti **160–161** All four: NHFF, photos by Jeffrey Kurtzeman **163** CHS **164** NHFF, photo by Jeffrey Kurtzeman **167** CHS **168–169** Bancroft Library, University of California, Berkeley **170** Fireman's Fund, American Insurancies Companies **172–173** San Francisco Commercial Club **176** Top: NHFF, photo by Jeffrey Kurtzeman. Bottom: Oakland Museum **177** Oakland Museum, Gary P. Encinas Collection **179** Culver Pictures **180–181** FMM, photo by Steve Heaver, Jr. **182, 183** BB **184** Top: FMM, photo by John Garetti. Bottom: FMM, photo by Steve Heaver, Jr. **186, 187** BB **188–189** Collection of Dale MaGee, Pasadena Fire Dept. **190** INA **191** Author's collection **192** Collection of Capt. Bob Foster, LAFD **193** Top: Collection of George Klass. Bottom: Author's Collection **196** Collection of Boston Sparks Association **199** Wide World **201** FDNY **203** U.S. Coast Guard **204–205** Photo by Hal Wakeman **207** Collection of Warren Redick **208** FDNY **209** Top: Author's Collection. Bottom: FDNY **210** United Press International **211** Top and bottom, **212** Top and bottom: FDNY **213** CFD **215** Collection of Warren Redick **216, 217** FDNY **219** Left: CFD. Right: Author's collection **220** CFD **221** Top: Snorkel Fire Equipment Company. Bottom: CFD **222–223** J. R. Eyerman **224, 225** LAFD **228, 229** LAFD **230–231** LAFD **232, 233, 236, 237** LAFD **238–239** Local 22 **240** Top: Philadelphia Fire Dept. Bottom left and right: Local 22 **242** Photo, courtesy *Philadelphia Evening Bulletin* **243** Local 22 **244** Photo by John J. Jankowski, Jr.

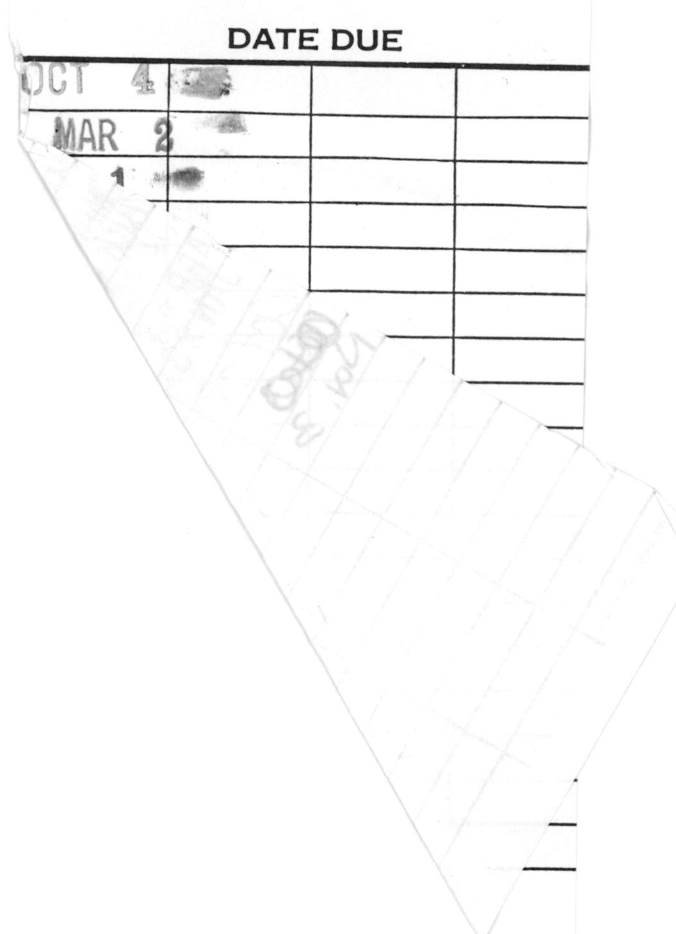
DATE DUE
OCT 4
MAR 2
1